No Curveballs

No Curveballs

My Greatest Sports Stories Never Told

Bill Werndl with Joe Vallee

Copyright 2016 Bill Werndl with Joe Vallee

Book chapter photos: Bill Werndl

Check us out at: www.nocurveballs.com

Facebook: www.facebook.com/BillWerndl

Twitter: @BillWerndl

Special thanks to West Chester Bayard Rustin High School's Chris Lunardi, for lending us some catcher's leg guards for the book cover, as well as West Chester Henderson
High School's Steve Mitten for letting us borrow some shoulder pads.

Cover photo and head shots: Aileen Bannon Photography

ISBN-13: 9780692757918
ISBN-10: 0692757910

Table of Contents

Testimonials

"EVERYBODY KNOWS BILL Werndl as "Philly" Billy, but I always called him "Wild Bill." And boy, did he have some wild ideas during his days on San Diego radio!

Back when I managed the Padres, Bill was never happy with the way I wrote out my lineup card, and he'd always offer suggestions on the radio as to how I should fill it out. So one day, before the Padres game, I walked out of the dugout and jokingly gave him a blank lineup card. We had quite a few laughs over that.

Even though we both eventually left San Diego, it's always great to catch up with Bill whenever I come to Philadelphia. I like and respect him immensely. Bill's stories are legendary, and his longevity and success in the world of sports are matched by very few."

-Bruce Bochy, Major League Baseball World Series Champion Manager

"Bill Werndl has been deeply involved in the sports world for a long time, especially in football on both the collegiate and NFL levels. Within this time frame, he's established a deep level of credibility that has allowed him to penetrate the inside of many unique experiences that he has now decided to share with all of us through this book. Thank you for sharing, Bill!"

-Dick Vermeil, Legendary Football Coach and Broadcaster

"Bill Werndl is an extraordinary man in two ways -- his knowledge of football and his passion for life. Bill has always been my go-to guy for draft information, which he provides with a fire in his belly and a twinkle in his eye. If you love sports -- and who doesn't? -- you will love Bill Werndl."

-Angelo Cataldi, *Angelo Cataldi and the WIP Morning Show (SportsRadio 94WIP- Philadelphia)*

"The first time I heard Billy, his voice and style made me perk up and listen. And the more I listened, the more it became clear that he is an absolute original whose passion for sports is tough to match in today's shallow soundbite sports culture.

As the sports media culture shifts to tired top 10 lists and one-click headlines, Bill Werndl headlines an increasingly rare company of interesting personalities who provide depth in storytelling and perspective. The idea of a sports-talk personality who has actual personality is increasingly rare. Bill Werndl's passion for sports and experience in the business make him the genuine article."

-Matt Vasgersian, *MLB Network*

Foreword
By Bill White

When I first arrived at Philadelphia's WFIL-TV/Channel 6 in the 1960s, I had no experience in television. As a result, program director Lew Klein decided to pair me with the station's best cameraman, Harold Hodgeman, along with their top soundman, a guy named Bill Werndl.

I was lucky I could depend on Bill to completely fill me in on the sports I wasn't that familiar with. I didn't know much about the 76ers, and I didn't know a damn thing about hockey. In fact, when I broadcasted some of the Flyers games on the West Coast, I would fly back with the tapes early the next morning and meet with Bill, who managed to cut the broadcast down to 45 minutes to an hour long. In the beginning, I would call the puck a ball and the arena a stadium, but Bill took out all my mistakes. He could do anything, including cutting tape. By the time he was done, everybody thought I was one hell of a hockey broadcaster!

It also helped that Bill knew every general manager and every PR guy on those sports teams. When Bill contacted them, I was never refused the opportunity to talk to any of the team officials. Although I knew a lot of the baseball players from having played in the major leagues, Bill had also built a rapport with them. Coming from St. Louis as a neophyte television broadcaster, and not knowing anything about Philadelphia except some of the people from the city, it was a great archway for me and a big plus. Bill knew everything. He knew more about baseball than I did!

I remember one time when I was assigned to do an interview for the station, but my cameraman got stuck in traffic. All the big Philadelphia sportscasters who were very popular in Philadelphia were also there for the same interview: Al Meltzer, Charlie Swift, and Pete Retzlaff. Of course, I was there and didn't know anybody! Bill, however, happened to know all these guys. Shortly after I arrived, former Philadelphia Eagle turned broadcaster Tom Brookshier, who worked at Channel 10, came over and asked us where our cameraman was. When we told him of our problem, Brookshier offered us his cameraman if our guy didn't show up in time. That's something you don't usually see. Back then, Channel 6 was battling WCAU-TV/Channel 10 in the ratings. Brookshier didn't know me, but because he knew Bill, he was going to let us use his cameraman. Not only did that make Brookshier a friend of mine for life, but it also showed how important, popular and resourceful Bill Werndl was at the time. And he was just a young kid back then!

I really have to give Bill credit. He made my transition from St. Louis to Philadelphia quite easy, and we became very close friends. When I would work occasional football games with Phillies broadcasting legend Harry Kalas, Bill was our spotter. When I worked basketball games with Kalas, I also made sure Bill was there. He knew everything there was to know about the Big 5. Bill was so well-prepared, if we had a game on a Saturday, he would start preparing for the game on the previous Monday.

In addition to my broadcast work with the New York Yankees, I was also doing work for ABC's *Monday Night Baseball* in the 1970s, and I brought Bill in as my statistician. As it turned out, a young broadcaster named Al Michaels, who I had previously worked with, saw how well-prepared Bill was, how he was on top of everything and how smart he made me sound! Al asked Bill to be his stat man, but Bill turned him down, telling him he worked for me. When he told me the story, I told him he was crazy! But that's friendship and respect for you. I really thought Bill made a mistake doing what he did, but I don't think he thought of it that way. He had that much respect for me knowing I needed his help, and I have always appreciated that.

Even after I retired from baseball's executive offices in 1994, Bill would always have me on his sports talk radio show in San Diego. He even had me stay with him and his wife when I would visit him out there. It was great to see Bill's radio success firsthand. He had worked behind the scenes for so long, and all of the sudden, he finally got a great opportunity to be one of the main guys. Bill made the show. He was extremely popular, extremely controversial and extremely knowledgeable in all sports. Not only that, but people respected him and they liked him. He had entree to anyone he wanted. Bill may occasionally rip them for something, but they would still go on the air with him, and that shows a lot of respect. One time, I went out to San Diego to present a plaque to a retired Major League Baseball umpire and I went on Bill's show. After the show ended, we went out to a restaurant and were taken to this big table. On the table, it said, in big letters: *RESERVED: "Philly" Billy*. He had made it.

During my 18 years with the Yankees as well as my days as National League President, I'd call Bill whenever I needed to clarify some sports information I wasn't sure of. I don't follow baseball or any other sport all that much anymore, but I still always ask Bill what's going on because he's still involved with everything. Because Bill is so opinionated, he and I disagree on things a lot of times. But he's tough enough, smart enough, and does his homework well enough that we can argue nicely. Most of the time, I go back to his side because he has all these figures in his head! We've had a relationship that has lasted almost 50 years and we've learned a lot from each other. I was his best man at his wedding, and we've often visited each other's homes and still do.

Lew Klein could have given me anybody to work with at WFIL, but he was smart enough to give me Bill, and that started me on my career. People have been good to me during my whole career, and I put Bill right at the top of that list. He's faithful, smart, aggressive, a hard worker and knows the intricacies of all sports. I really admire him and I appreciate his work.

Bill Werndl is one hell of a man.

- Bill White
July 2016

CHAPTER 1

In the Beginning

I WAS BORN on December 29, 1945 at Fitzgerald Mercy Hospital in Darby, Pennsylvania. My dad, William, who went by the name "Lodgie," and my mom, Mary, were very hardworking people from the Great Depression era who only went to school through eighth and tenth grade, respectively. Because of this, they believed it was paramount that I get an education. They were wonderful, tremendous individuals who really laid the foundation for me. I was an only child and people said I was a spoiled brat, but my parents could be tough at times. If you stepped out of line or got in trouble at school, you didn't want to tell them, because it would have been devastating for me when I got home.

I grew up in Sharon Hill, Pennsylvania. As a kid, baseball was my number one sport. I just loved it. After baseball, it was football and basketball. There wasn't really any hockey growing up, except for the Philadelphia Ramblers in the American Hockey League, but that was before my time. To a certain extent, I think my interest in sports came from my dad, who was a big boxing fan. Even though the Phillies were an abysmal, deplorable baseball team back then, we would go to a few games a year and we'd sit in deluxe box seats. It cost $4.25 per person back in the day, but my dad always wanted to have the best seat in the house.

Every summer during my youth, I would spend six weeks at my grandmother and aunt's house in Ohio. I loved going out there and still have friends there to this day. One time, the owner of a root beer stand down the street from their house, saw me talking to my buddies as I was answering some sports trivia questions. He ended up offering me a gallon of root beer for every five questions I would answer correctly at the stand.

With dad, mom and our dog, Queenie. December 29, 1949. My fourth birthday.

Since we were in Ohio, people would usually ask me questions about the Cleveland Indians or the Cleveland Browns. After about two days, he told me he couldn't keep me anymore because I racked up nine gallons of root beer!

When I wasn't answering trivia questions for soft drinks, I played baseball with my cousin Bob and his friends from about nine o'clock in the morning until about eight o'clock at night. We'd design all kinds of different games and had some great times. Because I never saw the Philadelphia Athletics play in person growing up, I saw my first American League game at Municipal Stadium in Cleveland, where the Indians played Harry "Suitcase" Simpson and the Kansas City Athletics. Then one time in 1961, my cousin Bob got tickets to a doubleheader between the Indians and the New York Yankees. Keep in mind this was the year Roger Maris was going for Babe Ruth's single-season home run record, so I was extremely excited. However, there was a catch to all of this. I had to paint my aunt and uncle's garage while Bob painted the house. Well, have you ever painted a wooden garage? It's brutal! The whole time I was painting, I asked myself 'Man, is a ticket to a doubleheader worth this?' I came to grips that it was, but I was so angry at doing that job and didn't want to do it any longer. I had a gallon of paint on the ladder, and I moved the ladder with the paint still on it. The ladder moved, the paint didn't, and the whole gallon came toppling down all over the place. My Aunt Maggie, who was a stickler for getting things done, was furious. It was the worst experience of my life, and I've never picked up another paintbrush to this day. I won't even look at one.

I went to high school at Sharon Hill High in Sharon Hill, Pennsylvania, where I was a member of the junior varsity basketball team. By that time, my nickname was "Whip," and the fans would just roar when I would come off the bench and into a game. I was a skinny forward, but I could shoot the ball. As a matter of fact, our team went to the state semifinals, but I didn't make the varsity team because the high school basketball coach brought up some older players who had been on the team longer. After the season ended, a couple of the guys pulled me aside and told me if I had been on the team, they would have gotten farther, because I was never afraid to shoot the basketball. I wasn't a good defender or a good rebounder, but I had some of the most unorthodox shots that would go in. It wasn't all fun and games, though. One time, I got my head split open by a guy nicknamed Baby Huey. I was bleeding profusely, and my good friend Jack Morrison, the brother of my best buddy growing up, Jim Morrison, called a time out.

"What the hell are you calling time out for, Jack?!" I yelled.

"You're bleeding!" Jack yelled back.

"Let's go. We don't play enough!" I snapped back at him.

I went back in and ran down the court, but the referee blew the whistle. They took me back into the locker room and wanted me to go to the hospital, which I refused. They just put an icepack on my head and I sat out the rest of the game.

Sometimes in life, you're lucky enough to find your calling at a very young age. As a kid, I would go out in the street by myself and play hoseball. For those of you unfamiliar with hoseball, you cut up an old hose into four or five inches long, take your broom stick and aim at the hose

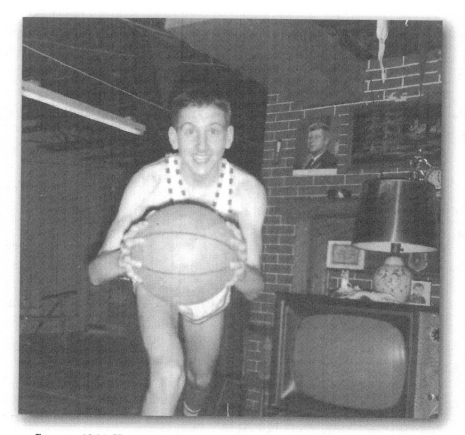

January 1964. You can see the picture of President Kennedy in the background. He was assassinated just two months before this photo was taken.

pieces pitched underhand to you. Usually, you have a pitcher, a hitter and an infielder. You play in the street. It was a fun game to play, and if there wasn't anybody around, I'd actually play by myself! I'd throw the ball up in the air and then go run and hit it. As I said before, the Phillies were really a bad team back then, but every time I played, especially by myself, I'd pretend to play for the Phillies and win the game. I would make the other team look awful. While I was playing hoseball, I would also do play by play. People in the neighborhood must have thought I was nuts, but you had to find ways to entertain yourself when you were an only child!

4

As it turned out, what I was doing eventually paid off.

We had a neighbor by the name of Mr. Gottschalk, who sat in his window and listened to me when I played hoseball in the street. One day, he saw my dad and called him over. Mr. Gottschalk told my dad that that he thought I was going to be a broadcaster someday. However, my dad stressed that getting an education was more important. He always said if I spent more time on math, science and English, I would be a lot better off than always looking at sports statistics. I knew I wasn't going to be a great athlete, and despite my dad's reservations, Mr. Gottschalk insisted that's what I was going to do.

Lo and behold, I would get my first opportunity several years later.

My broadcasting career started in October, 1965. That's when I decided to attend a four-month broadcasting school called Career Academy in Washington, D.C. After graduating from the school in February 1966, I applied to many radio stations all throughout the state of Pennsylvania: Central Pennsylvania, Western Pennsylvania and stations up in the Scranton area. You name it. No bites. Even though I wasn't having much luck, my mom happened to know a woman who worked for the Phillies who knew a gentleman named Clyde Spitzer. Clyde was a bigwig at WFIL-TV/radio and had a friend in Dover, Delaware who owned a radio station. I ended up going down there working at the station on weekends while staying at a rooming house. They had me do it all: news, sports, and I even spun some records.

Unfortunately, I screwed up some turntables one Sunday while on the job. I thought I was fired, so I never went back. Oddly enough, I wasn't ever fired. It took me 36 years to find that out, but that's another story altogether. Not long after the turntable incident, I saw an ad in the paper for a mailroom clerk job at a local radio/television station for $55 a week. As luck would have it, the station turned out to be WFIL. I applied and got the job! I'd take the trolley and the bus there during the week, and on Saturdays, my dad would give me his car because I had to be in work early.

In the meantime, the Philadelphia Bulldogs of the Continental Football League were looking for somebody to chart the team's plays. Coincidentally, WFIL ran the Bulldogs telecasts and hired me for ten dollars a game. The games were played over at Temple Stadium (the former home of the Temple University Owls football team), so I didn't have to travel at all. We had to edit a three-hour game down to an hour and a half for the broadcast, so we had to take out different parts of the game if it got too boring. Even though the games took place on Saturday night, they were broadcast along with NFL games on Sunday. You would never see that happen today!

After about eight months in the WFIL mailroom, people at the station started to take notice of my love of sports. And in December 1966, I was elevated to the newsreel as a sound technician.

As it turned out, one of my very first assignments was to interview an NBA legend.

CHAPTER 2

The Greatness of Wilt Chamberlain: My Very First Interview

AFTER AN ALMOST three-year absence from the City of Brotherly Love, the San Francisco Warriors traded former Philadelphia Warrior Wilt Chamberlain to the Philadelphia 76ers in the middle of the 1964-65 NBA season.

Wilt Chamberlain, of course, was no stranger to Philadelphia. He was born and raised in the city, having been a basketball standout at Overbrook High School. After spending his collegiate career at the University of Kansas followed by a brief stint with the Harlem Globetrotters, Philadelphia Warriors owner and original coach Eddie Gottlieb was able to secure Wilt's draft pick as a territorial pick in 1959, which was granted to NBA teams in hopes of helping franchises acquire popular players from local colleges throughout their respective areas. You're probably wondering how a player who played college basketball in Kansas managed to be selected by a Philadelphia franchise. Well, Eddie Gottlieb was a very powerful guy in the NBA. He even made up the schedule. Someway, somehow, the NBA agreed to give Eddie and the Warriors the rights to draft Wilt. It was allegedly based on the fact that there was no NBA team in Kansas at the time. Wilt's exceptional high school career in Philadelphia also helped matters.

Wilt spent several years in Philadelphia with the Warriors and established a reputation as a dominant force throughout the NBA. Wilt was never more dominant than he was on the night of March 2, 1962, when he had arguably the greatest single game of anyone in NBA history. That night against the New York Knicks in Hershey, Pennsylvania, Wilt scored

100 points in a 169-147 Warriors victory. To this day, Wilt's 100 points in a single game has yet to be duplicated by another NBA player! Following that season, however, Eddie Gottlieb sold the Warriors franchise. As a result, the team, including Wilt, relocated to San Francisco.

By the time Wilt returned to Philadelphia, my good friend Mike Iannarella, who had been the Warriors' ticket manager, now held the same position with the 76ers. Mike ran the office, along with Eddie Gottlieb and the team's legendary PA announcer Dave Zinkoff. Mike was a genius. He knew every seat inside Philadelphia Convention Hall, and years later, every seat inside the Spectrum. One day, Mike proposed an idea to the Sixers about having the team come to my high school, Sharon Hill High, for a scrimmage that would be conducted by Sixers head coach Dolph Schayes. Mike, who lived in Sharon Hill, was very familiar with the area. The Sixers agreed to come to my school, and Mike asked me if I wanted to be the PA announcer for the scrimmage. Needless to say, I jumped at the chance!

When I look back on it now, the whole story just seems surreal. Wilt, who was known to drink large quantities of non-alcoholic liquids, showed up and asked for a case of 7UP, so we went and sent somebody from the school all the way down to a local hoagie shop to get some for him. Then the game started and I was behind the microphone, trying to do my best Dave Zinkoff impersonation. After the game, Wilt was in our locker room and I talked to him briefly. The ceiling was pretty low and he had to duck. Here was this imposing man, sitting in this small high school locker room! Too funny.

So fast forward a few years later, when Wilt signed what was (at the time) the largest contract in NBA history. In fact, it was the largest contract any professional athlete had signed in any sport. WFIL didn't have anybody to cover the press conference (can you imagine that today?!), so Jack Hyland, the news director at the station, sent me down to the local Sheraton Hotel to interview Wilt.

I was nervous as all get-out, and Wilt knew it.

"Don't worry about a thing, kid," Wilt said. Most of my questions were about his contract and the team, and he went on to answer every one of them with class and professionalism. I can remember that moment as clear as day, and I was honestly still on cloud nine weeks after it happened! For a guy who just came into the money he did, there wasn't a trace of arrogance about him. Wilt was very gracious and nice—the exact same guy I met when I was in high school several years earlier. This didn't change over the years, as he always came off as a genuine person.

As much as Wilt was enjoying life on and off the basketball court, the Sixers were still not able to beat the Boston Celtics in the Eastern Division Finals in 1965 and 1966 to advance to the NBA Finals. One of the casualties of the Sixers' playoff failures was Dolph Schayes, who was replaced by Alex Hannum for the 1966-67 season. Alex was a tough, hard-nosed former NBA player. He wasn't the most talented guy on the court. He served more as a hatchet man, whose job was to physically intimidate players on the opposing teams.

Ironically, Wilt was coached by Alex when he played for the San Francisco Warriors and seemed to play well in his system. Alex did a great job of convincing Wilt that he didn't have to score 50 points a night for the Sixers to win games. As a result, Wilt's scoring average went from 33.5 points per game in 1965-66 to 24.1 in 1966-67. While his rebounding remained consistent (24.6 rebounds per game in '66 to 24.2 in '67), Wilt finished third in the league in assists with 630, an increase of 216 assists from the previous year! (414). If NBA statisticians kept blocked shots back in those days, Wilt would have finished with an average of seven or eight blocks per game.

The proof was in the pudding. The 1966-67 Sixers steamrolled over everything that came into their path that season. After their first 40 games, the team was 37-3! After finishing with a regular season record of 68-13, they beat the Cincinnati Royals in the Eastern Division Semifinals and finally beat the Celtics four games to one in the Eastern Division Finals. However, there was one more hurdle that stood in the way of Wilt and the Sixers winning the NBA title: The San Francisco Warriors, formerly the Philadelphia Warriors, as well as Wilt and Alex's former team. After the first four games of the championship, the Sixers had a commanding three games to one series lead. I was at Game 5 in Philadelphia, hoping that the team would clinch the title at home. However, Rick Barry scored 36 points against the Sixers in a Warriors win, so Philadelphia had to fly back to San Francisco for Game 6. Because I had to work at the station the next day, I couldn't stay up to try and see the Sixers win and only saw bits and pieces of the game. Keep in the mind the teams were playing in California, and games didn't start early back then to compensate for the time difference between the East Coast and the West Coast. Nonetheless, the Sixers won Game 6 by the score of 125-122 and were finally NBA champions! I was part of the camera crew the next afternoon at the Philadelphia International Airport when the team returned from San Francisco. Almost a half century later, the 1966-67 Philadelphia 76ers are still considered by many as the greatest NBA team of all-time, due in large part to the performance of Wilt.

Unfortunately, the Sixers' time as NBA champions turned out to be short lived. In the 1967-68 NBA Playoffs, the injury-riddled Sixers once again faced the Celtics in the Eastern Division Finals and even built a three games to one series lead against them. However, the team unraveled and lost the deciding Game 7 in Philadelphia, 100–96. There was a lot of controversy in the final game, as Wilt, for some reason, didn't take a single shot from the field in the second half. Following the Sixers' devastating playoff loss, Alex Hannum became coach of the Oakland Oaks of the American Basketball Association (also known as the ABA). Nobody knew it then, but Alex's departure seemed trivial compared to what happened next.

According to former Sixers general manager Jack Ramsay in his 2004 book, *Dr. Jack's Leadership Lessons Learned From a Lifetime in Basketball,*[1] Wilt mentioned to Ramsay and Sixers owner Irv Kosloff that he would be interested in being a player/coach now that there was a coaching vacancy on the team. Ramsay told him he'd give it some thought and would further discuss the issue when Wilt returned from a West Coast trip. Ramsay liked the idea and said he and Kosloff agreed to make a deal with Wilt to become the Sixers' head coach. Upon returning, however, Wilt apparently changed his mind. Not only did he not want to play in Philadelphia anymore, but he demanded a trade to the West Coast. If his demands weren't met, he would supposedly go and play for the Los Angeles Stars of the ABA. Ramsay then subsequently traded Wilt to the Los Angeles Lakers for Darrall Imhoff, Archie Clark and Jerry Chambers on July 9, 1968. That was the final nail in the coffin for the Sixers, who were just a little more than a year and change removed from reaching the pinnacle of basketball glory. Wilt's trade turned out to be one of the worst in NBA history. In the process, it set the Philadelphia 76ers back an entire decade.

To be honest, there are so many conflicting reports about what really happened in regards to Wilt's departure from the team that you're not sure who or what to believe. While some have blamed Ramsay for the trade, Harry Booth, former men's basketball head coach for St. Joseph's University and a friend of Ramsay's, has a different take on what transpired between Wilt and Ramsay.

"I think people had the wrong impression of what happened," Booth said about the trade. "Wilt got himself traded, really. For business reasons, he wanted to go west. Wilt basically put Jack in the position to where he had to trade him."

Al Meltzer, legendary Philadelphia sportscaster and my boss for 15 years as the sports director at WCAU-TV/Channel 10 in Philadelphia, was a friend of Wilt's. Al has the distinction of conducting the last exclusive interview with Wilt at his Los Angeles home in April 1999. The interview, which was broadcast on Philadelphia's Comcast SportsNet, is discussed in Al's 2012 book *Big Al*. During Wilt's sit down with Al, he offered a different side of the story as to how he left Philadelphia. Wilt claimed the Sixers fired Alex Hannum, and then Ramsay and Sixers owner Irv Kosloff offered Wilt the head coaching job. Out of the respect Wilt had for Alex, Wilt said he declined the job. Several circumstances were weighing on Wilt's mind at the time, as he then went to the West Coast to see his ailing father and to tend to some business. During this time, Wilt said he even considered retiring from the NBA. Then, Wilt met then-Lakers owner Jack Kent Cooke, who according to Wilt, convinced him that if he was going to continue playing basketball, he needed to be in Los Angeles. Wilt then said that *"when I told people back in Philly that I basically was going to retire, they had no choice but either to try to trade me or get nothing for me."*[1]

Personally, I think there's more to any of this than meets the eye. Shortly after Wilt returned to Philadelphia in 1965, Sixers' co-founder Ike Richman died of a heart attack during a game at the Boston Garden. As the Philadelphia Warriors' attorney, Ike had signed Wilt to his first contract with the Warriors and later became his personal lawyer. Ike loved Wilt, and Wilt trusted Ike more than anybody. It's been said that Wilt and Richman had an agreement in place that would have eventually given Wilt part ownership of the Sixers. However, Richman died before any agreement could ever be legalized. After Richman's death, Kosloff, who co-founded the Sixers with Richman, became the sole owner of the team. I don't think Kosloff remembered, or "didn't want to remember" the deal Wilt had with Ike. Either way, I believe Kosloff reneged on a possible deal at some point, and Wilt wound up in L.A. Since all parties involved have passed away, nobody will ever know what really transpired between Wilt and Ike Richman, Wilt and Irv Kosloff, or Wilt and Jack Ramsay.

After Wilt retired from basketball, there were several offers extended over the years for him to come back to the NBA. The most notable one was from former Sixers owner Harold Katz in 1982, but I think it was only semi-serious, since Wilt was usually busy with other ventures. One of the last times I saw Wilt was about a decade or so after the trade, when I ran into him as he stopped through Philadelphia for a visit to see Al Meltzer. After disputes with the 76ers organization had kept the team from retiring his number, Wilt agreed to return to Philadelphia in 1991 for an emotional number retirement ceremony. Although the bitterness seemed to have somewhat subsided, I thought Wilt, until the day he died, believed he was going to be part owner of the Sixers in some capacity, and that always stuck with him. Although Wilt had mentioned his reasons for going out west, I don't think he necessarily had to go to the bright lights of Los Angeles. He liked the California lifestyle, but could have always gone there in the summertime. I don't think he needed that.

Los Angeles remained Wilt's primary residence until he passed away in October 1999 at the age of 63. Despite all the hoopla that surrounded him, there were certain aspects of Wilt's life that were quite private. As a result, there was some speculation surrounding the exact cause of his death. One thing that was confirmed is that Wilt was suffering from some heart issues when he died.

"Wilt was having a heart problem, and they wanted him to have a pacemaker," Al Meltzer recalled. "And Wilt, because he's Wilt, didn't wanna do it. When you're the biggest man in the world, and you just can't buy the idea of having something in there making you work...it turns out that was the problem."

In retrospect, I find it ironic that my very first professional interview was with Wilt, and his final interview was with Al Meltzer, my former sports director. In another ironic twist, I got an opportunity years later in San Diego to develop a friendship with Wilt's former coach, Alex Hannum. I built up such a good relationship with Alex that I often had him on my radio show until he passed away in 2002. During our times together, Alex and I often talked about Wilt. In fact, I was one of the first people to interview Alex on the radio after Wilt passed away. Alex was very complimentary of Wilt. He thought he could do anything he wanted on a basketball court. Although Wilt was primarily a center, if he wanted to be a guard, he could have been a guard. If he wanted to be a forward, he could have been a forward. I miss Alex. He was a wonderful human being.

Everyone always talks about the athletic prowess of Michael Jordan, LeBron James and to a lesser degree Bo Jackson, but Wilt Chamberlain was probably sports' greatest athlete ever. Wilt could do anything on the basketball court and more. He ran track and field at the Penn Relays and was a high-jumper and shot put thrower in college. There was once talk of a possible fight between him and Muhammad Ali, he thought about playing football and also helped make beach volleyball what it is today. In fact, Wilt's contributions to the sport even earned him a spot in the Volleyball Hall of Fame! People sometimes don't realize just how much Wilt meant to the NBA. Yes, Bill Russell won all those championships with the Celtics, but Wilt was a person that people wanted to go out and see dominate. I remember a conversation I once had with former Celtics Hall of Fame guard Sam Jones, after a basketball game at the historic Palestra arena at the University of Pennsylvania.

"Sam, I know you played with Bill Russell and this is a difficult question to ask you, but who was the best? Chamberlain or Russell?" I asked him.

"Wilt Chamberlain was the most dominant player in the history of the game at that point in time," Sam responded point blank.

Sam would know. In 1960, Wilt set the NBA record for most rebounds in a single game with 55. His counterpart? Bill Russell. So much for all the people who say he always got the best of Wilt.

Wilt was not only a great athlete, but a tremendous businessman and philanthropist. He was one of the co-founders of the Rock 'n' Roll Marathon in San Diego, a 26-mile run which raises money for the Leukemia Society of America and other charities. Alex Hannum told me when Wilt passed away, that the majority of his multimillion-dollar estate was given to charities, including over a half a million dollars to his alma mater, the University of Kansas.

There was a certain aura around Wilt Chamberlain that was larger than life. He was just bigger than the universe. It was a pleasure to interview him and be in his company. I think I interviewed him a few more times over the years after that day at the Sheraton Hotel, but the first time was a pretty special moment. Starting my career off by interviewing Wilt Chamberlain is certainly something I'll never forget.

CHAPTER 3

Chuck Bednarik: The Last 60-Minute Man

THE FIRST TIME I met Philadelphia Eagles Hall of Famer Chuck Bednarik, I was working in the mailroom at WFIL. I saw this big, hulking man, mangled fingers and all, walking into the studio.

"Chuck, I always idolized you as a player," I said admiringly as I approached him.

"Argh," mumbled Chuck, and he walked away.

At the time, I thought Chuck would have been a bit more gracious. I didn't know it then, but as I later found out, Chuck was not a diplomat. He was a very gruff, tough, 6-foot-3, 235-pound steel mill worker and coal miner's son from Bethlehem, Pennsylvania.

And one particular incident soon after our first meeting confirmed the fact that he was indeed a menacing guy.

I started working with Chuck when he did sports on the weekends at WFIL. One time, we went up to the Yale Bowl in New Haven, Connecticut for a game featuring Yale and Penn. Chuck was going to be the color commentator, and Big 5 broadcaster Les Keiter was the play-by-play man. The game was to start at 1:30 pm. Keep in mind the Yale Bowl wasn't going to have 50,000 people in attendance. More like 15,000 to 18,000. As a matter of fact, Calvin Hill, future Dallas Cowboys running back and father of longtime NBA star Grant Hill, was playing in that game. I was the associate producer on the Penn broadcasts and charted all the plays. It was 10:30 am on the morning of the game and Chuck and I were sitting in a restaurant.

"I wanna go to the game right now," Chuck growled at me.

"Chuck, it's only 10:30," I said to him.

"I wanna go now! You and I are going to the Yale Bowl," he demanded. I wasn't going to answer back to Chuck Bednarik, so we hopped in a cab I agreed to go out there with him.

When we arrived at the stadium, there were some people cooking out and tailgating in the parking lot, but there was NOBODY in the stands except for some security guards! Chuck motioned for me to come with him into the stadium. After we walked inside, we saw these two little guys standing around. They must have been in their sixties and were probably retired. Chuck decided to go up to them.

"Giants or Jets fans?" Chuck asked.

"Giants," they responded.

"Giants fans. You guys had a great run in the late 50s and early 60s," he said.

Chuck then brought up 1960, the year his Eagles won the NFL Championship and beat the Giants in two key games that November. One of those games was at Yankee Stadium. Although the Eagles were winning 17-10, the Giants were threatening. After Giants halfback Frank Gifford caught a ball while running across the middle of the field, Chuck, running full speed ahead, slammed Gifford into the frozen turf, sealing an Eagles victory and forcing Gifford to miss almost two years of his career.

"1960. What happened to you guys?" Chuck asked.

"Well, we were driving for the game-winning touchdown, and the Eagles linebacker came across the middle and almost killed Frank Gifford. It was a cheap shot," yelled one of the guys.

'Oh boy,' I thought to myself. This is gonna get good.

"What was his name?" Chuck asked them.

"Bendners, Bodners. He was an insignificant player," one of the men replied.

Man oh man. By this time, I was thinking this was going to get really ugly. I was squirming, worrying about possibly having to call the police in about two minutes. Chuck once again baited them.

"What's the guy's name again?"

"Bodnars, Bernorik, Bondors," said one of the guys. They totally butchered his name.

At this point, Chuck's veins were jumping out of his neck.

"What was his name?" he asked one more time.

"Benders or something like that," replied one of them.

Chuck then pulled out his NFL Hall of Fame ring, put it right in their faces, and screamed at them.

"It was Chuck Bednarik. And it wasn't a cheap shot. Got it?!"

Oh yes, Chuck was an interesting character. The late Eagles defensive back and broadcaster Tom Brookshier once told me a great story about a joke he pulled on Chuck when the team was flying back to Philadelphia after an Eagles road game. Tom, who was a funny guy and a real prankster, got on the plane intercom pretending to be the pilot, and claimed both the left and right engines were on fire. Tom's back was facing the back of the plane, so he didn't see Chuck come down the aisle and grab him. Chuck, who flew on several combat missions over Germany while in the Air Force, emphatically told Tom if he didn't want to immediately "exit" the plane, he'd better stop doing what he was doing. Tom went back to his seat without saying a word.

Despite his gruff demeanor, Chuck was actually easy to work with. As a commentator, well, he was Chuck Bednarik. That's all I can say about that, but I never used a cross word or raised my voice with him, because I knew it could be curtains for me if I did. 'Everything is great, Chuck.' 'You want it, you got it, Chuck.' Just like that. That's the way it worked. As interesting as Chuck was, however, he was equally as scary. There was one time in the newsroom when we were working together, and an idea came into my head which clearly proved I wasn't thinking straight.

"Hey Chuck, would you demonstrate how you nailed Gifford?" I asked him.

"Yeah I'll demonstrate," he said.

Bad move. Chuck, with his mangled fingers (which were probably broken more than 11 times), gave me a forearm shiver to the chest and I wasn't even able to speak. I thought my chest was going to cave in.

"That's what I gave him, but you got a love tap, not the real shot!" he griped at me as he walked away.

Chuck worked at WFIL-TV/Channel 6 for about four years. I later saw more of him when Dick Vermeil made him an honorary coach with the Eagles back in the 1970s. Chuck would make the trips with us and was on the sidelines during the games. And yes, even in his fifties and sixties, he was still menacing. Years later, on one of the anniversaries of the 1960 Eagles championship team, I went up to his house outside of Bethlehem in Coopersburg, Pennsylvania, to do a story on him.

"Chuck, I need to get some shots of you for the story," I told him after I arrived.

"I'll give you some good shots," Chuck said. "Let's go out to the wood pile."

A few minutes later, we went out to this big wood pile in his backyard. By now, Chuck was probably around 65 years old, and he started splitting all this wood. He was knocking it down like it was nothing!

"That's enough, Chuck," I said.

"I'm not done!" he snapped at me. He kept on doing it.

Before Deion Sanders played regularly on both sides of the ball, Chuck was the last of the 60-minute men as they called them. Chuck took on "Neon" Deion when he matched his feat, basically saying that Sanders could never play with the same relentless intensity that he did. Whether it was Tommy Nobis or Bill Bergey, Chuck always reminded you that any current player was making a hell of a lot more money than he made in his career. And he was right. Today, Chuck probably would have been one of the top five paid players in football. I also thought Chuck got a raw deal when former Eagles president Joe Banner put the great Eagles players of yesteryear on the back burner during his tenure with the team. Banner, who arrived after Jeffrey Lurie bought the team in 1994, apparently thought the Eagles started when he arrived and seemingly wanted nothing to do with any past players. However, former Eagles coach Chip Kelly embraced team legends like Chuck. In fact, Chuck was the Eagles' honorary alumni captain for Kelly's first home game with the team in 2013. I don't know if Chip had anything to do with that or not, but it was nice to see Chuck appreciated like that.

Sadly, Chuck passed away while we were wrapping up this book. Personally, I think he was really struggling at the end. As great as he was, Chuck took a tremendous physical beating during his playing days. As tough as he was, there's no way that doesn't eventually take its toll on somebody. I saw him at Tom Brookshier's funeral, and he didn't remember me. Keep in mind that I worked with Chuck and knew him for a long time. That was eerie. However, if you told me I would be married for 67 years, have five children, 10 grandchildren, one great-grandchild and live for 89 years like Chuck did, I would definitely sign up for that. He certainly had one great run.

When you talk about great linebackers in the NFL, Chuck Bednarik has to go down as one of the top five to ever play the game. You can talk about Lawrence Taylor and Ray Lewis, but Chuck was absolutely fearless. He was big, had speed and could go sideline to sideline with anybody in the game. Not to take anything away from Sam Huff, but Sam got a lot of publicity because he played for the New York Giants. So did Ray Nitschke, who played on those great Packers teams. If Chuck had played on some better Eagles teams in the 1950s, they probably would have won a few more championships.

His nickname, Concrete Charlie, best describes him. And of course, everybody knows about those fingers. Whenever you talk about difference makers in the history of the NFL, you talk about Chuck Bednarik.

In my opinion, he was the greatest Eagle of all time.

CHAPTER 4

Bill White

IN THE EARLY days of my career at WFIL, working in sports was not my sole responsibility. I went out all over the city, covering everything from fires, shootings, riots and Philadelphia Mayor Frank Rizzo. All in all, I think I've tackled over 3,700 assignments during my days working the news. One of the most interesting stories of my career took place in 1968, when I was sent out to Chicago to cover the Democratic National Convention. On the day of the convention, we got word of police brutality towards activists and protesters outside the International Amphitheatre. Things had gotten so bad around the area that our hotel was allegedly tear-gassed. However, we were in the convention hall while all of this was taking place. When you really stop and think about it, that was probably the safest place to be in the entire area that day.

Despite having steady employment at WFIL in the late 1960s, I was still working side jobs related to sports in some capacity. I was in charge of television timeouts during University of Pennsylvania and LaSalle college basketball games. I had to run out on the court when the sponsors would take over the airways. I was making twenty five dollars a game, but I was nervous about doing this. A lot of the coaches didn't like it, despite the fact that I told them the station was paying a certain amount of dollars and there was nothing I could do about it. Around this time, I met a man whose immeasurable influence on my career has truly left an indelible mark on my life.

As a Philadelphia Phillies fan in 1964, I was rooting for the team in hopes that they would go to the World Series after playing 150 great games. However, the last two weeks of the season turned into an absolute disaster. The Phillies dropped 10 games in a row, and lost the pennant to the St. Louis Cardinals by one game. Two years later, I started working at WFIL in Philadelphia. Les Keiter was the sports director, and legendary Philadelphia sportswriter Stan Hochman was also a sports reporter. Rounding out the sports team was Chuck Bednarik and Philadelphia Phillies first baseman Bill White. Bill was on that 1964 Cardinals team who knocked off the Phillies on their way to beating the New York Yankees in the World Series. During the off-seasons while playing for the Cardinals, Bill had been working at KMOX radio in St. Louis under general manager Rob Hyland. By that time in his career, Bill was already a seven-time Gold Glove winner, eight-time All-Star and World Series Champion. But if you know Bill White, he's not a guy that just lives and dies for baseball. Bill loved the game and played it hard, but he was looking to further his career after he retired. Whether it's politics, business or family, you can talk about a myriad of things with Bill. He's a very knowledgeable, caring and bright individual. A lot of people might not know this, but Bill actually wanted to be a doctor, until he was offered a contract by the New York Giants (the baseball team that eventually became the San Francisco Giants).

After the 1965 baseball season, Bill was traded to the Phillies. Lew Klein, the Philadelphia-based revolutionary television programmer, knew that Bill worked in radio out in St. Louis, and gave him the opportunity to work weekend sports when the Phillies season was over. One day at a Phillies game, I was up in the WFIL auxiliary press box at Connie Mack Stadium and caught a foul ball that came into the box. Ironically, it was Bill who hit the ball. Little did I know that the two of us would soon develop a friendship that has now lasted almost 50 years.

A few months later on a cold November day, Bill, a cameraman named Hank Latven, and yours truly went on a fishing trip off Barnegat Light at the Jersey shore. I stayed overnight at Bill's house in Chalfont, Pennsylvania and we left for the trip the next day at four in the morning. A few hours into the trip, I turned to Bill as I was casting my reel.

"Bill, I hated you as a player," I said. "I hated you. You destroyed the Phillies in 1964!"

"Yeah I think I had 80 RBIs after June 1st, and I think 60 of them were against the Phillies," he chuckled.

Although Bill returned to the Cardinals to finish his playing career in 1969, he still kept his residence in the Philadelphia area. In addition to his sports duties at the station, Bill also served as a color commentator for Penn Quakers football at the University of Pennsylvania with the late George Michael for a few years. A guy named Bill Yerrick was a management trainee at WFIL, and they gave all the sports stuff to him. At the time, I was working as a sound technician, and felt I wouldn't get an opportunity to do any more than that because of the work they were giving Yerrick. When I bumped into Bill White when the Cardinals came to town that September, he remarked that he would see me soon, when we worked the Penn games together. I told Bill I probably wouldn't see him because Yerrick was most likely going to work the game. When the season started, I coincidentally found myself working the Penn games with the director and producer charting all the plays. Personally, I think Bill said something to Lew Klein about wanting to work with me. I got the opportunity to work on the broadcast, and Bill and I started developing a very strong bond. Right before the closing ceremonies at Connie Mack Stadium in 1970, I remember calling Willie Mays to interview him, but he had no time for me. All the sudden, Bill called him. The next thing I knew, Willie was on the phone with me for 20 minutes. That's all because of the impact Bill had.

Bill was such a tenacious worker. Whether he was covering baseball or reporting from the Brandywine Raceway, he always tried to work a story from a different angle. When Bill's former Cardinals teammate Curt Flood refused to accept a trade to Philadelphia, Bill flew out to St. Louis and got the first interview with him, which we used on the newscast. After Les Keiter decided to move to Hawaii, Bill became the sports director at the station. The pairing of Bill, meteorologist Francis Davis and my good friend Larry Kane behind the anchor desk made for a great team.

Eventually, Bill moved on to greener pastures, having a short stint on NBC's *Today Show* in the early 1970s, and a successful broadcasting career with the New York Yankees. Bill was paired with Hall of Fame shortstop Phil "Scooter" Rizzuto on WPIX/Channel 11. The two made for a great team, spending 18 years together in the broadcast booth. I remember going down to visit Bill in Ft. Lauderdale, Florida during his first spring training with the Yankees. He told me he didn't just want to be an analyst, he wanted to become a play by play man as well. Bill went back to his room after games and would evaluate and listen to tapes over and over again. Talk about somebody who is tireless! Before too long, the Yankees gave him the opportunity to be a play-by-play man. I never took advantage of Bill's standing with the Yankees, but whenever I needed tickets to a game at Yankee Stadium, he got them for me with no questions asked. After his run with the Yankees ended following the 1988 season, Bill was elected president of the National League, a position he held until his retirement in 1994. Bill is not a guy who lobbies for anything, but as a former player, broadcaster and National League President, his contributions are worthy of a spot in the Baseball Hall of Fame. I would be hard pressed to find anybody who has had the success Bill has had, on and off the field, in the history of Major League Baseball.

Next to my father, Bill White has had the biggest impact on my life.

You can roughly count on three or four friends in your life who will step up to the plate for you when the chips are down. Bill is one of those guys. If you're in a foxhole, you'd want him right next to you. When he was working *Monday Night Baseball* games, Bill called me up and got me the job of a statistician. Around this time, broadcaster Al Michaels called me and offered me the same job, but I turned him down out of my loyalty to Bill (more on that in another chapter). To this day, I'm glad I made that decision, because he is a true friend. When my father passed away in 1993, Bill drove from Washington, D.C. all the way up to Glenolden, Pennsylvania for the funeral. He was also there for me when my mother passed away. In happier times, Bill also attended my daughter's wedding. After I got laid off from my job in San Diego, Bill consoled me and went to bat for me more than anybody, even contacting Sirius XM in efforts to try and land me a job. Bill doesn't go to bat for people unless they are very competent. That being said, he's helped so many people along the way, and you'd never even know about it.

I try to see Bill three to four times a year and I still talk to him on the phone at least once a week. He told me three people call him on a regular basis: Sandy, Bob, and me. Sandy meaning Sandy Koufax, and Bob meaning Bob Gibson. Yep. Two Hall of Famers and me. Go figure. Bill's a very private person, but if I had the wherewithal in baseball, he would be my number one choice for baseball commissioner. If you're going to say I'm prejudiced, I'm absolutely prejudiced, but I've seen this man with people and he understands them. He had to deal with former Reds owner Marge Schott. He had to deal with Pete Rose from the very first day he stepped in office as National League President! Bill is now over 80 years of age, and he's still very active and in really good shape.

I'll never be able to repay Bill White back monetarily for what he taught me. He just takes everything to another level. I'll never forget the day when we were sitting in the newsroom at Channel 6, and he gave me some sound advice that always stuck with me.

"Bill, when you're making $20,000 a year, live like you're making $15,000. When you're making $40,000 a year, live like you're making $30,000. When you're lucky enough to make $60,000, you live like you're making $50,000. And if you're really fortunate to be making $80,000 to $100,000, you live like you're making $60,000. Never live above your means. Always live below your means because it's easier to adjust," he said.

I'm extremely lucky to have been around a man like Bill White. Next to my father, he has had the biggest impact on my life.

CHAPTER 5

Dick Allen: One of Philadelphia's All-Time Misunderstood Athletes

MIKE SCHMIDT, THE greatest player in the history of the Philadelphia Phillies, never hesitates to give credit to former teammate Dick Allen for mentoring him in the early stages of his career. In fact, it was Schmidt, Phillies second baseman Dave Cash and even broadcaster Richie Ashburn, who lobbied for the team's general manager, Paul Owens, to bring Dick back in the fold after a six-year exile. By that time in Dick's career, his numbers had declined, but he was still a respected, veteran ballplayer capable of helping any team with his bat. Dick's seemingly enigmatic personality has often made him a magnet for controversy. Nonetheless, I still think his presence on those Phillies teams was instrumental in helping them reach the postseason in 1976 for the first time since 1950.

I first got to know Dick pretty well during his first stint with the Phillies in the 1960s and he was always a gentleman. WFIL/Channel 6 used to televise the team's games on Saturdays and Sundays, and I would often go out to Connie Mack Stadium to watch them play. I once went out to Wampum, Pennsylvania and spent some time with Dick when legendary Philadelphia sportswriter Stan Hochman worked on his documentary called *Outta Sight*. When he first came up with the Phillies, Dick was such an unbelievable talent. He's arguably the greatest all-around offensive force I've seen in my lifetime who wore a Phillies uniform. Even better than Schmidt, although Schmidt was a better all-around ballplayer. Dick was such a force when he came to the plate that you had to stick around to watch him bat, regardless of what the score was! He hit for power, average, and ran from first to third as well as anybody. In fact, the only other player I've ever seen run better from first to third in my life was Willie Mays. From 1960 to 1969, only one player had better power numbers than Dick, and that was Hank Aaron. What makes this even more impressive is that Dick regularly faced pitchers like Juan Marichal, Sandy Koufax, Don Drysdale, Bob Gibson, Gaylord Perry and Nolan Ryan for the better part of his career. These are the greatest pitchers to ever play the game!

Of course, whether it's fair or not, trouble always did seem to follow Dick around. Philadelphia, and our country in general, was dealing with a tumultuous time in the 1960s as far as race was concerned. We had riots in North Philly, along with a number of incidents in the Greater Philadelphia area. Black people were treated like second class citizens in Philadelphia, and Dick was no exception. Before getting called up to the Phillies, Dick played minor league baseball in Little Rock, Arkansas, during the height of racial unrest in the United States. People slit his tires and called him all kinds of names. He had a very difficult situation on his hands. Dick was basically from an all-white neighborhood in Wampum, Pennsylvania. His buddy was Joe Namath. They played pool together! He didn't know racism until he was thrust into the Little Rock situation.

No matter what situation Dick experienced during his time at Little Rock or with the Phillies, he had a long memory. The late, great Stan Hochman, my friend, former co-worker and legendary Philadelphia sportswriter, experienced this firsthand.

"The Phillies called Dick up from the minors in September, 1963. The first road trip when he joined the team, he was wearing a tweed jacket with leather elbow patches, wing tip shoes that were almost orange colored and he was smoking a pipe," recalled Hochman. "I wrote a piece and said 'If the guy dresses like that, he'd better be able to hit, and this guy can hit.' 18 years later, I interviewed Dick in Kissimmee, Florida, where he was going to go to work as a minor league batting coach. We sat down on the bullpen bench in right field, and he said to me 'You made fun of my clothes.' This is 18 years later. He was still holding this inside of him. I reminded him of the punchline in the article, and he said 'No, you made fun of my clothes.' I apologized, but that sets the tone for Dick. He was sensitive. Besides being as strong as he was, swinging a 42-ounce bat, being tough, playing on a championship basketball team in high school, he was still sensitive. So why did he not conform? Why did he treat the Phillies the way he did? It's because of the treatment the Phillies gave him.

"The Phillies sent him to Little Rock in a time of racial tension. Fire hoses were being used on civil rights activists as well as attack dogs. They needed the National Guard to protect the kids integrating the schools. There were other clubs they could have sent him to. Were they trying to toughen him up to see if he could cope with this time of adversity? Somehow, the media is guilty for not pursuing it. We never got a clear answer from the Phillies as to why they sent him to Little Rock. There were people who analyzed Dick and said he didn't have a father figure, so he didn't like authority and didn't like to take orders. I'm not a psychiatrist and those people weren't either, but that was the image we had of Dick Allen: that he was a nonconformist and didn't owe the Phillies anything because of the way he'd been treated.

"Back when the Mets and Colt 45's were getting organized, each baseball team had to designate several players to a list where the two teams could choose from. Even though Dick was in the minor leagues, he was on the Phillies' 40-man roster. Dick was placed on the expansion list and the Phillies made no secret of it. The team badmouthed him, saying his eyesight was so bad that he'd never amount to anything, and neither team picked him. Even though that was a ploy by the Phillies, those are things that cause a guy not to be loyal to a franchise."

This behavior was not uncommon in Major League Baseball around this time. When Pete Rose was starting out with the Cincinnati Reds, Frank Robinson and Vada Pinson, two black teammates of Pete's, befriended him. They took Pete under their wing, showed him how to order room service, the whole deal. Well, a month into the season, Pete was actually called up to the Reds' front office by management, and was told it didn't look good that he was associating with Robinson and Pinson. When Robinson was traded to the Baltimore Orioles after the 1965 season, he was branded a "clubhouse lawyer" by the Reds. When in fact, all he really did was hang around one of the team's white guys and the Reds didn't like it. That was the mentality back then.

I recall one particular incident that took place in the middle of the 1965 season involving Dick and teammate Frank Thomas. For some reason, Thomas was calling Dick some rather insensitive names. Next thing you know, Thomas hit Dick in the shoulder with a baseball bat, and several teammates had to go over and separate the two. This is one of several incidents that perpetuated Dick's demise with the Phillies, who didn't handle the situation properly at all. Thomas was not a good guy, having bounced around a lot of clubs over the course of his career. Although Thomas was released shortly after the incident, the team was adamant that Dick not say a word about what happened. Because Dick never talked about it, a lot of fans took Thomas' side. It was really sad. What happened that day followed Dick around like a black cloud for the rest of his time with the Phillies in the 1960s, which really left a sour taste in my mouth.

"The Phillies told Dick he couldn't talk about the incident under the threat of a fine," said Hochman. "Thomas had started the incident. His nickname was "Big Donkey," as his own teammates knew how dumb he was. He was using certain references that got Dick so stirred up. The Phillies would not allow Dick to tell his side of the story. Thomas had his own following because he did occasional local radio shows. The fans took Thomas' side. Eventually, Thomas was released, and Dick had to bear the brunt of being the bad guy in that whole episode."

By 1969, the Phillies were getting tired of Dick, and the writing was on the wall that his days in Philly were numbered. This really bothered me. One of the most controversial figures ever to play the game was Babe Ruth. Although the eras which they played in were different, it's well documented that no matter what the Babe was doing off the field prior to a game, whatever team he was playing for made sure he was always on the field when the game started. They had his back. For whatever reason, I don't think the same could be said for Dick. When he was finally traded to the Cardinals, I think a lot of fans were more relieved than anything that all the drama surrounding him was over, and Dick probably was, too.

Of course, there was also a large portion of the Phillies' fan base who would long for his return, and they eventually got their wish. The day before Dick returned to the Phillies in 1975, I saw him over at Philadelphia Park. Dick loves horses and to this day owns several of them. When I walked up to Dick, he said two things to me. First, he didn't want me to report that he was at the track, and second, he was signing with the Phillies the next day. I kept that under my hat for him, and Dick always respected me because of that. Upon his return, the fans welcomed him back with open arms and gave him a standing ovation.

So, did Dick have a storybook ending in his second go-round with the Phillies? Well, not exactly, but I know for a fact that one particular incident he was involved in upon his return was blown out of proportion. A young player named Rick Bosetti was called up to the Phillies in September, 1976. On one occasion, he proceeded to get picked off twice in the same game. Bosetti, who was beyond distraught, was crying his eyes out walking up the ramp into the Phillies locker room. Right around this time, nobody could find Dick in the clubhouse, and the next day he was accused of leaving the ballpark early. As it turned out, Dick took Rick back to the grounds crew area and consoled him until about 2 am in the morning. That's the part of the story you didn't hear.

More controversy followed weeks later after the Phillies clinched the National League East against the Montreal Expos. Dick, along with teammates Cash, Schmidt and Garry Maddox, supposedly wandered off from the rest of the team and celebrated in a clubhouse broom closet. I'm not really sure why the players did this. Maybe they wanted to keep the celebration to a minimum because Pete Rose and the Big Red Machine were on the horizon in the National League Championship Series. Maybe they just wanted to get away from everything. Either way, it ruffled a lot of feathers, including management. Things got worse when Dick, who was very good friends with teammate Tony Taylor, declared he would not play in the NLCS unless Taylor was placed on the postseason roster. Dick was sticking up for his good friend and the Phillies compromised by making Tony a coach. Stan Hochman recalled the drama surrounding Dick after the Phillies clinched the NL East.

Without question, Dick Allen is one of Philadelphia's all-time misunderstood athletes. Spring Training, 1976.

"I was covering the division clincher in Montreal. After the celebration, I flew on a regular commercial airline back to Philly, and Dick was on the plane. He wasn't leaving with the team and wasn't going to their next stop in St. Louis. After much pleading and begging about what he was doing, Dick finally confided that he felt the Tony Taylor situation was an injustice. I thought 'My God. Things are going pretty smoothly. Why are you doing this?'"

After the Phillies were swept by the Reds in the NLCS, the team signed Richie Hebner to play first base for the 1977 season, marking the official end of Dick's tenure with the organization. He later signed with the Oakland Athletics as a free agent, but played his last major league game in July 1977 at the age of 35.

So why isn't Dick Allen in the Hall of Fame, you ask? Despite his impressive numbers, I think a lot of people felt Dick didn't live up to his true potential. Look at his lifetime numbers: a .292 lifetime batting average, 351 home runs, over 1,000 runs batted in, and a slugging percentage and OPS higher than Mike Schmidt's! His OPS+ is also better than those of Schmidt, Willie McCovey, Hank Aaron, and Willie Stargell, and is equal to Willie Mays'! All of those players are in the Hall of Fame, except for Dick. Also keep in mind the pitcher's mound was 15 inches high during the first five full years he played in the Major Leagues, and he still put up numbers that were astronomical. Don't tell me you have to play 20 years in order to be eligible! Look at Hall of Famers like Ron Santo and Jim Rice. Some of Dick's numbers are comparable or even better than theirs!

In December 2014, Dick drew consideration from the Golden Era Committee of the National Baseball Hall of Fame for possible enshrinement. He fell short. By one vote. One vote! This is a real disgrace. That alone goes to show you that the Hall is all about politics. Veteran media members should not be on the Golden Era Committee, because they had an opportunity to vote for some of these players on the ballot back when they were playing. They most likely didn't vote for them when they were eligible the first time. It's all an ego thing. Maybe only Hall of Famers should be voting for these players, and not executives, because there might be some hidden agenda. In addition to a player's overall statistics, factors such as character and integrity are supposed to be taken into consideration when players are elected to the Hall of Fame. I would like to know how these voters judge integrity, because the last time I checked, Orlando Cepeda was once convicted of smuggling drugs, yet he has a plaque in Cooperstown. Although Cepeda's entry into the Hall of Fame was most likely delayed because of what transpired, he was eventually enshrined in 1999. Almost ten years later, Cepeda found himself in hot water once again, when a police officer found drugs in his car. Dick, on the other hand, has never been associated with anything like that!

Another thing that goes beyond my level of comprehension is how a "baseball genius" like Bill James can offer an accurate assessment on the kind of person Dick was during his playing days. What gives a guy like Bill

James the right to say Dick was a disruptive force in the locker room? Did he know Dick? Did he cover him? What gives him the right to say this? Because he was once a stinking security guard who put together a comprehensive plan called sabermetrics? Can you tell me how many championships the Oakland Athletics have won since they started implementing sabermetrics? Why doesn't he talk to some of Dick's former teammates and ask them how it was to play with him. Mike Schmidt isn't the only Hall of Famer who holds Dick in high regard. Former White Sox teammate Goose Gossage not only praises Dick, but believes he is Hall of Fame worthy.[2]

I agree with Gossage wholeheartedly. People can say whatever they want, but in my mind, Dick Allen is and always will be a Hall of Famer. I judged him as a ballplayer and how he treated me as a person. I was a young guy breaking into the business and he could have easily turned his back on me, but he never did. I still enjoy talking to Dick to this day. He's good friends with Bill White. I'd love to have him on my radio show, but he's a hard man to get a hold of and there's practically a code to even try and get to him. I really wish the Phillies had understood him better during his time in Philadelphia in the 1960s. I think he could have had a longer and more productive major league career if they did.

Without question, Dick Allen is one of Philadelphia's all-time misunderstood athletes.

C H A P T E R 6

Howard Cosell "Showers" Eagles Fans on Monday Night Football

November 23, 1970.

THE PHILADELPHIA EAGLES were playing the New York Giants at Franklin Field on Monday Night Football. Man oh man, what a cold, cold, night that was. Eagles owner Leonard Tose decided to throw a big press party before the game. Broadcasting legend and Monday Night Football commentator Howard Cosell was covering the game and also happened to be at Tose's party. Tose, as Stan Hochman once said, never skimped on the pregame festivities.

"Leonard Tose always had a party and always fed the writers from Bookbinder's (a former seafood restaurant in Philadelphia), including steaks some nights and lobster some nights," acknowledged Stan. "They were the most generous meals for the media in the history of the Eagles."

Now I really don't know how I can politely phrase the following, but to put it mildly, let's just say Cosell wasn't feeling any pain by the time he went up to the booth to call the game.

This was not good.

During the first half, Cosell began to slur some of his words. Needless to say, he was not in good shape. Well, next thing you knew, it was halftime. There was an auxiliary bathroom at Franklin Field on the opposite side of where the writers were located, which was way upstairs. The radio and television booths were on the south side. I was up in the Eagles' play-by-play booth with team broadcaster Charlie Swift, when Cosell came out of the ABC broadcast booth and approached me.

"Young man, where's the bathroom?" he asked.

Before I could say anything, a bunch of people who were standing around pointed towards the big, grey door leading to the bathroom. Cosell managed to pull the door, but he didn't go in the bathroom. Instead, he reached down his pants, pulled out his "you know what," and proceeded to urinate on the crowd below. It was such a bitter, cold night that nobody probably even felt it.

As the third quarter began, Cosell went back into the booth to join his colleague, Don Meredith, who was wearing a new pair of ostrich-skinned boots. Just moments after "showering" an unknowing crowd of Eagles fans, Cosell then vomited all over Meredith's boots! That was the final straw for ABC. Somebody in the production truck phoned president of ABC Sports Roone Arledge in New York, and told him they were getting Cosell out of there. Soon after, several bodyguards came to the booth and removed him. Cosell was put in a limo and sent back to New York.

Although Cosell claimed he had the flu, I saw the actual chain of events unravel with my own two eyes.

"Cosell's disappearance was so noticeable and so notorious," Stan Hochman recalls. "If it wasn't Leonard Tose that told us he had too many martinis, it was somebody close to Tose who was able to remain anonymous, but let the media know that, indeed, he had too many pregame martinis. Cosell's alibi was that he ran laps with Tommie Smith (a former track & field athlete and wide receiver in the American Football League with the Bengals) before the game. Now, A. What was Tommie Smith doing at that football game? and B. Cosell never did anything athletic in his life. Why would he have run laps around Franklin Field?"

Ironically, Stan later got into an altercation with Cosell during the 1977 World Series between the New York Yankees and Los Angeles Dodgers.

"I got on a plane in Los Angeles and I'm sitting in an aisle seat," Hochman recalled. "Here comes Cosell coming down the aisle. Howard liked to describe writers as 'dregs of the earth.' He says it as he's approaching my seat. My only real previous interaction with Cosell was at a Super Bowl in Miami. I was at a pool in a lounge chair with Jim Barniak (a longtime member of the Philadelphia print and broadcast media), and NFL Films was following Cosell around. That's the first time I had heard the 'dregs of the earth' comment from him. They got it on film and used that in the documentary.

"Howard, you don't know what an honor this is to share this airplane ride with you," I said to him. "He reached in with his left hand and whacked me in the head three times. It was hard enough to make my head spin. It turned out he was wearing a heavy ring. After I got over the initial shock, I looked around and I saw Chet Forte sitting behind me and three other people from ABC sitting closest to me. They didn't see a thing. They weren't going to give me any kind of statement. An Air Force sergeant who was sitting two rows in front had turned around and he saw it. He gave me a statement saying exactly what happened. Baseball Commissioner Bowie Kuhn was in the last row of Business Class. He came up to me and said 'Stan, how about if Howard apologizes and we forget that this ever happened.' I said 'A. It's unlikely the son of a bitch will apologize, and B. I don't want to forget it. I'm gonna file charges against him.' I told the stewardess, I asked for an ice bag, told her I got hit by Cosell, and she goes to the cabin and tells the pilot. He came back and asked me if I really wanted to pursue this. 'Yes I do,' I said. 'He has no right to go around hitting people.'

"After we landed, I gave a statement to the New York Airport police. I asked for the seating chart, but they weren't going to give it to me. I came back to Philadelphia and we carried a story about it in the Philadelphia Daily News. A reporter from the paper interviewed me and wrote a story suggesting I'm looking for publicity. Looking back years later, I should have just sucked it up. It turned out the incident occurred on the ground in L.A., so if I wanted to file charges, I had to go back to L.A. The paper was willing to send me. The assistant district attorney was a young woman who was determining whether I had a strong enough case to go to trial.

"Cosell was represented by a big-time lawyer he later embarrassed while testifying in an antitrust case aimed at the NFL. He didn't show up to the hearing. He didn't want to turn it into a circus. He had a young lawyer get a deposition from Bruce Keidan, the Philadelphia Inquirer baseball writer, that put me in a negative light. But Keidan's name was spelled Kiden, and it said he worked for the Enquirer, not the Inquirer. I looked at it and it was shoddy work. Plus, Keidan suggested that I was looking for publicity, and he wasn't anywhere near the situation. He was upfront playing high-stakes bridge with the broadcast team. The young lawyer was a former law school classmate of the assistant district attorney and she referred to him by his nickname "Skip." The attorney the Daily News hired to represent me was overmatched in this situation. I saw I was doomed and it wasn't going to go to trial. I didn't understand that I could have filed a civil suit. I probably would have won, and the Air Force Sergeant would have been a good witness. But in any case, it was embarrassing. It embarrassed my daughter, who was in middle school at the time, it embarrassed my wife and it embarrassed me.

"Cosell was such a fraud. When he covered boxing in Montreal for the 1976 Olympics, he had an arrangement with the guy who looked at the scorecards. For example, if there was a guy from Ecuador fighting a guy from Poland, someone would tip Cosell off to the winner of the decision, and he would then predict the outcome on the air before the official announcement. He made himself look smarter by saying it on the air. He was a caricature of himself at the end. He got lucky with Muhammad Ali, who played along and made him a second banana. Cosell didn't do anything for Ali's career, but he liked to think he did."

The next time I saw Cosell after that Monday Night Football Game was at the NFL Draft in New York City. I was representing the Eagles, who would call me and tell me who they were selecting in the draft. I would then write the names of the players on cards and hand them to whoever was announcing the names at the podium. In other words, I pretty much knew who the Eagles were selecting before the commissioner or players did!

I remember this like it was yesterday. Cosell came walking into the building of the draft with NFL Commissioner Pete Rozelle. Cosell turned to Rozelle and said "Peter, slavery still exists in the National Football League. This is absolutely a farce perpetrated upon the American populace. The draft is illegal. These young men should have the right to pick the teams they want to go to, but this is unconstitutional. This is nothing but slavery in the 20th century." He continued to go on a tirade as he kept walking.

Yep. That was Howard Cosell for you.

CHAPTER 7

The Broad Street Bullies

I WAS WORKING as a soundman at WFIL-TV/Channel 6 the day the city of Philadelphia was awarded a National Hockey League franchise. The team would become the Philadelphia Flyers, and to be honest, people in the Tri-State area really didn't take too well to hockey during those early days. I remember tickets basically being given away, just to get people in the seats. I was at the game in 1968 when Red Berenson of the St. Louis Blues scored six goals against the Flyers, becoming the first and only (as of 2016) visiting player in NHL history to have that record. I would imagine the Flyers probably averaged around nine to 11 thousand fans per game during their first few years in the league. At the time, there certainly weren't any sellouts at the Spectrum, where the team played their home games.

Yes, it was a struggle for the Flyers in those years. During head coach Fred Shero's first season with the team in 1971-72, the team was eliminated from playoff contention on the last game of the season. Gerry Meehan of the Buffalo Sabres shot off an 80-footer with just seconds left in regulation. The puck got past Flyers goalie Doug Favell for a very unorthodox goal, resulting in a heartbreaking loss. The Flyers really didn't make their presence felt in the NHL until the next year, when they had their first winning season and beat the Minnesota North Stars for their first ever playoff series win. Even though the Flyers eventually lost to the Canadiens in the semifinals (now known as the conference finals), the team gained tremendous playoff experience.

Little by little, you saw signs of the Flyers improving. And in the 1973-74 season, everything finally came together.

I didn't cover the Flyers every day during the regular season that particular year, because I was still a sound technician. When the playoffs came around, however, I covered them extensively. In the first round of the postseason, the Flyers had an easy four game sweep of the Atlanta Flames and advanced to the semifinals against the New York Rangers. But despite going to the semifinals the previous year and having a regular season record of 50–16–12, the Flyers were still the underdogs against New York, in a series that came down to a seventh and deciding game. In the final game of the series, there was a brawl between Flyers winger Dave "The Hammer" Schultz and the Rangers' Dale Rolfe. For reasons only known to the Rangers, nobody on their team came to Rolfe's defense during that fight. There's been speculation for years as to whether the Rangers were or weren't intimidated by the physical presence of the Flyers. Nonetheless, the Rangers kind of limped out of the game, and the Flyers won the series four games to three to advance to the Stanley Cup.

The legend of the Broad Street Bullies really began to take hold during that series against the Rangers. Several years earlier, Flyers' owner Ed Snider and general manager Keith Allen made the decision to turn the Flyers into a tough, hard-nosed hockey team after being constantly outplayed from a physical standpoint by their opponent—notably the St. Louis Blues. The Flyers soon brought in such enforcers as Schultz, left winger Bob "The Hound" Kelly and defenseman André "Moose" Dupont. Simply put, the Flyers' brass didn't want to be pushed around anymore and wanted guys who would drop the gloves in a heartbeat. That's what those players did.

The Flyers' opponent in the 1974 Stanley Cup was the mighty Boston Bruins. Even though the Flyers were just one point behind the Bruins for the best record in the NHL that season, nobody gave them a hope in hell of beating Boston. With stars like Phil Esposito and Bobby Orr, the Bruins were just two years removed from their last Stanley Cup championship. Meanwhile, the Flyers were the upstarts. An expansion team who was accused of relying more on their fists than actual skill, which was ridiculous. To complicate matters, Boston had home ice advantage during the Stanley Cup. In their 19 previous games against the Bruins at the Boston Garden, the Flyers had lost 17 and tied them twice.

After losing the series opener in Boston, 3-2, things didn't look too good for the Flyers, and it looked even worse when they were trailing 2-1 in the closing moments of Game 2. But Andre Dupont tied the score with less than a minute left in regulation (and this was after Flyers goalie Bernie Parent was pulled!). Then, Bobby Clarke, the greatest Philadelphia Flyer ever, scored the game-winning goal in overtime. The Flyers won 3-2 and evened the series at one game apiece. After Game 2, the Flyers went on a roll, going back home to the Spectrum and winning Games 3 and 4 to take a shocking 3-1 series lead. However, the team went back to Boston and got promptly blown out in Game 5 by a 5-1 score. With a 3-2 series lead, the still-confident Flyers headed back to the Spectrum in Philadelphia for Game 6. In a nutshell, the team knew if they were going to win the series, they had to win that day. They did not want to have to go back to the Boston for a seventh and deciding game.

As it turned out, it wouldn't matter.

Early in Game 6, Dupont fired off a shot that Rick MacLeish tipped into the Bruins' net for a 1-0 Flyers lead. Two periods later, the score was the same, and that's how it stayed. I was in the runway of the Spectrum, and when the Bruins shot the puck down to the Flyers' side of the ice with just seconds left, it was over! The Spectrum erupted! The Flyers did it! They shocked the world! The team had become the first NHL expansion team in the post-Original Six era to win the Stanley Cup. Everybody stormed the ice, and I mean everybody! I was right out there with them, only I was a sound technician and had headphones on, while my cameraman was in front of me following the Stanley Cup around. Up until that time, I had never witnessed or been part of such a crazy fiasco, including the final game at Connie Mack Stadium!

After the celebration on the ice, we went into the Flyers' locker room, where it was just bedlam. Those players on that Flyers team were a special breed. All of them were Canadians and like most Philadelphians, just regular, down-to-earth guys. While they were celebrating, all of the Flyers were talking to the local sportscasters, calling them out by name. "Hey, Joe Pellegrino!" "Tom Brookshier!" "Al Meltzer!" Meanwhile, there I was, sitting there as a lonely producer, thinking to myself 'One of these days, I'll know every Flyer by name, just like those guys do.'

I had the honor of putting together a half-hour special for the Flyers' 1974 Stanley Cup parade. And as luck would have it, I put together another special when the team won the Stanley Cup again in 1975! This time, they beat the Buffalo Sabres in six games. I was in Philadelphia when the team got off the plane after winning the Cup in Buffalo. I remember either a lady or a man climbing a flagpole at the Philadelphia International Airport and they were stark naked. It was a wild scene. After celebrating two parades in as many years, the Philadelphia Flyers were officially the toast of the town. By the end of that season, I made good on that promise to myself and had every phone number of every player on that team. Those guys embraced me, and I really appreciated them.

Bobby Clarke, the captain of that Flyers team, was terrific: a catalyst in the truest sense of the word. Some guys are given the moniker of "captain," but Bobby was a true leader. He wasn't a vocal leader, but when he spoke, people knew Bobby Clarke meant business and he was the ultimate competitor. Whether it was a regular season game or in the Stanley Cup, Bobby did not like to lose. You had to play the Bobby Clarke way if you were a Philadelphia Flyer. When he walked in the room, he had a certain presence about him. Bobby was a diabetic and constantly trying to maintain his sugar level. Because of this, many had reservations as to whether he would even last in the National Hockey League. So much, in fact, that he fell to the second round in the 1969 NHL Draft. Needless to say, Bobby most likely surpassed the expectations of a lot of people.

Bobby was a tough cookie. One game, he suffered a cut from the bridge of his nose all the way down under his cheek. When the Flyers returned from a road trip and I went down to interview him at practice, the blood was still oozing out of his cuts. It was pretty intense. When I put the footage of his injury on the six o'clock news, my news director went ballistic. "You can't do that, Bill! People are eating dinner!" he screamed. I was able to cover up some of the footage with some B-roll, but that was quite a gash. In addition to his toughness, Bobby was a tireless worker who never wanted to come out of a game. He wouldn't sit out because he had a back issue or a tweak here and there. Bobby typified the spirit of the Broad Street Bullies. They weren't better than the Boston Bruins, but his grit and determination enabled the Flyers to beat them.

Sometimes, Bobby was accused of being a dirty player. I think some people might misconstrue that. Bobby pushed the envelope, but so did Gordie Howe. Great players will always push the envelope. That's the way he played hockey. Hard-nosed. You have to play with that sense of intensity. Some people say Pete Rose was a dirty player, but he played all out, all the time. If you go all out, all the time, you're gonna do anything to win. Sometimes, that means pushing the envelope because you're the ultimate competitor. Former Eagles quarterback Norm Van Brocklin didn't have the most talent around him when the Eagles won their last championship in 1960. But Van Brocklin, like Bobby, was able to get the most out of every individual on that squad. Fred Shero was a great strategist and motivator, but the Flyers never would have been successful if they didn't have Bobby on the ice. I'm thoroughly convinced of that. Every player revered him. Bobby Clarke was the heart and soul of that Flyers team, and everybody knew it.

One day, Bobby asked me if I could get him two Eagles season tickets he could purchase. Being that I had access to the Eagles, and I knew the team's general manager, Jim Murray, that wasn't a problem. About a month later, I was at the skating rink at the University of Pennsylvania, where the Flyers used to practice. Bobby called me over and told me to follow him over to the Spectrum, which I did. When we got there, Bobby opened the trunk of his car. It was filled with clothes.

"What do you want?" Bobby asked me.

"What do you mean what do I want?" I asked him back.

"Pick anything out that you want in the trunk," he said.

There was a nice brown leather jacket, so I picked that.

"No, Bill. Take all the clothes," Bobby insisted.

I was just astonished. At the time, Bobby was doing commercials for Jack Lange, a men's clothing chain, so I'm sure he had his pick of the litter regarding his wardrobe. There must have been three to four thousand dollars' worth of clothes in that trunk, and Bobby gave me everything. Suits, jackets, it was incredible. Some might say I compromised my integrity by taking what he offered me, but back then, stuff like that was harmless. It was never intended to be anything more than what it was. One day, Rick MacLeish was avoiding me at practice when I was looking to do an interview. I asked to speak to him a few times and he refused. Then one day, I was at the Spectrum during a team skate, and MacLeish asked me out of the blue if I wanted to do the interview. I was floored. He blew me off twice before. I later found out that Bobby told Rick to do that interview with me.

Bobby gave me an entree to the Flyers by laying the groundwork, and the rest of the guys followed suit. Reggie Leach, who came to the team after they beat the Bruins in the Stanley Cup, was great with me, as were brothers Jimmy and Joe Watson. They were favorites of mine and I built up a really nice bond with them. In fact, those two still come on my radio show to this day! One time in 1976, Joe and I drove to Yankee Stadium and watched Mark "The Bird" Fidrych pitch for the Detroit Tigers against the Yankees. We were about halfway through the game and we both smelled something funky behind us. It was some guy smoking marijuana in the seats. Right behind us in broad daylight!

I also got to know Flyers Hall of Fame goalie Bernie Parent, who suffered a devastating eye injury several years after the Flyers won their second Stanley Cup. While he was being treated at Thomas Jefferson University Hospital in Philadelphia, Bernie called my house and told my dad to tell me he was being released the next morning at 8:30 am, and to have a camera crew there. As a result, we were the only local news station to get coverage of Bernie leaving the hospital. Unfortunately, none of us knew at the time that Bernie would never play another game in the NHL. I'm not sure if he knew this either, but for him to be nice enough to call my house and do what he did during a very tough time in his life spoke volumes.

As much as they were loved in Philadelphia, however, the Philadelphia Flyers were booed by hockey fans in every NHL arena not named the Spectrum. They were absolutely hated by the rest of the league. If an opposing player took a shot at Clarke or MacLeish, believe me, Fred Shero would send Schultz or Kelly over the boards and that was it. They were the

*Interviewing Flyers legend and NHL Hall of Famer
Bill Barber, during my days at Channel 6.*

policemen, and nobody messed with those guys. As much as the Flyers were predominantly loathed around the NHL, however, the general public's animosity towards the team changed briefly on January 11, 1976, when they faced off against the Soviet Red Army Team in Philadelphia. During the first period of the game, Flyers defenseman Ed Van Impe speared Soviet player Valeri Kharlamov, which almost caused World War III. The next thing you knew, the Soviets walked off the ice! Flyers owner Ed Snider then warned the Soviet team that if they didn't come back and play, they wouldn't get paid. After the Russians had a caucus, they went back on the ice. The Flyers ended up winning the game, 4-1. For a brief moment, they were embraced by hockey and considered heroes because they brought down the Soviet team. After the game, Flyers' assistant trainer Jim McKenzie, who's become a dear friend of mine, told me to go into the Soviet's locker room. It was empty. The team took their towels and soap, put it in their bags, and left. They were in and out of there like rats. The Soviets never even showered after the game! I don't know whether this is coincidental or not, but for many years, the Flyers were not a team that drafted or signed many Russian players.

The Flyers may have beaten the Russians, but they couldn't beat the Montreal Canadiens for a third straight Stanley Cup the following May. Parent and MacLeish were injured, and the Canadiens swept the series four games to none. Every game was decided by one goal, except Game 4, which the Flyers lost at the Spectrum, 5-3. Although Flyers fans stood up and applauded their team for their accomplishments over the previous two seasons at the end of the final game, there was a lot of disappointment because everybody was expecting a three-peat (although they didn't use that term back then). Canadiens goalie Ken Dryden played tremendous hockey against the Flyers that series. He stood on his head and just played out of his mind. You can't take that away from him.

After the Flyers' Stanley Cup loss in 1976, Dave Schultz was traded to the Los Angeles Kings and the identity of the Broad Street Bullies began to change. Despite having solid regular seasons in 1977 and 1978, the Flyers failed to return to the Stanley Cup. The team reached the semifinals during those years, but lost both times to the Bruins, who in turn lost back to back Stanley Cups to the Canadiens. Right around the end of the 1977-78 season, rumors started circulating that Fred Shero was contemplating resigning as the Flyers head coach. I think Fred was possibly talking to the New York Rangers through a third party at the time. He may have seen the writing on the wall and thought he took the team as far as they could go. Whether those certain rumors were true or not, by late May 1978, Fred had turned in his resignation. Although he denied talking with any NHL teams at the time, he was soon named general manager and head coach of the Rangers.

I got along well with all of the Flyers and the members of their organization- except for Fred Shero, who was rather standoffish to me. Fred would often refer to me as "That skinny little *blankety blank*" whenever he'd see me at practice. He was a little paranoid and couldn't figure out who I was. At the time, only newspaper guys were covering the team on a regular basis, while I might have been with them once or twice a week. Even though I didn't have to deal with him anymore, the loss of Fred was the end of a great era in Flyers hockey, and a tough pill to swallow for Bobby Clarke. I think Bobby felt very betrayed when Fred left. He probably didn't understand why Fred would take the team as far as he did, only to leave them for the hated Rangers. Nobody understood it, really, especially the guys who were the remnants of those Stanley Cup teams. It took the air out of the balloon for a lot of them. Fred was getting a bundle of money to go to New York, but the Flyers couldn't relate to that. Despite the fact that they accomplished as much as they did, they weren't money-grabbing players. Through it all, they seemed just like you and me, and a story that took place on the night of Fred Shero's resignation proved just that.

There was once a restaurant in Roxborough, Pennsylvania called Speedy Morris's Drop in the Bucket, which was owned by future La Salle University college basketball coach Speedy Morris. Speedy asked me if I could get Flyers winger (and current team president) Paul Holmgren to ask Bobby Clarke if he would make an appearance at his establishment for two hundred dollars. Before coaching at LaSalle, Speedy coached at Roman Catholic High School in Philadelphia, and I got Paul his first assistant coaching job with Speedy in a summer league. Paul ended up asking Bobby and he said yes. According to the fire marshal, I believe the capacity for 'Drop in the Bucket' was 160. You know how many people were in Roxborough the night Bobby came out? Over one thousand! They were waiting in the streets to see Bobby and to get his autograph. I had to introduce Speedy to Bobby Clarke to complete the transaction. Instead of taking Speedy's money, however, Bobby tore up the check and put it in the waste basket.

"That pays for the beer for all my players," Bobby said.

Not only did Bobby show up, but so did Paul and about ten other Flyers.

Even though the Flyers continued to draft young players like Mel Bridgman, Ken Linseman and Behn Wilson in the mid to late seventies, it was the same result at the end of each year: no Stanley Cup. In addition to the departure of their head coach, players were slowly but surely moving on as well. Center Orest Kindrachuk was traded to the Penguins, Don "Big Bird" Saleski and Joe Watson were traded to the Colorado Rockies (then a hockey team), and Parent had to retire after that horrible eye injury. The Flyers hired Bob McCammon to coach the team after Fred Shero left, and he was fired midway through the 1978-79 season. He was replaced by the late Pat Quinn, whom I got along with famously. Years later, Pat went to law school and got his degree from the Widener University School of Law in Delaware, which I did a story on with Al Meltzer. Going into the 1979-80 season, some of the faces had changed, but Pat was once again at the helm as the Flyers embarked on one of the most memorable and surprising seasons in club history.

From October 14, 1979 to January 6, 1980, the Philadelphia Flyers had a 35-game unbeaten streak. With a record of 25–0–10 during that stretch, they didn't lose a single game! In the process, the team set a North American sports record that still stands to this day. I remember interviewing Pat at the airport when the team came home from Buffalo after setting the record. The younger players were blending in nicely with the veterans, as rookie Brian Propp excelled playing with Bobby Clarke and Reggie Leach. With a final regular season record of 48-12-20, the Flyers'

116 points in the Patrick Division dwarfed the second place New York Islanders' 91 points. After losing to Fred Shero's Rangers in the 1979 quarterfinals, the Flyers got their revenge by beating them in a quarterfinals rematch. After beating Minnesota in the semifinals and advancing to their fourth Stanley Cup in seven seasons, the Flyers were favorites against the New York Islanders.

However, what seemed like a storybook season up to that point turned into a nightmare of a finish.

After a stunning overtime loss in Game 1 at the Spectrum, the Flyers evened the series 1-1 in Game 2. However, history would not repeat itself the way it did in 1974. In fact, the exact opposite happened to the Flyers this time around. The Islanders dominated the Flyers in Games 3 and 4 to take a 3-1 series lead. The Flyers won Game 5 in Philadelphia, and the team travelled to the Nassau Coliseum in Long Island, New York for Game 6. The contest, which took place on the Saturday afternoon of Memorial Day weekend, featured a terrible, terrible botched offsides call that is one of the biggest blown calls in the history of hockey. I watched all of this unravel from the press box, and it wasn't pretty. With the score tied 1-1, the Islanders scored on an offsides play that referee Leon Stickle allowed, despite furious protests from the Flyers. The momentum of the game clearly changed on that play. The Islanders eventually built a 4-2 lead. The Flyers came back and tied the score at 4-4, but Islanders winger Bobby Nystrom scored an overtime goal which won the Islanders the game and the Stanley Cup, 5-4.

After the game, Flyers owner Ed Snider was beside himself. He went outside the officials' dressing room, ready to take on Stickle and anybody else. He was not happy. Don Tollefson, a colleague of mine from the news station, instructed me to go down to the Flyers' locker room and gather players to interview while he prepared for his live shot. I went in there, and it was like a morgue. Just absolutely morbid. The Flyers were stunned. They couldn't believe it. Being down 3-1 to the Islanders, the offsides call that Stickle blew, losing the Cup after such a successful season. Everything. The Flyers never got back to the Stanley Cup with that group of players. Game 6 against the Islanders was Bob Kelly's last game as a Flyer, as he was traded to the Washington Capitals prior to the 1980-81 season. The next year, Rick MacLeish would be traded to the Hartford Whalers. What started to disintegrate after their Stanley Cup loss to the Canadiens was unofficially made official after their loss to the Islanders: The Broad Street Bullies were no more.

The Philadelphia Flyers were not only the first team to openly embrace me, but they were probably the first team that wholeheartedly embraced the city of Philadelphia. Here was a sports fan base once lukewarm, if not completely skeptical, of hockey coming to our city. But after the Flyers adopted the personality of Philadelphia, that all changed. Everybody related to them. Their community work endeared them to the fans, who hung out at bars and had drinks with them. Philadelphia needed a champion. The Phillies hadn't won a pennant since 1950. The Eagles were in the doldrums, and even though the Sixers weren't that far removed from winning a title in 1967, they were in the process of coming off a terrible year that saw them go 9-73. The landscape of sports was changing dramatically in the 1970s. People were covering sports more and more and it exploded in Philadelphia. That's why I got my job! Right after the Flyers started winning, the Phillies had one of the most successful eras in their history, the Eagles hired Dick Vermeil as their head coach, and the Sixers got Julius "Dr. J" Erving.

Of course, the fee would be much higher now, but could you see a present day athlete ripping up a check like Bobby Clarke did that night in 1978? Exactly! By winning back to back Stanley Cups, the Broad Street Bullies raised the bar and set the standard for everyone that followed in their path.

They're the most beloved Philadelphia sports team of all time.

CHAPTER 8

Bill White, Bob Gibson and the Historic Night That Never Was

AT LONG LAST, all my hard work seemed to be paying off in dividends. In September 1974, I officially became the first full-time sports producer in the city of Philadelphia. WFIL was bought by Capital Cities Broadcasting and became WPVI-TV/Channel 6. We had a great team: sportscasters Joe Pellegrino, Steve Levy (not to be confused with the ESPN sportscaster), Don Tollefson and quite a few others along the way. Those guys gave me free reign to do all the interviews with the Eagles, Flyers, Phillies and Sixers. Speaking of the Sixers, I was there the night the team signed Julius "Dr. J." Erving in 1976. With the recent success of the Flyers and the emerging Phillies starting to put the pieces together, it was a fun time to be a sports fan in Philadelphia.

Then one day in 1977, Bill White called me and made me an offer to be his statistician on ABC's *Monday Night Baseball*. I was honored that Bill even thought of me and I took the job without hesitation! When Bill wasn't doing play-by-play, I would work with his partner, Jim Lampley.

The first time I worked a Monday Night Baseball game was on July 25, 1977 in a contest featuring the Cincinnati Reds and the St. Louis Cardinals. Bill told me to dress for success, so I flew out to St. Louis wearing my best suit. I was ready. The game was only going to be seen on the West Coast, as the Yankees and Red Sox both had games that night (although not against each other). For some reason, Lampley was unavailable, so Bill was paired with his old Cardinals teammate, Bob Gibson, for the game. When I got wind of this, I realized something special would be taking place that evening, and I turned to Curt Gowdy, Jr., the lead producer during the production meeting, and informed him of it.

49

"You know, we're going to make history tonight," I told him.

"What do you mean?" Curt asked.

"Do you realize we have two black announcers who are going to be broadcasting this game to part of the nation? This is a historic event," I said.

Of course, they didn't build up something like this back in the day, although Curt took a little notation down of it. When we arrived at the ballpark, however, we were informed that there was rain on the East Coast, and that the network would be flying broadcaster Al Michaels in for our game. As a result, Bill and Bob would now be the color commentators, and Michaels would be the play-by-play guy.

I didn't have a computer back then, but I had all these stats. I mean stats upon stats. If Pete Rose had a certain batting average during a certain time of the day in 1976, I had it, and I relayed these stats to Michaels during the game. I did so well that Michaels turned to me after the game and said "You did one hell of a job, kid."

I took an early flight back to Philadelphia the next morning and went to work at Channel 6. When I got home that night, my mother told me there was a message for me from a Mr. Michaels. He left a phone number and I called him at his home in California. The call went something like this.

"Al, this is Bill Werndl."

"Hi Bill. I want you to be my statistician on Monday Night Baseball from now on," Michaels said.

Yep. So in one of my worst decisions of all time from a career standpoint, I informed Al that I had the upmost respect for Bill White, and that I wouldn't be able to take the position. I told him I really appreciated the offer and it was awfully nice of him, but I was committed to Bill and Jim Lampley. Al said he understood and that was that.

Afterwards, I called Bill and told him what happened. He couldn't believe I did such a thing and wondered why I stayed with him. He emphasized how Michaels was on the rise and that I had to take that job! I was loyal to Bill because he gave me an opportunity to work on Monday Night Baseball and I felt an obligation to him. To this day, Bill still reminds me that it was not a good call, but Al Michaels knew where I was coming from.

While I have absolutely nothing against Al Michaels, he shouldn't have even been at that game in St. Louis to begin with. I was very disappointed with the network because there was no doubt in my mind they were a little reluctant to have a game televised nationwide featuring two black broadcasters. You have to remember we'd just gone through a very tumultuous time in our society. The 60s were a turbulent time of racial unrest, and I believe ABC was afraid of the possible reverberation that could happen at that time. The mindset we have today is a lot different than it was almost 40 years ago. ABC would've made a historic move in race relations if they let Bill do play-by-play and Bob Gibson do color commentary that night. It would have put a stamp on it. I'm not blaming Curt Gowdy, Jr. for this. He had to answer to Roone Arledge, the president of ABC Sports. I think it was a natural reaction to get their number one play-by-play man

Working with Bob Gibson in 1977, on the night history was almost made.

in Michaels to call the game, but I also think they were afraid and worried about public reaction.

I'm not blasting ABC, and Michaels is outstanding, but they should have made a statement that they were moving forward. And regardless of whatever happened in the past, they were shifting into first gear and not neutral. I don't recall a chance like that ever happening again to the best of my knowledge, and it's a real shame. It would've been a perfect scenario to break down those racial barriers that have been present in our society for so long.

CHAPTER 9

Stanley "The Hammer" Burrell: The Eyes and Ears of the Oakland A's

STANLEY BURRELL WAS a "batboy" for the Oakland Athletics at Oakland Alameda County Coliseum from 1973 until 1980. Stanley would entertain and regularly dance outside the pavement when the A's fans would enter the stadium. Now despite their success in the first half of the 1970s, keep in mind the A's never really drew many fans to begin with, so it probably wasn't a large crowd Stanley would dance to, but I digress.

Back in August 1978, I just so happened to be working the Game of the Week for ABC out in Oakland, and I saw Stanley's act in person. During my travels as a producer and soundman at Channel 6, I had the pleasure of meeting Jim Essian, a former Phillies player who was now playing for Oakland. The A's were taking infield practice, and I looked up and saw this kid who looked about 16 years old, in a full green and gold A's uniform, taking ground balls at shortstop.

"Hey Jim, who's the guy at shortstop?" I asked.

"He's the second most powerful guy in the organization," he responded.

"What?!" I asked in disbelief.

"He's the eyes and ears of Charlie Finley," Jim said.

Charlie Finley was the colorful (if not clueless) owner of the A's. Finley, who wasn't exactly what you would call a conventional owner by any stretch, took a liking to Burrell. The next thing you knew, Burrell was given an honorary position as the club's executive vice president! He was only a teenager! Hey, I said Finley was unconventional. Whenever Finley stayed in his primary residence in Chicago, Burrell, after working out with the team, would sit in Finley's owner's box, which had a telephone installed, and he'd take calls from Finley's offices! So ABC came up with the idea to put a microphone in Finley's box. There was no internet or satellite television back then, so Burrell was literally Finley's play-by-play guy and he would relay what was going on during the game to wherever Finley was.

ABC happened to record the interactions between Burrell and Finley, and used some excerpts from the game. For example, Burrell would tell Finley 'Hey, this pitcher is losing his stuff. We need to get somebody up in the bullpen,' or 'Our guy was a little slow getting to that ground ball at second base.' Then Finley would say 'Get someone else in at second base. Call down to the manager.' Burrell also had a phone to the dugout, and he'd go and tell the team's manager whatever Finley wanted. I also got the impression from Essian that Burrell would also report on players he didn't like, and that you'd better be nice to him.

Burrell left the A's after graduating high school and later spent several years in the Navy. If by some small chance you're wondering what ever happened to him, don't worry. He achieved worldwide fame and fortune about a decade later under his better known stage name: M.C. Hammer. But back in 1978, he was indeed Charlie Finley's guy.

He literally had the hammer.

CHAPTER 10

Dick Vermeil: Philly's Most Influential Coach

AFTER THE PHILADELPHIA Eagles severed ties with head coach Mike McCormick following a disastrous 1975 season, Eagles owner Leonard Tose and general manager Jim Murray had their sights set on Penn State head coach Joe Paterno. Despite rolling out the red carpet for Paterno, they struck out with him. The two then decided to go out to the West Coast to try and recruit a young, upstart head coach named Dick Vermeil, whose UCLA Bruins just upset the undefeated and number one ranked Ohio State Buckeyes in the Rose Bowl.

Dick Vermeil represented the state of California through and through. He was born in northern California and he was coaching college football in southern California. The West Coast was his love. Trying to convince Vermeil to come to Philadelphia was not easy and a little bit of a gamble. The Eagles had run amok. So much to the point that Murray told Vermeil that the fans would give him a standing ovation if he just won the coin toss! After a seven week search, Vermeil officially became the Eagles' 14th head coach in team history on February 8, 1976.

Vermeil's task of turning around the Eagles was probably a tougher job than most NFL head coaches ever had. Due to trades involving quarterback Roman Gabriel and middle linebacker Bill Bergey, the Eagles did not have a draft choice until the fourth round of the 1976 NFL Draft and the fifth round in 1977. Most of the talent Vermeil acquired was through trades or required some level of creativity. Some players, like cornerback Herman Edwards, signed with the team as an undrafted free agent. Keep in mind there was no free agency or multi-million dollar deals in the NFL back then. The Eagles had nothing, but Dick was not a guy who was going to roll over and play dead. Never once did he complain that he didn't have the resources that the Dallas Cowboys or New York Giants had.

One defining moment early on in Vermeil's coaching career with the Eagles came during his first training camp in the summer of 1976. The Eagles had a cornerback named Joe Lavender, who refused to report to camp. Vermeil, who wanted to establish an 'all for one and one for all' culture with his new team, gave Lavender a one week ultimatum to report to the Eagles. When Lavender decided to push the envelope, he was traded to the Washington Redskins for tackle Manny Sistrunk and three draft picks. The Eagles used one of these draft picks to select running back Wilbert Montgomery, who was a sixth round pick in the 1977 NFL Draft. With the Lavender trade, Vermeil was slowly changing the mindset of the Philadelphia Eagles. He was so focused and obsessed with getting a job done that one time he screamed at somebody to stop the fireworks going off outside his window during the Fourth of July. Keep in mind that was our country's Bicentennial!

I met Dick for the first time around March of 1976. Dick was a very active runner back in the day, and I did a story on him running around Veterans Stadium getting ready for the season. In the next few months, I also saw him during Eagles training camp at Widener University. Being a spotter for the Eagles, I would go on to see Dick every weekend the Eagles played football for the next seven years. You can throw the laid back, California stereotype out the window with Vermeil. Tunnel vision to the umpteenth degree. One time, I interviewed Wilbert Montgomery, and asked him whether he thought he should eventually be converted from running back to wide receiver to prolong his career, much like the Redskins' Charlie Taylor did. I ran the story on the six o'clock news that night and shortly after the broadcast, I got a call from Dick. Needless to say, he was not enamored with the story or my idea. I'll leave it at that. Another time, I appeared on middle linebacker Bill Bergey's radio show with Bill and Eagles' play-by- play announcer Charlie Swift. Prior to that show, I got a report that the Baltimore Colts were interested in Bergey. I gave the tip to my guys at Channel 6 and they reported it. Although the trade never happened and Bergey ended up staying with the Eagles for the rest of his career, Dick was not happy with me in the least after that story was reported!

Then there was the Eagles' 1980 season opener against the Denver Broncos. My colleague at Channel 6, Steve Levy, called me at home and asked me if we had any video of the Eagles' recent practices he could show during his sports broadcast. I had video in my drawer and told him where it was. Little did Steve or I know that the Eagles were practicing a spot pass that week, and little did we know that the Broncos flew in that weekend and might have been watching our news broadcast! The Eagles never used the spot pass in the game and still blew out the Broncos, 27-6! After the game, Eagles public relations director Jim Gallagher told me the coach wanted to see me. When Dick asked me why I would use that footage, I completely took the blame. I told him it was my fault, and that if he waved me off that day at practice, I never would have shot or aired the video. Being that the Eagles won, he just kind of looked at me and smiled, but I made sure not to let that happen again.

Later that season, we travelled to Seattle to play the Seahawks. After we arrived at the team hotel, Dick was on his way to a team meeting when he was verbally accosted in an elevator by four white guys. Those "gentlemen" used some pretty vicious terms that were so derogatory I probably couldn't even print them in this book.

"Hey Dick, you have too many n*****s on your team!" yelled one guy.

That was all it took for Dick to go nuts. He was so livid, you could see the veins popping out of his neck. He was fit to be tied. I had to calm him down along with the late Eagles' statistician Jack Edelstein, because he was incensed and was going to kill those guys! Whether his players were black, white or hispanic, Dick loved each and every one of them equally. Some have even accused Dick of holding on to a few of them for too long out of loyalty for making him a successful coach. You can make whatever you want out of that, but whether you were the 45th player or first player on the roster, Dick Vermeil didn't treat his players like pieces of meat. They were family to him, and he was going after those guys in the elevator as if someone hurt a member of his family. He was that mad!

Even though Dick previously spent three seasons as an assistant coach for the Los Angeles Rams, Eagles fans were initially a little skeptical regarding his hiring. Here was this California guy coming from the college ranks, which wasn't something too common in those days. The Eagles were a team that fell on hard times and the fans rightfully didn't have much faith in anybody! In the beginning, there were some lean years, but right around his third season with the team in 1978, the foundations he was building began to take shape. That season saw the Eagles finally return the playoffs for the first time in 18 seasons. Unfortunately, they lost the Wild Card game to the Atlanta Falcons, 14-13. The Eagles had a 13-0 lead going into the fourth quarter, but the kicking team was suspect after they lost kicker Nick Mike-Mayer at the end of the regular season to a rib injury. His replacement, Mike Michel, was really a punter masquerading as a kicker, and he missed a game-winning field goal with seconds remaining. The Eagles also made the playoffs in 1979. This time, they squared off against the Tampa Bay Buccaneers. Late in that game, kicker Tony Franklin ignored Vermeil's order for a long kick, and decided to go for an onside kick. Vermeil was not happy about that at all! The attempt failed, and the Eagles lost, 24-17.

After several seasons of disheartening playoff losses, the Eagles and Dick Vermeil finally made believers out of everybody in 1980. They came out of the gate with all guns blazing. On the Sunday the Phillies beat the Kansas City Royals in Games 5 of the 1980 World Series to take a 3-2 series lead, the Eagles beat their fierce rivals, the Dallas Cowboys, 17-10 at Veterans Stadium. A month later, the Eagles beat the Oakland Raiders at home, 10-7, in a knock-down, drag-out affair. With that win, the Eagles' record improved to 11-1, and the team was feeling really, really good about things. After seeing how far this team had come over the previous four years, it was amazing to watch. The team finished with a regular season record of 12-4. In the NFC Divisional Playoffs, the Eagles beat the Minnesota Vikings rather easily, 31-16. The only thing that now stood between the team and their very first Super Bowl appearance was an NFC Championship Game showdown against the hated Dallas Cowboys.

Philadelphia's dislike for the Cowboys is basically a birthright, and here's a brief history lesson as to *why* the Cowboys are so despised in the city. Back in 1967, the Eagles played the Cowboys in a late season game in Dallas. During the game, which turned out to be a Cowboys rout, Dallas middle-linebacker Lee Roy Jordan delivered a cheap shot to Eagles running back/kick returner Timmy Brown. The hit left Brown with a fractured jaw and six loose teeth. While Brown was left seeing stars on the ground, Jordan stepped over him and was doing a lot of trash talking. Brown was a very popular player in Philadelphia, and that's when the hatred towards the Cowboys really built up.

While Eagles fans were hopeful as the big game approached, I don't recall them being overly confident that their team was facing off against "America's Team" on that cold, cold, Sunday afternoon in January 1981. Some fans didn't think the team stood a chance at all. The same can't be said for the Eagles themselves. As they stood in the tunnel waiting to take the field that day, they knew they were going to beat Dallas. The energy at Veterans Stadium was palpable from the outset, and when Wilbert Montgomery rushed for a 42-yard touchdown early in the game, the crowd of 71,000 at Veterans Stadium was going berserk! The Cowboys were the best scoring team in the NFL that year, but they were absolutely helpless against the Eagles defense. The final score was 20-7, Eagles. The team was now on their way to New Orleans to face the Oakland Raiders in Super Bowl XV.

Unfortunately, this story doesn't have a happy ending. The Super Bowl, which I spotted working alongside Eagles broadcaster Merrill Reese, was a disaster. Eagles quarterback Ron Jaworski, who had a shaky NFC Championship Game against Dallas, threw three interceptions that were picked off by Oakland linebacker Rod Martin. The Eagles were never able to get anything going, and the Raiders routed them, 27-10. I'll never forget that day as long as I live. I honestly thought the Eagles were going to win that game. However, if you ever watch the footage of the team coming out of the runway in New Orleans prior to Super Bowl kickoff, the team collectively looked like a pack of deer caught in the headlights. Over the years, I've heard some fans and commentators blame Dick for overworking the team in the weeks leading up to the Super Bowl. You can't say they were overworked, but they had a few weeks to think about where they were headed, and it seemed like they were surprised to be there. In retrospect, the Eagles beating the Cowboys for the NFC Championship was really their Super Bowl.

The 1980 season was as good as it would get for Vermeil and those Eagles teams. The following season in 1981, they suffered a disappointing loss in the NFC Wildcard Game to the Giants at Veterans Stadium. Then there was an NFL player's strike in 1982, which took a lot out of Dick. Linebacker John Bunting, who was the Eagles players' representative for the NFL Players Association and a member of the Executive Committee, took an active role in the strike.

Just before the work stoppage, I approached John in the Eagles locker room. Knowing the team was going to strike very soon, I thought I'd give him my two cents about what I thought the players should get out of a possible new agreement with the NFL owners. First off, it was my opinion they needed to eliminate AstroTurf, because it was ruining a lot of players' careers. Second, they needed a better pension fund that was almost comparable to baseball's. Maybe not as great, but close. Third, the players needed medical insurance after their playing days ended.

John had been talking to Tom Condon, then a Kansas City Chiefs offensive lineman who's now arguably the most powerful agent in football. Tom thought free agency was more of a priority than medical insurance. I think it was wrong they sidestepped that issue. That had to be addressed back then. I knew John well and still do. To this day, I feel very badly that I wasn't more forceful with him about that. I don't think Dick ever held a grudge against John for his role in the strike, but I think by this time, he was just mentally and physically spent. Whether it was the first day of training camp or a meaningless final game of a season, Dick was in full force all the time.

To a certain extent, his players might have been exhausted, too. During training camp that year, three-time Pro Bowl defensive tackle Charlie Johnson could no longer deal with Dick's program and asked to be traded. When the team returned after the strike in November 1982, they were in lousy physical shape. Also that season, Carl Peterson, Dick's administrative assistant and future chief executive officer of the Kansas City Chiefs, left the Eagles after an offer to be part owner and president of the Philadelphia Stars of the USFL. The years it took Dick to get the Eagles back to respectability, combined with the tough Super Bowl loss, the playoff loss to the Giants, the strike and all these other intangibles most likely took its collective toll on him. A week after the season ended, the Eagles called a press conference. Citing burnout, a tearful Dick resigned, claiming he needed a break from coaching. I don't recall anybody seeing this coming or reporting a possible resignation before it happened. As I recall, the press conference was kind of thrown together quickly. Despite what happened since the Super Bowl, Dick's resignation definitely came as a surprise to everybody. Here was this great coach who was so beloved in this town, and suddenly, he was gone.

After leaving the Eagles, Dick got into broadcasting with ABC and CBS and found plenty of things to do to keep himself busy. There was talk that Dick and Eagles' owner Jeffrey Lurie once discussed his possible return to the Eagles, but for the most part, everybody thought he was done coaching for good. That all changed in 1997, when Dick returned to the NFL as head coach of the St. Louis Rams. The NFL was a different league than it was in 1982, and Dick had to adjust. In his first two seasons, the Rams struggled mightily, and I thought he wasn't going to make it. Then, in his third season, Dick turned things around. The Rams drafted wide receiver Torry Holt and acquired running back Marshall Faulk in a trade with the Colts. In addition to wide receiver Isaac Bruce, the Rams became "The Greatest Show on Turf." Led by quarterback Kurt Warner, Dick finally won the Super Bowl that had eluded him since that dreadful Super Bowl loss to the Raiders in New Orleans back in 1981. What he did in just three seasons with that Rams team was unbelievable. I was so happy for Dick, and so was the majority of the Delaware Valley. As a result of his efforts, he was named NFL Coach of the Year for the 1999 season.

However, days after the Rams' Super Bowl victory, Dick announced he was stepping down from coaching the team. He was walking off into the sunset as a Super Bowl-winning coach. It was perfect. Almost too perfect.

Without naming names, I think several members of the Rams organization were politicians making noise behind the scenes and they wanted Dick out of there. He had two years left on his contract and returned to coaching a year later with the Kansas City Chiefs. What does that tell you?! He still wanted to coach! The Rams, with Dick's talent, returned to the Super Bowl two years later, and lost! If Dick was coaching, they would have won! This is my opinion, and I'm gonna stick to it!

Despite last coaching the Eagles over 30 years ago, Dick Vermeil never left Philadelphia, and that's why he's still loved there. He's kept a home in the Philadelphia area and is always giving back. He's been involved with countless charities over the last several decades, including the Boy Scouts of America. Every year for the last two decades, he's hosted the Dick Vermeil Invitational Golf Tournament in Pennsylvania, hosted by the Chester County Council. He is so widely regarded by his players that many of them readily show up at the event without hesitation. Not too long ago, I called Dick and asked him if he would be able to speak to my students at Widener University, where I teach a class. I knew he was busy and it was short notice. It didn't matter to Dick. He cut me off in the middle of my sentence and asked me what time I wanted him there! That's the kind of guy Dick is. He showed up and spoke to my students for 55 minutes. They were absolutely captivated and enthralled by him.

Dick Vermeil's legend only grows as time goes on. Looking back, the way Dick established character on his Eagles teams isn't dissimilar to what Chip Kelly is trying to do with this current Eagles squad. However, Dick didn't have the resources and free agency that Kelly has. Back then, if a player got cut, then you could sign him, but that was it. The late Eagles owner Leonard Tose would have spent a bundle on free agency if it had existed back then. This is why, in my opinion, Dick Vermeil should be a member of the Pro Football Hall of Fame. I know John Madden was a television darling and he has all the video games and notoriety, but look at the players he inherited from John Rauch after he took the Raiders head coaching job. Art Shell and Jim Otto are Hall of Famers. When Dick took over the Eagles, he had Roman Gabriel, Bill Bergey, Charle Young, Jerry Sisemore, Stan Walters and Mike Boryla. That's about it. These guys were

I spotted every game Dick Vermeil coached in his seven
seasons with the Philadelphia Eagles.

good players, but not Hall of Famers. No other coach would have been able to take that Eagles team he inherited in 1976 and have them in the Super Bowl four years later. He built a team from below the ground up. To the people out there who say Dick doesn't belong in the Hall of Fame, you'd better do your homework! You'd better do your homework!

To this day, Dick Vermeil is the most influential sports coach or manager I've ever been around in Philadelphia sports.

CHAPTER 11

The 1980 Philadelphia Phillies:
The Team That Wouldn't Die

1980 WAS JUST an unbelievably historic year for Philadelphia sports, and I was right in the middle of it.

The Flyers played in a controversial Stanley Cup against the Islanders, the Sixers reached the NBA Finals and were almost singlehandedly defeated by Los Angeles Lakers rookie Magic Johnson, who stepped in for an injured Kareem Abdul-Jabbar and scored 42 points in the series' final game at the Spectrum. I actually interviewed Magic and his teammate Jamaal Wilkes before and after that game. The Eagles also played for a championship that season and reached their first Super Bowl.

And last but not least, there was the 1980 Philadelphia Phillies.

Being around that Phillies team in spring training, you could tell there was something special about them. Even though their core group was aging and they were coming off a disappointing 1979 season, spring training had a certain feel to it. After taking over the Phillies in September of the previous season, new Phillies manager Dallas Green had evaluated the team and was not afraid to ruffle feathers or replace veteran players with youngsters who could get the job done.

I first met Dallas Green when he was the Phillies' farm director. He was originally signed by the team after graduating from the University of Delaware, but was just an average pitcher. I remember one time going out to his farm in Southern Chester County and interviewing him on a tractor. Dallas told it like it was, never pulled any punches and would answer questions directly. That team was in shock when they first met him. Danny Ozark, the Phillies' former manager, was low key and really laid-back, but Dallas shot from the hip. There was no nonsense with him.

Greg Luzinski was a very popular player for the Phillies and a favorite of team president Ruly Carpenter, but his numbers had declined and Green would frequently start rookie Lonnie Smith in his place in left field. Keith Moreland would take longtime catcher Bob Boone's place behind the plate for most of that summer as well. Both Smith and Moreland turned out to be key components of that team, and rookies Bob Walk and Marty Bystrom stepped in when injuries depleted the Phillies' starting rotation. Bystrom was just lights out. Nobody thought he could do what he ended up doing. He's the greatest September call-up in baseball history.

Then there was the Phillies' bullpen, which included youngsters Kevin Saucier and Dickie Noles. I just so happened to be in a bar with those guys one evening in Clearwater, Florida during spring training. I was talking with a young lady, when her boyfriend came in and shoved me. I was innocently talking with this girl, but her boyfriend wanted to make a big deal out of it. Well, Saucier and Noles happened to see this from the other side of the bar, and they walked over to the guy. Dickie, who was pretty tuned up after a few beers, was going to lay this guy out. He was gonna kill him.

"Hey man, he's our friend. Get outta here!" Dickie warned the guy, and he was gone. I still tell this story to Dickie and we have a good laugh about it!

Even though those Phillies teams during that time were sometimes perceived as a surly bunch of guys with a chip on their shoulder, I really enjoyed them. After the games, players like Garry Maddox and Bake McBride would go over to the Holiday Inn next to Veterans Stadium for a few "pops." Maddox, Noles, Smith, Boone, Walk, Bystrom, Pete Rose and Larry Bowa were all guys that would talk to you with no issues. I always got along very well with big Ron Reed, the team's 6'6" setup guy. Second baseman Manny Trillo gave you limited answers, but that was more of a language barrier than anything. Mike Schmidt could be kind of distant, but you could get comments out of him. Overall, I cannot say any of those guys gave me a hard time, and Phillies reliever Tug McGraw was on a whole other level. Tug was great. Just tremendous. One night after a game, I had a problem with my car. Knowing I lived near him in the Philadelphia suburbs of Media, Tug readily offered to give me a ride home. When he dropped me off, I asked him if he wanted to come inside for a drink. Next thing you know, Tug was leaving my house at 4:30 am in the morning. Tug McGraw was a nice, nice man. He had his demons and issues, but I guess we all do, really.

Now back to the season. To say I knew the Phillies would end up in the 1980 World Series would be an absolute lie, but the vibe coming out of spring training was one of urgency. Time was ticking for this team, and there was an overwhelming feeling that, when all was said and done, they really wanted to accomplish something special.

"Even though we had so many great players who were fairly young who had all grown up together, the clock was running on that team. I think that's a good way to put it," says Chris Wheeler, a broadcaster for the 1980 Phillies. "The number one thing at that time was that the Phillies made the decision things weren't going to happen with Danny Ozark as the manager. In those days, you could actually have somebody go down and manage that could take over and run things with an iron fist. That doesn't happen anywhere in sports today for a variety of reasons. Paul Owens had Dallas Green sitting there. They had the perfect guy in place. They also knew Dallas would have a short shelf life with the way he does the things that he does, but they felt 'Why not? Let's take a shot with Dallas.' The rest is history. It worked."

The assessment Chris offers is accurate. It wasn't all sunshine and rainbows between Dallas and the players. It wasn't quite like the scuffling Oakland A's of the early 1970s, but it was close enough. There was some jealousy amongst certain players, and the relationship between Dallas and most of the team was anything but warm and fuzzy. While Bowa was a very chirpy-like guy, a player like Schmidt was more refined. However, once the team took the field, it was all for one and one for all. That team had a Memorial Day fight against the hated Pittsburgh Pirates that was the stuff of legends! Look it up!

While the 1980 Phillies sometimes took their aggressions out on the field, it didn't always translate into wins. In early August, the team lost four in a row in a weekend series against the Pirates. I remember interviewing some of the players at the airport prior to the trip, and they weren't exactly the most positive bunch. With the exception of the first game of the Pirates series, none of the other games were close. By the time the series ended on Sunday, the Phillies were six games out of first place. A lot of people thought the team was dead. Even by the middle of September, they were still two and a half games out of first place. Then suddenly, the Phillies somehow caught lightning in a bottle. The last weekend of the season saw the team travel to Montreal tied for first place with the Expos. The Phillies won the first game on Friday to take a one-game lead in the National League East standings. The next day was a Saturday afternoon/ early evening game that saw the Phillies trailing 4-3 and down to their last out in the ninth inning, before Bob Boone tied the game with a base hit. In the top of the tenth inning, Schmidt hit a two-run blast that put the Phillies up 6-4. Three defensive outs later, the team won their fourth division title in five years.

Because the Eagles' season had started, I wasn't able to spend much of my time with the Phillies during the National League Championship Series against the Houston Astros, but I do remember interviewing Astros outfielder Terry Puhl after the Phillies' Game 2 loss at Veterans Stadium. Puhl had one heck of a series, winding up with a .526 batting average. He was a very gracious guy and undoubtedly would have won the NLCS MVP if the Astros had prevailed, but the Phillies finally got over the hump and beat them three games to two in what was probably the greatest and most intense NLCS ever played in the history of Major League Baseball. The Eagles were playing the New York Giants in New Jersey that day, so I wasn't there when the team arrived back from Houston after the clincher. I know it seems like I'm skipping over the whole series, but a few sentences can't properly describe those five games or give it proper justice. If you haven't seen the highlights of that series, watch them! The tension throughout that series was palpable! Everything was on the line for the Phillies. Without question, it was the biggest obstacle the team faced that entire season. Two days after knocking off the Astros, the Phillies played the Kansas City Royals in Game 1 of the 1980 World Series, where the big lingering question remained: Can the Philadelphia Phillies FINALLY win it all?!

Back then, it was a completely fair assessment. Out of all the original 16 teams in Major League Baseball, the Phillies were the only team who had yet to win a title. Oddly enough, that fact was never brought up by the media. The team came into the league in 1883! That's 97 years without winning a championship. The Royals were not unlike the Phillies, having lost three straight championship series in the 1970s as well. They had some real nice players in Amos Otis, Dennis Leonard, Hal McRae, and their top gun, third baseman George Brett, who hit .390 during the 1980 season. After splitting the first four games, the Phillies edged out the Royals in a nail-biting, come-from-behind win in Game 5 to take a 3-2 series lead. The team headed back to Philadelphia with Steve Carlton, the best pitcher in baseball, ready to take the mound in Game 6. During this time, the city was absolutely electric. We were confident, but we all wondered aloud: Are we finally going to get over that hump? There was a lot of pent-up emotion over years of heartache and frustration: the 1964 collapse, not getting past the Big Red Machine in 1976, Black Friday in 1977, losing the pennant again to the Dodgers in the 1978 NLCS, falling to fourth place in 1979 despite signing Pete Rose. The fans were fed up with all of that. They were ready to celebrate. Veterans Stadium was abuzz, but I was nervous. There was always that underlying feeling that something could go wrong. Right until the very last pitch.

However, the Phillies did not disappoint. Schmidt drove in the team's first two runs in the bottom of the third inning and the Phillies never looked back. By the top of the eighth inning, they had built a 4-0 lead and were six defensive outs from finally winning it all! Carlton was in complete command for most of the game, striking out seven in seven innings before Dallas Green took him out for Tug McGraw, who was practically unhittable since recovering from a bout with tendonitis earlier in the season. By the top of the ninth inning, the Royals cut the lead to 4-1 and McGraw managed to load the bases.

With two more outs to go, Royals second baseman Frank White hit a pop foul over towards the Phillies' dugout. Bob Boone and Pete Rose approached the ball, which popped out of Boone's mitt and fell into Rose's glove for the second out! It's one of the most miraculous plays in World

Series history! One more out to go! Only Royals' left fielder Willie Wilson stood in the way of the Tri-State area going absolutely crazy. Despite having a horrendous series, Wilson had 230 hits and batted .326 during the 1980 regular season. Like I said, there was always that underlying feeling something bad could happen. I wasn't a member of the organization and I didn't have money on the game. I was simply a lifelong fan. As a member of the media, we were all huddled in a tunnel behind home plate watching the game on a small television. Then it happened. Four pitches later, McGraw struck out Wilson and the Phillies were finally World Champions! It was jubilation!

It was fitting during the locker room celebration that Dallas Green, general manager Paul Owens, and Ruly Carpenter were standing at the podium with the World Series trophy. Those three guys helped transform a team that was once the laughingstock of Major League Baseball into champions. Not only was I happy from a fan's perspective, but I just loved Ruly. His family had experienced so many emotional highs and lows with that team for almost 40 years and they deserved to win more than anybody. Anytime you needed an interview, you could call the Phillies' offices, and Ruly would let you come down whenever you needed him. Despite growing up being former Phillies owner Bob Carpenter's son, Ruly's father made him learn every part of the Phillies' baseball operations from the ground up. As a result, he knew how to run a successful organization.

When the Carpenters owned the Phillies, it was a family-like atmosphere with everybody. How he isn't a member of the Phillies Wall of Fame is a disgrace. Many organizations, including the Atlanta Braves, took Ruly's blueprint in developing a team and incorporated it into their own success years later. Ruly was such an unassuming guy and so devoid of ego that he would sit with the grounds crew behind the home plate tunnel and watch the game wearing a flannel shirt and khakis. Ruly was the same age as most of the players, and his relationship with them was a strong one. I will say this until the day I die: If Ruly Carpenter continued to own the Phillies instead of selling the team in 1981, they would have been a dynasty, just like the New York Yankees of the 1990s. Do you think they would have traded players like Julio Franco and Ryne Sandberg?! No way! Ruly was into player development. Simply put, he was the best owner of any Philly sports team in my lifetime. It's too bad he didn't stick around, but he didn't want to deal with baseball's escalating salaries and changing infrastructure, and who could really blame him?

Ruly was also a guy who thought "outside the box." Many people are unaware of this, but he was one of the first owners to implement a strength and conditioning coach. A man by the name of Gus Hoefling was a conditioning coach with the Eagles back in the 1970s. Knowing my affiliation with the Eagles at the time, Ruly pulled me aside, asked how well I knew Gus. I eventually introduced the two of them, they struck up a relationship and Ruly hired Gus as the Phillies' strength and conditioning coach. I remember when Gus started Steve Carlton on an intense, martial-arts training program. He had him spend time in a small, tiny chamber known as the "Mood Room," which channeled positive thinking. Maybe it's just a coincidence, but Carlton won three Cy Young Awards while working with Hoefling. Bob Boone gives Gus a lot of credit for helping him play as long as he did. Until his record was broken by Carlton Fisk and Ivan Rodriguez, Bob had caught more games than anyone in baseball history. During one off-season, I remember filming Bob working out using a rice bathtub, which I think he used for about 15 minutes a day or maybe longer. Carlton would twist his fist all the way to the bottom of that bathtub. These guys were unbelievable. Gus' legendary work with the Phillies made him a fitness guru, and I take some pride in knowing I had a hand in this.

Gus was one of many individuals in that locker room on the night of October 21, 1980 who were instrumental behind the scenes in helping the Phillies win their first championship. I interviewed a number of players that night, none that I can specifically remember, but it was euphoric. There was no more hostility or edginess. They were just very delighted to win it all. They validated their place in baseball history, and it was a very special night.

I remember driving home later that evening and saying to myself, 'They did it. They finally got over the hump.' After decades of frustration and coming close several times, the Philadelphia Phillies were finally World Champions.

CHAPTER 12

A New Decade, A New Job, A Legendary Team

SHORTLY AFTER THE Phillies won the 1980 World Series, I received a pay raise at Channel 6. Problem was, it was only for $50 a week, and I was doing a lot of work there. I wasn't married yet and was always trying to get as much done as I possibly could. I had previously gone to the station's news director, Alan Nesbitt, and asked for a $100 pay increase from $400 to $500 a week. I had been there a long time and was a dedicated employee, but all they could muster up was $50.

Around the same time, I was at a local event and bumped into 'Big Al' Meltzer, who by now was working as a sportscaster at WCAU-TV/ Channel 10 (then the local Philadelphia CBS affiliate), which was right across the street from Channel 6. I knew Al from his days on WFIL radio, when I first started out working in the mailroom. Whenever I'd see Al, he'd always say the same line to me: "Someday kid, we'll work together." Although our paths occasionally crossed when we worked several football games together, it was never anything full time. When I told Al that I was frustrated about my financial situation at Channel 6, he told me he would look into things for me at Channel 10 and see if there was a possible job opening. Shortly after talking with Al, Bill Lawlor, the former news director at Channel 6 who had moved over to Channel 10, came up with an unbelievable offer that almost doubled my salary, not including overtime. You're talking close to $17,000 or $18,000 more a year. I couldn't turn that down. On my final day at Channel 6, I got called into general manager Larry Pollock's office. Larry offered me one more dollar than Channel 10 was offering me, just to stay at Channel 6. I told Larry that it wouldn't be fair. They had the opportunity to do this before, they didn't deem it necessary, and I would just be going back and forth between the two stations.

I would have stayed at Channel 6 if they initially offered me $500 a week, including overtime. They didn't do it.

Even though Channel 10 offered me a lot more money, it was very difficult for me to make the decision to leave Channel 6. They gave me my start and I had a certain amount of allegiance to them. I'm not a "take the money and run" kind of guy. I had mixed emotions. Nonetheless, on February 4, 1981, I worked my last day at Channel 6. Three days later, I became the senior sports producer at Channel 10. In addition to already knowing Al, my friend Larry Kane, who formerly worked at Channel 6, was also working at Channel 10 after a brief stint in New York. Al, Larry, and Jim "Sports" Kelly (not to be confused with the Buffalo Bills Hall of Fame quarterback) all made it a comfortable transition for me. Channel 10 (which later switched over to NBC 10 in 1995) would be my home for the next 15 years

In addition to my new place of employment, things were also going well in my personal life. On June 12, 1982, I married my first wife, Nancy. But as always, sports is never too far off my radar. Four days before my wedding, the Philadelphia 76ers lost another championship to the Los Angeles Lakers. This was the team's third Finals loss in six years. I felt particularly bad for Julius "Dr. J" Erving, the Sixers' top gun and the 1981 NBA MVP. Doc was just an unbelievable ambassador for the game of basketball, and the fact that he hadn't won an NBA championship by that time in his career was a crime. Despite what happened regarding certain circumstances off the court in the years since his retirement, I still think Doc is a classy guy. One time, there was a young cancer patient who wanted to meet with Doc after a Sixers game, which ended around 9:45 pm. When the locker room opened at 10 pm, my camera crew was nowhere to be found and I started to raise all kinds of hell. I found out my crew wouldn't be there until 10:45 pm. When I told Doc of the predicament, he took a shower and waited an hour and ten minutes after the game ended to meet this young girl. That's what always impressed me the most about Doc. He spent time with everybody and never blew you off. That's one of the many reasons why the man never got booed in Philadelphia.

The hoopla surrounding Doc's impending NBA arrival back in 1976 was tremendous, and Philadelphia was ecstatic! The ABA was folding, and

Doc's team, the New York Nets, had to pay merger fees with the NBA in order to join the league. To make a long story short, the Nets could no longer afford Doc and his increasing salary. Sixers then-general manager Pat Williams strongly encouraged and eventually convinced then-Sixers' owner Fitz Dixon to purchase Doc's contract from the Nets and the rest is history. The team held an introductory press conference at the Holiday Inn, right across the street from the Spectrum, where the Sixers played their home games. In Doc's first season with the team, the Sixers went to the NBA Finals and squared off against Bill Walton and the Portland Trail Blazers, who were coached by former Sixers general manager Jack Ramsay. During the NBA Finals, I convinced Doc's teammate Lloyd Free (now known as World B. Free) to run up the Philadelphia Art Museum steps and raise his hands up like Sylvester Stallone did in the movie *Rocky*, which was released a few months before. As I recall, Sixers' head coach Gene Shue really didn't appreciate that.

In the finals, the Sixers went up two games to none on the Blazers. Then, Portland rallied back and won four straight games to take the title. After losing 73 games in 1973, the Sixers had come a long way, but fans were still disappointed. Their team was right there to get the brass ring and they didn't come up with it, which is probably one of the reasons why the team's motto for the 1977-78 season was "We owe you one." However, the Sixers would go on to lose in the Eastern Conference Finals against the Washington Bullets that season. The dilemma the Sixers faced during Doc's first two seasons with the team was the presence of George McGinnis. Both Doc and George liked to control the basketball. I liked George's game, but he didn't keep himself in the best of shape. When McGinnis was traded in 1978, the offense was now centered around Doc, but the Sixers still came up short in the playoffs, losing a seven-game series to the San Antonio Spurs in the 1979 conference semifinals.

After a three-year absence, the Sixers returned to the NBA Finals in 1980. This time, however, they fell to the Los Angeles Lakers, who were led by a 20-year old rookie named Earvin "Magic" Johnson. In the deciding Game Six, Magic, subbing for an injured Kareem Abdul-Jabbar, scored 42 points, grabbed 15 rebounds and dished out 7 assists, as the

Lakers won the title on the Sixers' home court at the Spectrum. The next year in 1981, the Sixers were up three games to one against the Boston Celtics in the conference finals, but lost the next three games, and the series, in ugly fashion. Boston then faced Moses Malone and the 40-42 Houston Rockets in the finals and won the championship in six games. The next year, the Sixers again faced the Celtics in the conference finals and had another three games to one series lead. However, Doc and the gang proceeded to lose Games 5 and 6, and were forced to go back to the Boston Garden for another Game 7. This time, history didn't repeat itself, and the Sixers moved on to face the Lakers for the title. Just like in 1980, however, they lost in six games. After the final game in Los Angeles, Doc was crying in the locker room. He thought the window of opportunity had closed for him to get a ring and was taking it very hard. Nobody knew it at the time, but Doc would get another chance to try and bring a championship to Philadelphia, and the 1982-1983 basketball season would be a ride that none of us in the city would ever forget.

That following fall, I embarked on my final season spotting Eagles games with the great Merrill Reese. However, the NFL strike resulted in a work stoppage that lasted almost two months. While it may have been quiet on the football front, the Sixers were about to make some serious noise. After their championship loss to the Lakers, it was apparent that changes needed to be made to the team's roster. The main problem was at center. The team had the late Caldwell Jones and Darryl Dawkins in the middle, but as colorful as he was, Darryl never lived up to his potential. Jones was solid, but the team needed a dominant inside presence who could combat Kareem Abdul-Jabbar and compliment Doc as well. That's when new Sixers owner Harold Katz made the bold move to acquire center Moses Malone from the Houston Rockets.

Malone was coming off another MVP season in Houston, but he was a restricted free agent, which meant he could test free agency, but the Rockets would be allowed to match any offer he'd receive from another team. I think Malone needed a change of scenery. After looking at the Sixers' roster and seeing players like Doc, Bobby Jones, Andrew Toney and Maurice Cheeks, who wouldn't want to play on that team?! The road to making a deal with Malone, however, was a complicated one. He ended up signing with the Sixers, but the Rockets matched their offer. After a few weeks of negotiations, the Rockets traded Malone to the Sixers on September 15, 1982 for Caldwell Jones and the Sixers' 1983 first-round draft pick. The addition of Malone officially made the Sixers a formidable force to contend with, and the city of Philadelphia felt extremely lucky to land a player of his caliber. He was just tenacious and a defensive force, especially on the offensive boards. Dennis Rodman could grab the offensive rebounds, but he never had the inside moves Malone had.

As Malone and the Rockets showed in 1981, anything was possible in the postseason. Despite coming up short against the Celtics in the finals that year, Malone led that sub-.500 Houston team all the way to the threshold of a championship with basically no supporting cast. Malone was also familiar with the Lakers. In the first round of the '81 playoffs, his Rockets upset Los Angeles in a best-of-three series. As happy as Sixers fans were that Malone was coming to Philadelphia, their team would most likely have to face the Lakers again if they were lucky enough to get back to the NBA Finals. Although there were some initial concerns as to whether Doc and Moses would be able to play together, the Sixers came out of the gate that season taking no prisoners and never looked back. By December 8, the team was 17-3. On February 3, they were 40-6, and at the beginning of March, they were 50-7! Looking back, it sounds ridiculous that some people didn't initially think the 1982-83 Sixers were capable of doing what they did. Near the end of the regular season, however, many believed the team would surpass the 1966-67 Sixers' regular season record of 68-13. There was even talk as to whether they were the best team ever assembled in Philadelphia history. Everyone was excited, but that team could have gone 82-0, and if they didn't win a championship, it would have meant nothing.

In the end, the Sixers didn't win more games than the Wilt Chamberlain-led squad of 1966-67, although they still finished with an astounding 65-17 record. They probably had a chance of winning 70 games if they didn't finish .500 over their last 16 regular season games. Going into the playoffs, Stan Hochman asked Malone to make a playoff prediction. He responded with one of the greatest quotes in Philly sports history: "Fo' Fo' Fo'," meaning the Sixers would sweep through the NBA Playoffs in 12 games. Malone came close with his quote. After sweeping the New York Knicks in the first round, it took the Sixers five wins in the conference finals to beat the Milwaukee Bucks, and a rematch against the Lakers was all set.

As far as the 1983 NBA Finals was concerned, it was no contest. The Sixers swept the Lakers in four games, winning Game 4 in Los Angeles for their first championship since 1967. Simply put, Moses Malone was the difference. He got the ball in the low post and went strong and went hard, averaging 25.8 points and 18 rebounds per game in the sweep. He put a whooping on Abdul-Jabbar, outrebounding him in the series, 72-30. Even though Malone thought the Sixers would win and the team was up three games to none, I honestly didn't think the Sixers would win Game 4. Look, it's one thing to sweep the Lakers in Philadelphia, but in LA?! At the Forum?! Are you kidding me?! That was wild! By the way, "Fo' Fi' Fo'" was inscribed inside the players' championship rings. I was in the locker room for the emotional post-game celebration. The person I was happiest for was Doc. Nobody deserved that championship more than him. Channel 10 asked Harold Katz if we could put a microphone on him for the Game 4 clincher. To my surprise, Katz agreed to our request with no problem. To this day, I'm really surprised he allowed me to do that. If the Sixers had lost Game 4, he probably would have been really dejected and I'd have to delete some expletives from the tape. I was taking a big chance. Some people had problems with Katz, but he was always nice to me and my relationship with him was a good one. Keep in mind this was when he was still in the good graces of the city.

I'm not trying to rain on the Sixers' parade, and I might be wrong and tick off some Philly fans in the process, but the fact that Lakers forward James Worthy suffered a fractured leg in the season's final weeks and missed the entire playoffs was a plus for the Sixers in that series. I think the Lakers would have extended the Sixers to at least six games if not for Worthy's injury. The Lakers were still deep enough to make another run, but even though he was a rookie, Worthy was one of the greatest forwards of his time, as well as one of the best players in NBA playoff history. He was very quick, a good shooter, and complemented Magic Johnson and Abdul-Jabbar very nicely. There's a reason why his nickname was "Big Game James" and he's an NBA Hall of Famer. I don't want to use the word "tainted," but you can't help but wonder what would have happened if he had played. But then again, the Flyers lost the 1976 Stanley Cup to the Canadiens when Bernie Parent and Rick MacLeish were out with injuries. It happens.

Unfortunately, there would be no encore for the 1982-83 Sixers. In the first round of the 1983-1984 NBA Playoffs, the team was upset in five games by the New Jersey Nets. Michael Ray Richardson, who was such an off-the-court train wreck that they once did a documentary on him, scored 24 points and six steals in the deciding Game 5 at the Spectrum. I was there, and the crowd was stunned. I could not believe it. Michael Ray Richardson?! Coming off a championship the year before, people were so excited to see if the Sixers could repeat. What happened was an embarrassment. Just like the 1967 squad, the Sixers' lone title from that era was their crowning achievement.

Despite the opinions that I voiced in the above paragraphs, I still think the 1982-83 Philadelphia 76ers will go down as one of the greatest teams in NBA history. No doubt about it. You look at what they did that season and it was just an amazing, amazing accomplishment. The team's 12-1 record in the NBA Playoffs set a record for highest winning percentage ever in the playoffs, until the Lakers went 15-1 in 2001. Oddly enough, that same Lakers squad beat the Sixers in the NBA Finals that year. Keep in mind, however, that the Lakers set this record after the expanded playoff format, which began in 1984. I think that sometimes, people tend to look the other way when it comes to Philadelphia teams and they don't want to give them their just due. People get caught up in the Lakers and the Celtics, and you still have that stigma of Philadelphia.

During the Sixers' championship parade, which took place a few days after sweeping the Lakers, Harold Katz, ever the businessman, did not help himself when he addressed the crowd and asked everyone if they were season ticket holders. I don't think too many people were happy about that, because they interpreted it as Katz trying to get more money from them. The timing was terrible. Couldn't that have waited? Little did we know at the time that this would be a sign of things to come for the Sixers franchise.

Sadly, the player who had the biggest impact on that classic Sixers championship team was the first one to lose his life. On September 15, 2015, Moses Malone was found dead in a Virginia hotel room, after failing to show up for breakfast on the morning of a charity golf tournament he was scheduled to play in. The cause of death was cardiovascular disease. Moses, who was apparently wearing a heart monitor when he died, was diagnosed with an irregular heartbeat shortly before his death. He was 60 years old.

On the same night NBA legend and Lower Merion High School graduate Kobe Bryant played his last game in Philadelphia against the Sixers in December 2015, the Sixers honored Moses during a special halftime ceremony. Doc and Clint Richardson, former Sixers teammates from their championship team, spoke on his behalf. After Doc and Clint spoke, it was announced by Moses' son that the Sixers organization would finally retire his father's No. 2 jersey during the 2016-17 NBA season, two decades after Moses' last game in a Sixers uniform (he returned to the team for the 1993-94 season). While it's a very nice gesture, and no player has worn that number since Moses, I never understood why this wasn't done over the course of the last two decades. I once heard that Moses didn't want his number retired unless all his Sixers teammates from the championship season could be there in person to take part in the festivities, but I can't confirm that this is 100% accurate.

If this is true, however, it wouldn't have surprised me in the least. While a lot of the Philadelphia media didn't understand him, Moses, while quite different, was still a gracious guy. He was really a big kid who loved the game of basketball. I remember going to Saint Joseph's University to watch him work out after he suffered a pretty serious eye injury at the end of the 1985-86 season. Moses couldn't say much to me regarding the injury when I arrived at the facility, but he promised me an exclusive story if I came back the next day. True to his word, I returned to Saint Joe's 24 hours later, and Moses, who ended up missing the rest of that season as well as the playoffs, gave me an update on his condition that none of the other networks had. That's the Moses I remember fondly. If he liked you, he wasn't tough to cover at all. Moses just went out there and played the game of basketball. When he led the Sixers to the title, he was not going to be denied. Moses was an absolute force on the offensive glass. He is currently one of only four players to accumulate 25,000 points and 15,000 rebounds in his NBA career. The other three are Wilt Chamberlain, Abdul-Jabbar, and Elvin Hayes, who played with Moses in Houston.

Following his retirement from basketball, I ran into Moses Malone several times, including the NCAA Tournament when I was working out in San Diego. Moses was not a man of many words, but he was a nice person and always greeted me warmly. Even though Charles Barkley and Allen Iverson gave Sixers fans many memorable moments during their years with the team, they were never able to duplicate what Moses and that 1982-83 Sixers squad accomplished.

And judging by the current state of the franchise, it looks like we're not going to see that happen again anytime soon.

CHAPTER 13

Andrew Toney and the Fall of the Philadelphia 76ers

WHILE THE PHILADELPHIA 76ers remained competitive several years after their 1983 championship season, it didn't last. Despite the addition of forward Charles Barkley from Auburn in 1984, the Sixers came up short in the 1985 Eastern Conference Finals to Larry Bird and the Celtics. After the 1985-86 season, Moses Malone, who had apparently worn out his welcome with Sixers management, became associated with arguably the worst day in the history of the franchise on June 16, 1986. It was on this day that Malone and teammate Terry Catledge were traded to the Washington Bullets for center Jeff Ruland, forward Cliff Robinson and two first-round draft picks. If that wasn't enough, the Sixers, who had the first pick in the 1986 NBA Draft (which they acquired in 1979 after trading Kobe Bryant's dad, Joe Bryant, to the San Diego Clippers), traded the pick to the Cleveland Cavaliers for forward Roy Hinson. The Cavaliers turned that pick into Brad Daugherty, who had a solid career in the NBA.

Moses, who was 31 years old and still had a few good years left in his career, was deeply hurt by the trade. He had some problems with the team during his final season in Philadelphia, but he wanted to stay with the Sixers. I'll never forget when he returned to the Spectrum for the first time since being traded. He called me over in his big, bellowing voice and said "Hey, you tell that guy with the big CI-gar that Moses is back!" Of course, that guy with the big CI-gar he was referring to was Sixers owner Harold Katz, who was not Moses' favorite person in the world at that time.

As for the players the Sixers received? Well, Hinson turned out to be a bust and was eventually traded to the Nets, Ruland made five appearances with the team and eventually retired due to a knee injury (although he briefly came out of retirement a few years later to play a handful of games with the team), and Robinson never played more than 62 games a season during his time in a Sixers uniform. I don't know who thought any of these moves were good ideas, but whoever did set the Sixers franchise back for decades. Some say the team has never recovered. In addition to those disastrous moves, Bobby Jones and Julius Erving retired following the 1986 and 1987 seasons, respectively.

Another reason for the Sixers' decline in the late 1980s was in large part to the sad story of Andrew Toney, who was a great, great, NBA player during those Sixers playoff teams of the early 1980s. Known as the "Boston Strangler" because of his dominating performances against the Celtics, the Sixers' chief nemesis actually acquired defensive specialist Dennis Johnson from the Phoenix Suns just to try and stop him! After averaging nearly 20 points per game for the 1983 championship team, the Sixers rewarded Toney with a seven-year, $4.73 million contract in 1984. Not too long after signing that contract, however, Toney started having injury problems with his feet, so he went to Temple Orthopaedic Surgery and Sports Medicine on North Broad Street in Philadelphia for treatment. Sixers owner Harold Katz was not at all happy with the lack of progress his newly minted superstar was making while trying to return to the starting lineup. The problem was that Temple was trying to get Toney back on the court and could not detect the stress fractures he had in his feet. One day, Katz asked to speak to the trainer at Temple. The trainer had picked up the phone, and Toney apparently overheard Katz make several derogatory remarks about him. Needless to say, Andrew wasn't happy with what he heard on the other line.

According to my longtime colleague and former Sixers beat writer, Stan Hochman, Katz had suspicions regarding Toney's injury.

"Harold cast doubt that it was serious," Hochman recalled. "I don't know the exact quotes, but he made it clear that he didn't really believe Andrew was hurting. His teammates were sympathetic. They knew his character. They understood that if Toney wasn't hurting, he would've been happy to play and play hard. They knew he wanted the ball at the end of games. They knew that he was tough. What came down was really nasty.

81

I was not a big Katz fan, so of course I sided with the player. If he says he's hurt, he's hurt. Nobody really knew Andrew. He came from Southwestern Louisiana (now the University of Louisiana at Lafayette), was pretty introverted and not a big city kind of guy. He kept to himself. He was close with Mo Cheeks, his best friend on the team. But I trusted Andrew. If I had to make a choice of who to believe, I'm going to believe in Andrew saying that he's too hurt to play, and I'm not believing Katz. It was bad."

Toney's stress fractures were eventually discovered by another doctor. Several weeks later, I saw Andrew at St. Joseph's University Fieldhouse, where the Sixers practiced. I flat out asked him whether he thought he was being treated like a raw piece of meat by the Sixers. He responded yes, and we used his sound bite on our newscast that night. About two weeks later, I was back at practice, and Sixers coach Matty Guokas was meeting with reporters. I walked up to Matty and I asked him what the deal was with Andrew.

"What?!" Matty yelled. He went ballistic. Getting really, really, incensed and backing me into a corner.

My camera man was right there, but for some reason he wasn't rolling when the incident happened. It would have been great video. That was our story. To this day, I'd confront Matty about that incident. He wasn't happy about me asking that question. At all. I had an okay relationship at best with Matty, and I obviously struck a nerve with what I asked. Eventually, he lost his job as Sixers coach. I tried to get some information from Sixers general manager John Nash prior to Guokas' firing, but John was avoiding me. So I went down to the Sixers' offices and saw Zach Hill, who is now the director of communications for the Philadelphia Flyers. Back then, Zach was a young assistant for the Sixers. I went to the front door and asked to see John. Zach told me he wasn't coming out. I had a feeling this was going to happen, so I parked my car right behind John's Cadillac and told Zach I wasn't leaving until I talked with him. They threatened to call the police. I was ticked off. An hour later, John eventually came down and talked to me. After the whole Toney fiasco, John would often come up to me and drop that infamous quote I used when I spoke to Andrew that day at practice: "Raw piece of meat, huh?" John is a good friend of mine and still is to this day.

Apparently, there were other issues behind the scenes regarding Toney and the Sixers that nobody even knew of, because Toney supposedly kept quiet about it. Sixers management reportedly forced Toney to play in the 1985 playoffs, despite the fact that he missed several games at the end of the season due to severe pain in his feet. After that season ended, Toney was forced to take a random drug test by the NBA, which he passed. While this incident may seem coincidental that the Sixers were at odds with Toney at this time of the test, Katz and the Sixers denied having any association with it. Nonetheless, rumors started circulating throughout the NBA that Toney was a drug addict. Just prior to the 1985-86 season, a year which saw Toney appear in only six games, he and his agent met with Matty Guokas, who according to Toney, discussed the possibility that he may have a drug problem.[1]

In a nutshell, I think the Sixers had some convoluted idea that Toney was getting his money and didn't want to play. The trials and tribulations of the Toney debacle lasted several more seasons and offered additional subplots that seemed to go on and on. Toney thought the Sixers tried to force him to retire so they could get some insurance money, which Katz has also denied. After Toney's retirement was made official in February 1989, Maurice Cheeks was the only player left from the Sixers' 1983 championship team. As it turned out, Cheeks would be traded several months later in what was another embarrassing scenario for the franchise. Cheeks was told by sportscaster Michael Barkann (now of Philadelphia's Comcast SportsNet) that he was getting traded to the San Antonio Spurs upon arriving at his home one afternoon. He found out he was getting traded from the Sixers by a reporter for crying out loud! It was the official end to arguably the greatest era in Sixers basketball. I always thought that team could have made one more run, but injuries and age caught up with them.

Although shots were fired from both sides, Andrew Toney was so hurt over the Sixers' treatment of him that he avoided having any association with the team for years. After the way his career ended, nobody could really blame him. It was truly sad. And although Katz sold the team in 1996 and the grudge Toney held against the Sixers now seems to have been somewhat buried, decades of estrangement and hurt feelings make you wonder if time will ever completely heal those wounds.

CHAPTER 14

The Philadelphia Stars: The Class of the USFL

THE SIXERS' 1983 title would be the last championship the four major sports teams of Philadelphia would see for the next 25 years. Even though the Phillies returned to the World Series the following October, they ran out of gas after a great September and lost to Cal Ripken Jr. and the Baltimore Orioles in five games. The Eagles, moving on without Dick Vermeil, floundered under new head coach Marion Campbell and wouldn't start showing signs of life again until the end of the decade. The Flyers, under new head coach Mike Keenan, advanced to two Stanley Cups in 1985 and 1987. Unfortunately, Mike and the Flyers couldn't get past Wayne Gretzky and those great Edmonton Oilers teams, losing to them in both trips to the finals. Despite his icy reputation, I had a great relationship with Mike. Whenever I needed a player to interview after the game, Mike always readily got one for me.

My greatest accomplishment away from sports during this time, however, was the birth of my daughter Ashleigh on March 9, 1985. I take great pride in the fact that I helped raise a very nice girl who has given me two wonderful grandkids, McKenzie and Mitchell.

While the big four might not have been able to bring us another parade, there was an emergence of another football team in the city: the Philadelphia Stars of the up-and-coming USFL (United States Football League). The brain trust behind the Stars included Carl Peterson, the former Philadelphia Eagles' personnel director who was the Stars' president and general manager, and Myles Tanenbaum, a real estate developer who developed Pennsylvania's King Of Prussia Mall.

Peterson and Tanenbaum had some very good ideas to keep player salaries within reason and put a tremendous game plan together for evaluating talent, which included a 5'9" linebacker named Sam Mills. Pound for pound, Sam was one of the toughest guys to ever play the game of football. They also brought in Chuck Fusina, the former Tampa Bay Buccaneers quarterback out of Penn State, and Kelvin Bryant, a rookie running back from North Carolina who would become the 1983 USFL MVP. The team also had some former Eagles in wide receiver Scott Fitzkee, tight end Ken Dunek and linebacker/coach John Bunting. Along the way, I struck up a great relationship with the team's punter, Sean Landeta. I spent a lot of time with Sean because punters and kickers had special teams practices, which lasted around 20 minutes. I would stand on the sidelines and talk with Sean. He was a very engaging guy and still is to this day. Peterson, Tanenbaum, Terry Bradway and Bill Kuharich all worked in unison to put together one of the best franchises in USFL history. In fact, Peterson, who later became the president, general manager, and chief executive officer of the NFL's Kansas City Chiefs, gave me my first break as a radio color commentator for several Stars' broadcasts when I filled in for former Eagle Vince Papale.

The Stars head coach was Jim Mora, who later went on to have a very successful NFL coaching career. I would go down on a Tuesday or Wednesday and see Mora watching film on his projector. He assembled a great coaching staff. Every player in the locker room was so happy they were being covered. There wasn't one guy that was obnoxious and they were all great to deal with. They either knew their time playing football was limited, or they could possibly take things to the next level in the NFL.

"I've always said that what made the Stars special was that it was initially built with players like myself, Chuck Fusina, Sam Mills, Steve Folsom. Guys that had a chance at the NFL, but things didn't work out as well as we had hoped," said Stars' tight end Ken Dunek. "This was really a second chance for us to continue to do what we loved to do, so we took it very seriously. There were a lot of other people who were very good football players, but the NFL is the ultimate numbers game. We were talented players, but we got caught in a numbers crunch. This gave us another chance to play professional football. Carl added some very talented rookies like Kelvin Bryant, Irv Eatman and Sean Landeta. That second year, he brought in guys like William Fuller, George Jamison and Michael Johnson. Also, Scott Fitzkee and John Bunting joined the team, so we had a really good group of core veterans who appreciated the opportunity to play, and the rookies bought into that.

"There were no egos. We really appreciated the fact that every day, we were able to do something that we loved to do. We didn't worry about the money. Nobody was making a whole lot of money in those days, anyway. I had a base salary between $35,000 to $65,000 a year, but I think even the big names were only making $200,000 to $300,000, so there wasn't that much money to get jealous over. Character wise, we had good guys. Carl took a page out of Dick Vermeil's playbook and was very good in bringing in character people. I can't really think of a bad seed that was on the team. Ninety nine percent of the time, everybody got along and we enjoyed each other's company. The Stars were a really talented football team who came to play every day. Because I also played for the Eagles, a lot of people have asked me who would have won a game during that time between the Eagles and the Stars. You can never really know who's going to win a football game, but my answer has always been this: When you played the Stars, you had to buckle your chinstrap, because the Stars were going to come at you. I think that would have been a really good game between the 1985 Eagles and the Stars of that era."

When the Stars first came into town, a lot of people had reservations about them. A rival football league was tried before with the original World Football League (WFL) in the early 1970s, which never got off the ground. The team was going to play at Veterans Stadium (which was at the time the home of the Phillies and Eagles) in the spring. Spring football? Was that going to make it? Even though the Eagles were in decline, the Stars still had to compete with them. I don't think they ever got 50,000 fans a game, but people started taking a liking to the Stars and they were fun to watch. While the Sixers were on the threshold of a title, the Eagles wouldn't be competitive for another few years, Bobby Clarke was soon retiring from the Flyers, the Phillies were nearing the end of their great run and fans were looking for another option.

On the field, the Stars were an absolute juggernaut, compiling a 15-3 record during their first season in 1983. In the playoffs, they came back from a 21-point deficit in the semifinals against the Chicago Blitz to win 44-38 in overtime. The Stars then advanced to the league's title game, where they lost to the Michigan Panthers, 24-22. Despite the frustrating loss, people still believed the Stars were so good that they could compete with some of the weaker teams in the NFL. That's how solid of a squad they were. The Stars avenged their championship loss from the previous season and rolled over everybody in 1984, going 16-2 as they returned to the USFL Championship Game. This time, they annihilated the Arizona Wranglers, 23-3, to win the USFL Championship. A tremendous parade followed the victory.

"It was terrific," Carl Peterson said of the parade. "That was a culmination of a lot of hard work by a lot of talented people, coaches and players. Jim (Mora) and his staff had done a marvelous job. Like anything, you have to put it all together and make it work. We were able to do that. It was such a highlight to have been with the Eagles in 1980 and to have defeated Dallas to win the NFC Championship that year. I certainly knew Philadelphia and their passion for pro football. When the Eagles went to Super Bowl XV, I continued to see how Philadelphia not only supported our team, but the Sixers, Flyers and Phillies. Even with that, I was still taken aback by the great turnout and parade down Broad Street, as were our players, coaches and staff. We could see the excitement, the loyalty and the fan base growing. Our first year was a great start. We averaged about 18,500 a game. The second year, we averaged close to 28,000. It was going in the right direction without question."

Behind the scenes, however, there was trouble on the horizon. When the USFL's New Jersey Generals signed Heisman Trophy winner Herschel Walker out of the University of Georgia, his contract value doubled that of the league's salary cap! The owners were caught between a rock and a hard place. Feeling the need to compete, the salaries of the league increased. As a result, no salaries were kept in check and it wasn't cost efficient. Things totally got out of control.

"That kind of changed the philosophy of the USFL," Peterson admitted. "After the conclusion of the second season in 1984, the thought process began to change."

Carl Peterson went from general manager of the Eagles to president and general manager of the Philadelphia Stars of the USFL. He later became president, general manager, and chief executive officer of the Kansas City Chiefs.

When you factor the increase in salaries, along with team equipment and travel expenses, those costs add up very quickly. I think there were lots of teams just keeping their heads above water, although the Stars weren't one of them.

"The Stars didn't have any financial difficulty, because Myles Tanenbaum had very deep pockets and was totally committed to the project," Dunek insisted. "I never saw one instance of the team skimping on anything at all. The team did little things like give us a free catered lunch at practice. I heard other teams were charging their players or taking it out of their paycheck. The Stars never did that. Our checks always cashed.

There were other teams in the league that were not as doing as well as we were, but we always had faith that there was big money behind this. All these Heisman Trophy winners were signing with the league, they had television contracts and we just figured the league would eventually succeed. Of course, Donald Trump got involved with the league and kind of ruined the whole thing, but we never felt one iota of financial pressure or hardship with the Stars franchise."

Although the Stars didn't struggle financially, Trump tried to convince the majority of the USFL owners that their league could force a merger with the NFL if they played their games in the fall instead of the spring. It was his thought that the NFL would have no choice but to admit several USFL teams into the league, and then the owners' original investment would skyrocket. Most of them were apparently convinced. In the fall of 1984, the majority of the league's owners sided with Trump's idea and voted in favor of the USFL playing their games in the fall at the start of the 1986 season. The decision had dire consequences for the Philadelphia Stars, as the reigning USFL Champions were forced to move to Baltimore.

"After that, we knew we could not remain in Philadelphia," Peterson said. "If we were going to move to the fall, we'd have to share Veterans Stadium not only with the Phillies, but obviously with the Eagles. We probably would have to play our first eight games on the road.

That was the end of it for us. We knew we had to leave, so we began to search for another city that would welcome the Stars and the USFL, and we certainly found that in Baltimore.

"The mindset of the USFL changed because of two people: Donald Trump, who owned the New Jersey Generals, and Eddie Einhorn, who acquired the rights to a Chicago franchise. Myself and Myles (Tanenbaum) certainly voted against it, but over two thirds of the league went with their thoughts that, if we moved to the fall, one of two things would happen. Either they would absorb some USFL teams into the NFL, which was certainly what some USFL owners wanted, or we'd prove that the NFL violated the Sherman Antitrust Act. It was not a happy league meeting for us. I didn't like the idea of going directly against the NFL. The original plan was to crawl before we walked. We originally thought that five years in the spring would give us a pretty good idea where the league was, what our relationship was with the NFL and how we were doing ratings-wise on television. Frankly, we were doing well. Networks never had ratings like that in the spring. We really thought there was a place for us there, but Donald and Eddie were very impatient. It was disappointing, and it obviously made us turn in another direction."

In the lawsuit, the USFL basically claimed the NFL was monopolizing the market and conspiring to control professional football. The USFL looked for $1.32 billion in damages and asked the court to declare the NFL's relationship with the three major television networks at that time to be illegal, claiming that it prevented the USFL's attempts to gain access to a network television contract. There were several other claims involved in the lawsuit, but that was the gist of it. Meanwhile, the pending changes to the league affected the Stars immensely, on and off the field.

"I can't imagine a pro team having more hardship than the 1985 Stars," Dunek said. "We were playing and practicing in Philadelphia, and our home games were a three and a half hour drive to College Park, Maryland. We couldn't get Memorial Stadium in Baltimore because the Baltimore Orioles had a locked-up lease and wouldn't let us play there. It was actually easier for us to go to away games than it was to drive to home games, because the Philadelphia Airport was only a half an hour drive. Then we got kicked out of Veterans Stadium because of a city dispute midway through the season, so we had to pack all of our stuff up on a Monday when we should have been looking at game film. The team then went over to the University of Pennsylvania, where our offices were in the ROTC building. We were having position meetings in each corner of a classroom with desks that were made for coeds, all while looking at film on the classroom wall. We were hanging our clothes on nails that were hammered into the wall, just to change our uniforms. It was an absolute disaster.

"We got off to a really bad start that year because of all the distractions. Then we had a team meeting with about eight or nine games to go, where we just said 'Listen, we've had everything in the world go against us here, but we know we have a team who can turn it around. Let's just concentrate on football and turn this around.' We won nine of our last 13 games to get into the playoffs, where we ran the table and beat the Oakland Invaders to win the last USFL title. Oakland had players like Bobby Hebert, Anthony Carter and Albert Bentley. They were a really good football team. I think it's one of the great accomplishments in pro sports how our team overcame the adversity that we did to win the championship."

Unfortunately, the Stars' second consecutive championship marked the end of a great run. The team's victory against Oakland would be the very last game ever played in the league. The USFL and NFL got into heavy litigation. Teams were folding and owners were scrambling. While a jury found that the NFL had violated the antitrust law, it ruled against the rest of the USFL's claims, basically stating that most of the problems the league faced were a result of their own deviation from their original game plan, and that their overall mismanagement led to their undoing. The USFL was awarded only $1 in damages. They eventually received a check in 1990 for around $3.76.

"Had the league continued to go on playing in the spring, I have no doubt in my mind it would have been a big success," lamented Dunek. "When the Stars won the title in 1984, we were drawing about 28,000 fans a game. Had we been able to come back in 1985 and play in Philadelphia, I think we would have drawn 40 to 50 thousand a game, but it wasn't meant to be. Interestingly enough, the team kept a core group of players in 1986 and paid us not to go to the NFL. I think they gave me a $15,000 or $20,000 signing bonus that year not to sign with any NFL team. I took that and finished my Bachelor of Arts in Broadcast Journalism. When the league folded in 1987, I just decided to retire."

"It was excruciatingly difficult for me and a lot of other people because we all had to go on with our careers," Peterson said. "Just a disappointing end to a terrific opportunity for an awful lot of talented players and coaches. What the USFL showed very quickly was that there were a number of cities that could and would support pro football in the spring. If we stayed in the spring for five years, you might have seen a scenario where the NFL thought a lot of the league and that it was a great place to develop players. Then, they might have wanted to purchase the league, or wanted to expand and purchase a number of teams to come into the NFL. That's ultimately what they ended up doing by expanding in Jacksonville and North Carolina. I think if we just stayed with our original business plan, I think the USFL could have very well survived in some form, if not in its entirety. Between the draft, combine, and Senior Bowl, you have the NFL working on year-round exposure to pro football. They do a great job of marketing all of that."

It was so unfortunate what happened to the Stars and the USFL. The team built a strong fan base and I really hoped the league would make it. But for me, it wasn't a surprise when they went under. The NFL beast was really starting to roar, and several players from the Stars as well as the USFL moved on to great success there. Sam Mills went on to play 12 seasons with the New Orleans Saints and Carolina Panthers. Nobody thought Sam could play in the USFL let alone the NFL, but he proved a lot of people wrong. He wanted to play, and he played at a very high level. You can't measure a guy's heart, and Sam Mills had a heart as big as the universe. Sadly, Sam passed away of cancer in 2005. Running back Kelvin Bryant was later part of the Redskins' Super Bowl winning team during their 1987 season. Center Bart Oates won two Super Bowls with the New York Giants and another with the San Francisco 49ers. Sean Landeta also won two Super Bowl rings with the Giants and had two separate stints with the Eagles, who signed defensive end Reggie White after the USFL's collapse in 1985. Quarterbacks Jim Kelly, Steve Young and offensive tackle Gary Zimmerman also started their careers in the USFL. Those players are now all members of the Pro Football Hall of Fame.

I think a lot of people forgot about the Philadelphia Stars because they were a stepchild of Philadelphia. They weren't the Phillies, Flyers, Sixers or Eagles. To a certain extent, they've become more appreciated as time has passed, but I don't think they get the recognition they deserve. The team's three-year record of 48-13-1 still holds as the best record over a three-year span in the history of pro football. From top to bottom, that was a well-run organization. They brought fans a lot of excitement, because they really were a very, very good team.

CHAPTER 15

Ourlads' Guide to the NFL Draft

FROM 1973 TO 1982, I presented the Philadelphia Eagles' NFL Draft card to NFL representatives during the draft. The names of the Eagles' draft picks for that respective season would be on a card I was given. The player's name was then announced by the representative when it was the Eagles' turn to draft a player. The very first year I was there, the Eagles drafted offensive lineman Jerry Sisemore and tight end Charle Young. Both players made the Pro Bowl multiple times in their careers. Young even won a Super Bowl with the San Francisco 49ers in 1982.

One year at the draft, I met Tom Hepler, who along with his son, Phil, both attended the event annually. Tom was the owner of Base-line Systems Corp., a company based in South Jersey that specialized in computer processing, as well as data preparation and processing services. Back in the 1970s, Tom began storing NFL players' statistical information on one of his computer programs. It was sort of like a hobby for him. Even though there was a drugstore list and a few other draft guides popping up at the time, the NFL Draft got bigger, and the need to know certain information about the players increased. Former Eagles' offensive tackle Stan Walters never failed to remind me how I put way too much emphasis on the NFL Draft. "We don't play the season for the NFL Draft!" Stan always used to say. Although I didn't entirely agree with Stan regarding those particular sentiments, it always brought about some friendly arguments. Personally, I think the foundation of any sports franchise is built through the draft. Although there's always an exception to the rule, the majority of successful football, baseball, hockey and basketball teams have been assembled this way.

By the early 1980s, Tom had stored so many NFL pro football player statistics on his computer that he and Phil handed out printed sheets with information on close to 400 players to fans who attended the draft. After meeting him in New York, Tom became aware of my standing with the NFL due to my work at Channel 10 and my association with the Eagles. Shortly after our initial encounter, I would meet regularly with Tom and put together mock drafts. Tom fronted the money, provided the printing, and assembled the needs for every NFL team, while the late Jim Sabo was an expert in print and electronic media. The database Jim built for the depth charts of every NFL team was vital to our computer draft algorithm. Jim was the first guy to incorporate who was on each roster, the specific needs for every team, the whole deal. With our team in place, *Ourlads' Guide to the NFL Draft* was born! Here is Tom Hepler's recollections on the beginnings of *Ourlads'* and how our relationship came to pass.

Tom Hepler: "I started going to the NFL Draft in 1979, which was the last year it was held at the Waldorf-Astoria Hotel in New York City. The Waldorf was bad for crowds. Everybody sat at the same level and you didn't see much. We would stand in line for tickets. That was the year of Dick Vermeil's initial first-round draft pick, even though he had been the Eagles' coach for three seasons. Then in 1980, the draft was again moved to the New York Sheraton, in Midtown Manhattan. The Sheraton had a balcony and it worked better for crowds. That was the first year the draft was telecast on ESPN.

My first encounter with Bill was during the 1981 draft. One of my business clients was CBS News, so by that time, I was able to get floor passes. In those days, the draft went until eight in the morning until three thirty or four in the morning. After the first round, people thinned out. By the time you got to rounds five or six, it was in the evening, and you were able to make your way around. I happened to walk over and talk to Bill, who was manning the Eagles table. We exchanged phone numbers and stayed in touch.

The 1982 NFL Draft, which turned out to be Bill's last draft, was fun. I ended up sitting at the Eagles table in New York with Bill. The Eagles drafted Mike Quick with the 20th pick in the first round. By this time, I was getting together with Bill in the off-season and we started our mock drafts. We knew we had the potential to do something interesting, but for the most part, we did it for our own benefit. I had a computer-based company, and I started doing mock drafts based on files I would build each year on NFL players. I would probe the software programs over the years, then Bill came onto the scene and we added a few more wrinkles to it and were able to get a little more information. In those days, there wasn't a lot of information going around, and NFL games weren't as plentiful to watch.

About a week before the next draft in 1983, I was coming home from a business trip in New York, and it occurred to me that fans of the draft needed some kind of scorecard when the draft was taking place. They needed something in their hands and needed to know the players and how they were rated. They needed an alphabetical index, an index by rating, an index by position, an index by school, so when you're sitting with a program, you can follow things. That weekend, I printed out about 400 of those books. It was rather crudely done by today's standards, but it was still pretty good. I went to the draft the next week, and I started handing out those books to the guys I used to stand in line with. As a matter of fact, the police came by because they thought I was doing something illegal! I received some additional inquiries from people who saw what I did, and they encouraged me to continue printing the guides. I approached Bill, Jim and my son Phil, and said 'You know what? Let's do this for real next year.' In 1984, we printed our first spiffy looking guide and offered it for sale. We didn't get many customers because nobody knew us! We sold 67 copies the first year, but the next year we sold 244. We weren't in it for the money, but we were definitely getting more attention! The following year, we multiplied our sales by four times the previous year's amount. It kept going up each year."

After several years, *Ourlads'* was growing legs, and a particularly interesting story that took place around the time of the 1985 draft actually resulted in one of my nicknames.

That year, the Philadelphia Eagles had the ninth pick in the draft. Even though the team needed an offensive lineman, I've always contended that as an NFL franchise, you have to take the best player available on the draft board. However, Eagles' head coach Marion Campbell thought otherwise. Marion was a great defensive coordinator who could deploy an NFL defense very well, but as a head coach, he was in over his head. After the Eagles selected offensive tackle Kevin Allen out of Indiana University, Campbell and assistant coach Lynn Stiles took to the podium at a press conference to discuss the pick. After noticing that better talent was still available on the board, I was not happy with the pick. I stood up and went nuts.

"Are you kidding me, Marion?! Are you kidding me?! You're picking Kevin Allen?! Really?!" I yelled.

There were four guys on the board who I thought were better picks than Allen. Wisconsin wide receiver Al Toon (who turned out to be a pretty good player for the New York Jets) and Eddie Brown (another wide receiver who had some nice years with the Cincinnati Bengals) were just two of the players still left in the draft. There was also Jim Lachey, who was projected to be a guard when he was drafted by the San Diego Chargers, but later became a very good tackle and won a Super Bowl with the Washington Redskins. And finally, you know the first guy the Eagles had an opportunity to pick? The greatest wide receiver in NFL history.... Jerry Rice!

As I was going ballistic, it just so happened that John Schulian, a writer from the Philadelphia Daily News, was taking notice. The next day, John wrote in his Daily News article how there was this "Loon" buzzing around the press conference who was out of control when the Eagles announced the Kevin Allen pick.

After my rant, I turned to somebody at the press conference and stayed true to my convictions.

"Mark my words. I'll be vindicated," I said.

And I was right.

In the first game of the 1985 Eagles season, Kevin Allen lined up against New York Giants Hall of Fame linebacker Lawrence Taylor, who used him like a rag doll. Eagles quarterback Ron Jaworski looked like he went through a meat grinder and a pizza machine at the same time. He was just mutilated. After four games that season, Allen was benched. Overall, this pick was a disaster from the start. One day after the Eagles selected Allen, he apparently failed a drug test. Then in 1987, he pleaded guilty to raping a woman on a Margate, New Jersey beach the previous Labor Day, and spent several years in jail. Kevin Allen never played in the NFL again.

Although my predictions regarding Allen were in reference to his on-the-field work, Stan Hochman did a great article on me years later with the headline "Don't dismiss this loon." Somebody gave me a plaque of the article and I still have it on my wall at home. That's how I got my nickname "The Loon."

As the years went on, *Ourlads'* just got bigger and bigger. By 1990, we had over 4,000 subscribers. By 1996, we had about 5,600 subscribers. You might think that because of my standing with the Eagles and ESPN that my opinions carried more weight than those of some of the other guys, but that couldn't have been further from the truth. Everybody had a certain amount of input. We all had the expertise, but Ourlads' was really Tom's baby.

"A typical draft weekend would start in my offices in Mount Laurel, New Jersey around 8:00 in the morning," recalled Hepler. "We'd go get our coffee and basically commiserate over the needs for every team in the draft, all that stuff. It was me, Bill, my son Phil, Jim Sabo and his son Steve, who is now the head of college scouting for the Atlanta Falcons. Steve would be the one sitting at the keyboard while we worked the mock drafts. For example, if it was the Minnesota Vikings' turn to select a player, the computer would make a selection based on an algorithm. We may or may not override it, but we would let her rip. Sometimes we'd run out of time, and the computer might finish rounds three through seven by itself. If that ever happened, we'd print them out, look them over, take them home and come back the following week. After the draft, we'd go out to lunch somewhere and recap what we did. We would even have guests sometime. Longtime Eagles general manager and team president Harry Gamble would usually stop in about two weeks before the draft. Harry liked our work. Not that we had any influence on him, but he knew that we were serious about what we did. One time, former Eagles running back Wilbert Montgomery stopped by to see us!"

*That's how I got the nickname "The Loon." I'll be forever
grateful to Stan Hochman for writing this article on me.*

With the exception of Tom's son, Phil, and Jim's son, Steve, we all had
full-time jobs. We started putting the guide together at the end of the football season in January and worked all the way through April. Throughout
the process, we would look at tons of tape and film. In addition to my job at
Channel 10, I was also working for ESPN at the time, so I saw some of the
top players. From Aundray Bruce to Bo Jackson, we rated and analyzed everybody! All of those players were looked at. We made some mistakes on some
guys and had some real doozies. One guy I didn't make a mistake on, however, was Zach Thomas. Zach turned out to be a much better player than his
fifth round selection in the 1996 NFL Draft would suggest. I'll always look
on that draft with fondness, as it was my last draft before I left for San Diego.

"Being in the radio and television business, Bill really understood how
to promote things," said Hepler. "He did a lot of radio stuff for us. As a
matter of fact, that's how he ended up in San Diego! Before Bill got the
job full-time, he occasionally travelled out there. I liked to joke with Bill
by telling him to get as far away from us as possible, because we'd be stuck

doing so many mock drafts I didn't even want to look at him! Then, the group in San Diego liked him so much they offered him a job!"

I've been telling people for years that you can easily talk about the NFL Draft on a radio or television show during the Fourth of July, and the phone lines would still light up like a Christmas tree. It's a phenomenon I can't put my finger on. I think the NFL Draft has enhanced the success of the NFL because people now feel they need to know about all of these players. I started doing radio shows in Pittsburgh, Cleveland, Cincinnati, Baltimore and all over the country! That's how Chris Visser discovered me in San Diego! Little did I know that a booklet we put together would lead to one of the biggest breaks in my career. Unfortunately, it would have been pretty tough to keep working on *Ourlads'* from my end across the country. Although the guys were disappointed I had to move on, they knew I wanted to do talk radio. All was not lost, however. My new job actually got *Ourlads'* more press, as I was able to have the guys on my show in San Diego.

Every weekend for over a decade, all of us associated with *Ourlads'* sat in Tom's office, talking about players and evaluating them, doing a back and forth of 'I don't like this guy,' 'You like that guy' or 'I don't think the Eagles should pick this guy.' We'd let the computer run wild as it made its projections and printed out its analysis. Other times, we would do several rounds manually on our own, and the final decisions were always done by ourselves. When all was said and done, I'm glad I was part of the building blocks of such a great publication. Tom, Phil, Jim and Steve were an awesome group. Tom Hepler agrees.

"I retired in 2004 and handed things off to a gentleman named Dan Shonka in 2005, but every weekend leading up to the draft for basically 13 years, our group got together. I really, really miss that."

There's no doubt in my mind that *Ourlads'* was instrumental in keeping fans interested in football year-round. It was a great, great experience, and it helped me out an awful lot.

CHAPTER 16

How I Helped Launch Mike Schmidt's Broadcasting Career

MUCH LIKE HIS former teammate Dick Allen, Phillies Hall of Famer Mike Schmidt, the greatest third baseman in the history of Major League Baseball, also qualifies as one of Philadelphia's all-time misunderstood athletes, albeit for different reasons.

Throughout the course of his 18-year career, I never thought Mike was fully awarded the adulation he deserved from the fans of Philadelphia. Mike was a 6'2" natural athlete who was expected to be Mr. Superstar day in and day out, game in and game out. The fans thought Mike should have won the National League MVP every year. In the beginning, Mike had his struggles. A product of the massively talented Phillies farm system of the 1970s, things weren't so easy for the guy who would later make the game look real easy. Mike hit just .196 in his first full season in 1973. However, Phillies owner Ruly Carpenter, general manager Paul "The Pope" Owens, and then-farm director Dallas Green knew Mike had great potential, so they stuck by him, even during the times when he was in Phillies manager Danny Ozark's doghouse. In fact, early in Mike's career, Ozark once said he would basically trade him for a wagon load of pumpkins!

To complicate matters, Mike is an introverted Midwesterner from Dayton, Ohio. Not exactly the type of guy Philadelphia fans gravitate towards. Philly is a blue collar city that relates more to a guy like a Pete Rose or Larry Bowa, who had to work extremely hard for everything he ever achieved on the baseball diamond. Every January 2, Bowa would be down in the Veterans Stadium tunnel, working on hitting with coach Billy DeMars a month before spring training started. Mike was there as well, but the game came easier for him. While Bowa and Rose were out there front and center and in your face, the fans and media could never figure Mike Schmidt out, and that was a shame.

I don't think fans realized at the time how hard Mike tried to be the ultimate superstar. He not only strived to be the best player in Phillies' history, but also one of the best players of all-time, which he turned out to be regardless! Sometimes when you looked at Mike on the field, however, it seemed that he struggled to enjoy playing the game. He put tremendous, undue pressure on himself, and it wasn't until Pete Rose came to town in 1979 that somebody convinced Mike that he was one of the game's elite players and to just be himself. It's no coincidence that Mike had the best years of his career when Pete was his teammate. He loosened Mike up and took a lot of the heat off him whenever times got tough.

Despite having a fellow home run hitter like Greg Luzinski in the Phillies lineup, Mike always thought he had to carry the team on his shoulders. As a result, his postseason performances in the 1976-1978 NLCS were less than spectacular. In fact, Mike's ability to come up big in clutch situations was in question until 1980, when the Phillies played the Montreal Expos on the last weekend of the season as the two teams were tied for first place in the National League East. The Phillies won the first game of the series, 2-1, thanks to Mike's home run and two runs batted in. The Phillies then went into Saturday afternoon's game needing just one more win to clinch the division. With the score tied 4-4 in the top of the 10th inning, Mike drilled a pitch off Expos reliever Stan Bahnsen deep into the left field seats to give the Phillies a 6-4 lead that won them the NL East. In my opinion, that was the biggest home run of Mike's career. Even though he had a shaky NLCS against the Astros, he rebounded to have a great World Series against the Kansas City Royals, hitting two home runs and driving in the winning runs in the final game. For his efforts, Mike won the World Series MVP as the Phillies became first-time World Champions!

Despite winning the World Series in 1980 with an aging team, the future still looked bright for Mike Schmidt and the Phillies. Carpenter, Owens, and Green were still at the helm running the operation, the team's minor league system was still strong, and they were poised to make another World Series run in 1981. Then, in the beginning of that year, we were all hit with a bombshell. Without a question in my mind, it was the worst thing that has ever happened to the Phillies franchise.

One afternoon in spring training, Ruly Carpenter gathered all of us together and announced he was selling the team. It seemed Ruly would have had to make some difficult decisions along the way in order for the Phillies to move forward. I'll never forget him crying at the press conference when the Phillies sold Greg Luzinski to the Chicago White Sox a few weeks later. To make a long story short, Ruly didn't like what was in store for the future of baseball, and the looming work stoppage that would wipe out most of the summer's games didn't make things any better. Even though the baseball strike statistically put a dent in what would be another MVP season for Mike, many people are unaware of the fact that this is when he technically started his broadcasting career.

And I was the one who gave him his shot.

Prior to the strike, I went to the news director at Channel 10 and suggested we should bring one of the Phillies players aboard for the newscasts until the teams resumed playing again. I thought Mike would be perfect, but he wasn't exactly a popular choice among my co-workers, who really didn't interact with him as much as I did. After you talk to Mike, you find out that he's a very articulate and sharp guy. I thought he'd do very well in the role if he agreed to do it. Eventually, we asked Mike and he said yes. It was a 15-minute sports show on Sunday nights, and he did a good job! I remember taking him to the Eagles training camp in West Chester, Pennsylvania, where he threw a 60-yard pass in the air! Dick Vermeil was coaching the Eagles at the time, and Mike blew him away by putting on a pretty good show. Mike drove me home a few times after we worked together at Channel 10 and he treated me very well. Eventually, the strike ended, and Mike went back to baseball.

The 1981 Philadelphia Phillies were a great ballclub. After the strike, however, the team never regained their momentum. I think the wind was taken out of their sails and they didn't seem to have that desire like they did in 1980. Pete Rose did, but collectively, something was missing. Because of the new playoff format that was established, the teams that were in first place at the time of the strike were guaranteed automatic playoff berths. If that Phillies team played a full year, they would have finished strong and would have won big in the postseason. Instead, they faced the Montreal Expos in the very first National League Division Series (this format was officially adopted 14 years later in the 1995 postseason). Montreal was out for blood after the Phillies edged them out for the NL East crown the previous year. In the best of five series, the Phillies dropped the first two games in Montreal, but won Games 3 and 4 at Veterans Stadium. The series was tied at two games apiece, and the stage was set for Phillies ace Steve Carlton vs. Expos ace Steve Rogers in a deciding Game 5. Unfortunately, there would be no encore for the 1981 Phillies, as Rogers bested Carlton, 3-0. The Expos celebrated on the Phillies' home turf and moved on to the NLCS to face the Los Angeles Dodgers. The fans of Philadelphia were absolutely looking for a repeat, and the wind was taken right out of their sails.

"In 1981, the monkey was off the Phillies' back, the team was playing great, the fans weren't booing, everything was going well for them, and then the strike happened," recalled former longtime Phillies' broadcaster Chris Wheeler. "I really thought that was a hell of a team. That was the last hurrah for that bunch. Think of the turmoil that occurred after that season. Ruly sold the team, Dallas Green left for the Cubs and a lot of our scouts went with him. All kinds of things happened. Unfortunately, that was the end of that era. The Phillies went to the World Series in 1983, but how we won the pennant with all the older players on that team was off the wall. It was a one-year thing."

I agree with Chris. No question about it. After their Game 5 loss, the wheels started coming off the Phillies franchise. After Ruly Carpenter officially sold the team several weeks later, a group of investors headed by Bill Giles took over, signaling the beginning of several turning points during the decade of the 1980s. Rumors started surfacing during the NLDS that Phillies manager Dallas Green could be leaving the team, thus ending the possibility of him becoming the Phillies future general manager after Paul Owens retired. Meanwhile, the labor stoppage had made things tense between the Phillies and catcher Bob Boone, who was very active in player negotiations during the strike. By the end of 1981, Boone was sold to the California Angels. He went on to win five more Gold Gloves and played nine more seasons, before retiring with the Royals in 1990. It was also around this time that Larry Bowa became extremely vocal about his contract and got involved in a war of words with Giles. Shortly after the issue became public, Bowa was dealt to Dallas Green's Cubs in early 1982 for shortstop Ivan DeJesus. And by the way, to compensate for the age difference between Bowa and the younger DeJesus, the Phillies sweetened the deal by throwing in a prospect by the name of Ryne Sandberg.

Granted, Bowa was 36 years old at the time and Boone had some knee issues, but the Phillies shipped Boone off because of his role in the player's union. Don't let anybody tell you otherwise. Some of these players may have been on the flip side of their careers, but they were still integral parts of the team. The Phillies also traded key players such as Keith Moreland and Lonnie Smith, and they were some of the younger guys! This isn't Russia. Do you want a bunch of guys who fall in line, or a bunch of tigers who would play their asses off to win games? You have to put your personal feelings aside about players and find a way to make them part of your organization for life.

Bob Boone should be the Phillies general manager. Look at the great job he did putting the Washington Nationals together! Under Giles' watch, the Phillies' drafts were awful. They didn't land anybody! They made bad, bad personnel decisions. And to add insult to injury, the team let Dallas Green fleece them with every trade he made with them, and there were many. By 1984, Green and the Cubs found themselves on the doorstep of the World Series, playing in the NLCS against the San Diego Padres while fielding practically all ex-Phillies. In 1983, the Phillies went back to the World Series, but soon started a steep decline that took them decades to recover from. After Owens made the decision to take over as the team's manager in the middle of the 1983 season, it was understood that longtime Phillies coach Bobby Wine would eventually succeed Owens. However, Wine never got the job and left the organization on bad terms. Owens was replaced by John Felske. How did that work out?

By the late 1980s, only Mike Schmidt remained from those glory years. He had seen every player come and go from those teams. He watched the Phillies' minor league system, once full of prospects, poached of all its talent, with some of those players going on to have All-Star and even Hall of Fame careers. Every year, the Phillies sank further and further behind other clubs. Near the end of his career, I interviewed Bill Giles about Mike, and whether he would eventually be accorded the same respect in the Phillies organization that Willie Mays, Ted Williams, Hank Aaron, and Stan Musial had with their organizations. Giles assured me that was going to be the case. However, right after Mike won his third and final National League MVP Award in 1986, I interviewed him for 20 minutes at fitness guru and former Sixers owner Pat Croce's rehabilitation center in Broomall, Pennsylvania. Mike may have been relatively quiet as he watched everything unravel over the years, but that didn't mean he wasn't standing back and taking notes on what was going on around him. When I asked Mike the same question I asked Giles regarding his future with the Phillies, he flat out told me that he didn't think Giles would ever let him be part of the team's front office or have a say in any of their operations. When Mike's comments were made public, he was not too pleased with me. Oh well. It wasn't the first time that I'd pissed off an athlete in Philadelphia.

Now, Mike could very well deny this, but I think in the back of his mind, he wanted to be a general manager after he retired. I think he wanted to right the Phillies' ship, which was stranded so far out to sea by this time that it wouldn't have been found on the world's best radar screen. Keep in mind that until the end of his career, the majority of the Phillies teams Mike played on were contenders. He knew how Carpenter, Owens, and Green built that franchise when he was coming up in the early 1970s, because he was part of it! He knew the game plan they used. On the flip side, Mike also got a firsthand glimpse of the complete deterioration of the team. Bill Giles, for all his promotional experience, wasn't any more of a general manager than I was. Mike's frustration was evident in another interview that took place around the time he hit his 500th home run in 1987. In the interview, Mike pulled no punches, saying how the once-proud Phillies organization had hit rock bottom. He took shots at the team's front office, minor league system, and even the conditions at Veterans Stadium, which by that time had become a rat-infested dump. He took shots at Giles, the lack of any accountability in team's front office, the team's depleted minor league system, and overall lack of pride regarding the Phillies' brass.

And everything he said was 100 percent spot on.

Mike Schmidt was never one to show his emotions, but he cared deeply about the Phillies organization and badly wanted things to get back on track. In a business that has zero loyalty, a franchise like the Phillies should have felt fortunate to have their greatest player ever care the way he did. I recall Mike eventually apologizing for those remarks, but I think that was more damage control than anything. A first ballot Hall of Famer should really be allowed to say whatever he wants if it makes sense. You don't want a guy who's going to sugarcoat things, and that's one thing Mike won't do.

"I think one of the problems was that Mike wanted to jump into a major role right off the field, and they weren't ready for him to do that," said Chris Wheeler. "If you remember, he did go down to Clearwater and try to manage in the minor leagues, and he decided that wasn't for him, as opposed to what Ryne Sandberg did. Now, that's not to say other organizations don't take a player and put him right in the dugout. In this case, the Phillies decided Mike was not a guy to step right in and be named manager or general manager of the team. I'm not the one to say why. While some people understood that, it didn't sit well with other people.

"I don't think Mike would have ever been a good assistant. I think he wanted to be *the* general manager, and that he would go in, make some trades, and go home at night. I think he learned as time went on, what an all-consuming job a front office position is. I think he was much better served going out and playing golf, relaxing on his boat in Florida, and to just gear back a little bit and do what he's doing right now. I know he's really enjoying himself. The Phillies just felt they weren't going to go that way and did not think that was the role for him at the time. It's probably one of the best things that ever happened to him, because when you get into that job, you're going to get fired. I used to tell Whitey (Richie Ashburn) that all the time, because he wanted to be the Phillies' manager. They wouldn't have had that funeral for him at Fairmount Park if he was a manager or general manager, because he wouldn't have had the same luster that he previously had. Look at the way Mike is revered right now. I think the same thing would have happened to him."

Whether Mike would have been successful in the Phillies front office or not, one thing that I know for certain is that Bill Giles and his regime absolutely ruined that team. Ruined it. Giles had a perfectly well-oiled machine in place to contend for years if the Phillies kept the good baseball men they had when he bought the team in 1981 with that group of investors. Instead, Phillies ownership forced out good people like Owens, and they allowed Green to leave the team and run the Chicago Cubs, who literally gave him everything but the kitchen sink in their attempts to pry him away from the Phillies. If Owens stayed on as an advisor and Green took the reigns as general manager, the Phils would have been like Secretariat in the 1973 Belmont Stakes!

By the late 1980s when Mike's career was winding down, everybody knew he wouldn't have a chance to win another World Series with the Phillies. Around this time, he was almost coaxed by Pete Rose to go back to his birthplace of Ohio and play for the Reds. Pete mentioned to me a number of times when he was managing the Reds that he told Mike he could be his first or third baseman if he wanted to come to Cincinnati. Rose contends that if Mike played the last three or four years as a member of a winning team like the Reds, he would've ended up with 600 home runs! The Reds were on the doorstep, but the Phillies had nothing. That's another reason why Mike retired. As we all know, Pete was subsequently banned from baseball by the time the Reds won the 1990 World Series with Lou Piniella as their manager, but Mike would have been a great asset to that team. Even though the Phillies won the 1993 National League pennant just four years after Mike retired, only some of those players were homegrown.

To be honest with you, I always thought that Mike should have left the Phillies and gone to the Reds to try and win another championship.

Some of the greatest baseball players of all time played for multiple teams. Babe Ruth, the greatest Yankee of them all, finished his career with the Boston Braves. Willie Mays finished his career with the New York Mets, Hank Aaron played his final big league game with the Milwaukee Brewers in 1976, and Ty Cobb finished his career with the Philadelphia A's. Stan Musial was going to be traded to the Phillies for Robin Roberts, but he threatened to retire if the trade happened. One time, the Yankees even contemplated trading Joe DiMaggio for Ted Williams! At the end of the day, Mike got cold feet and he ended up staying with the Phillies. He retired on Memorial Day 1989, when the Phillies were on the road in San Diego. Oddly enough, I took a picture of him and my daughter together, shortly before he retired when the Phillies had a game at Veterans Stadium. What transpired several years earlier with him in that interview was water under the bridge.

A few years after Mike retired, he was golfing in a celebrity tournament in San Diego and my radio station scheduled an interview with him. He was glad to see me and was very gracious. I even saw him a few summers back at Phillies Alumni Weekend, and he was busting my chops telling me to lose some weight. As of this writing, he's back broadcasting with the Phillies on their weekend home games and I think he really does a great job. Mike understands everything about the game and I think he would have been a tremendous broadcaster if he stuck with it after he retired! I smile when I see him on the air and have a sense of pride. I was happy to be able to give him the opportunity I did at Channel 10 all those years ago.

As good as Mike is as an analyst, however, he was too valuable to just be a broadcaster. He should have been part of the regime that eventually turned the Phillies around. I always enjoyed Mike's company whenever I conversed with him. If Ruly Carpenter still had the club, he would have been with the franchise forever and wouldn't have disappeared to Florida. It could have been a great PR move for the Phillies. Instead, he was in exile all those years, almost like he was cast off. Mike's not a happy-go-lucky type of guy, but there's ways of finessing people. He's very knowledgeable and insightful, and could have easily been appointed as an assistant or

With my daughter, Ashleigh, and Phillies legend Mike Schmidt, shortly before his retirement in 1989.

special advisor to the president or general manager of any Major League Baseball club.

In my mind, Mike Schmidt will always hold a special place among Philadelphia's greatest athletes, and I don't think people realized how spectacular he truly was until his career was over.

CHAPTER 17

A New Decade, A New Town, A New Career

THE RETIREMENT OF Mike Schmidt marked the end of an era in Philadelphia sports, as well as the end of the 1980s. In addition to my work at Channel 10, some additional opportunities were also coming along. As the 1990s got underway, I was approached by *Sports Radio 610 WIP* Program Director Tom Bigby, who wanted me to work their Eagles show on Sundays. Only thing was, it was the same time of the actual Eagles games on an opposite station. WIP had lost their football contract to WYSP, and I wasn't at all comfortable with the situation. Next thing I knew, Eagles play-by-play man and former colleague Merrill Reese got wind of this and offered me seven minutes a week on his Eagles pregame show. What was originally supposed to be a brief cameo turned into a full-time hosting gig with former Eagle John Spagnola, Super Bowl champion Johnny Sample and my good friend Tom Cardella. On top of that, former Eagles quarterback Ron Jaworski wanted me to work on his post-game show with him. Both shows were really popular with the fans and got great ratings.

What was originally a tough spot for me ended up working out pretty well, and I began to wonder if there was something else out there for me in the world of sports besides a producer's job. I had several conversations with the late, great Philadelphia sportscaster Gary Papa that really opened my eyes regarding a bigger picture than I perhaps originally envisioned. Gary would always tell me I should try sports talk radio, and that I was wasting my time behind the scenes. I was apprehensive at first because I'd basically been a sports producer and only dabbled in other areas of the business from time to time.

Then in 1991, I wound up meeting a sports producer named Chris Visser, who was the brother of sportscaster Lesley Visser. Chris' track record in helping establish sports talk radio in San Diego is legendary, and his accomplishments would probably take up an entire page. Chris wanted me to come out and work at a San Diego radio station over the course of four days, so I went out and auditioned during my vacation from Channel 10. One day I worked the morning show, next day the midday show, then the drive time show, and the final day I did the night show as their NFL Draft expert. The station's owner, John Lynch Sr. (father of former Tampa Buccaneers safety John Lynch), sent the station's general manager Tom McKinley out to speak with me. Tom liked what I did on the air, but thought I only knew football. When I told him what I did back east, he offered me a contract for $60,000 to join *XTRA Sports 690 AM*. As tempting as it was, my parents were elderly and I couldn't leave them behind. I was also in the middle of a divorce and overall the timing just wasn't right. I have to be honest here. More often than not, a career in sports is not conducive to a great marriage. It's a very tough life. Both of you have to work at it, and I think more so the man than the woman. The sports world runs 24/7, and sometimes, I think maybe I never should've gotten married. The greatest part about all of it was that I brought a daughter into the world.

As far as our local sports teams were concerned, there wasn't really much to embrace. The Flyers and Sixers were rebuilding and the Eagles were beginning their decline. However, the 1993 Phillies were taking Major League Baseball by storm, becoming the sport's Cinderella story of the year. In the process, they became one of the city's most popular all-time teams—from a fan's perspective, not by the media. They weren't so beloved if you had to cover them. Players like Jim Eisenreich, Terry Mulholland and Tommy Greene were great guys, but the team as a whole was tough to deal with and most of them wouldn't even give you the time of day.

The reason Philadelphia embraced them was because they were the underdog: a blue collar team who lost 92 games the year before and weren't expected to do anything in 1993. Then, those "special vitamins" that centerfielder Lenny Dykstra was ingesting really helped propel them. Dykstra was a very complex guy. Only a few people got close to him and he was a difficult person to deal with. A lot of times, you'd have to interview the back of his head after the game as he sat in his locker. Third baseman Dave Hollins was a pretty intense guy, and pitcher Danny Jackson, along with first baseman John Kruk, were particularly tough with the media. There were moments when John was cooperative, but other moments when he wasn't. I had spent a lot of time in the off-season with catcher Darren Daulton back in 1986, when he was rehabbing from a severe knee injury. Darren was okay with me, but he was the leader of that team and he changed a little bit after being around that group of guys. I loved their manager, the late Jim Fregosi, but overall, it was tough to be fond of that team.

I honestly don't know why they had such hostility towards us. Maybe it was an "us against them" type of mentality. They kept their distance and it was very hard to try and break through to them. They had their inner circle and that was it. Maybe that was deliberate. It wasn't like the 1980 Phillies, who were a fun bunch of guys to be around, at least from my perspective. They could be tough at times, but I enjoyed Pete Rose, Larry Bowa, Mike Schmidt, Greg Luzinski, Lonnie Smith, Keith Moreland and those guys.

I think a lot of people contend that several players on that Phillies team were taking those "special vitamins" I referred to earlier in regards to Dykstra, who had an awesome 1993 postseason. After winning the NL East, the Phillies upset the Atlanta Braves in the NLCS before losing in the World Series on a walk-off home run by Toronto Blue Jays outfielder Joe Carter. My former colleague at Channel 10, Al Meltzer, was in Toronto and interviewed losing pitcher Mitch Williams after the Phillies' Game 6 loss. Whether you like him or dislike him, Mitch was always a stand-up guy and was gracious enough to do an interview after throwing the pitch that lost the World Series. Some of those players were not too happy that Al got access to Mitch so quickly after losing the game. I was in Miami spotting a football game when they lost. I remember getting back to my hotel room, turning on the television, and seeing the replay of Carter's home run. The 1993 Phillies were a one-shot deal. After that season, the team wouldn't even sniff the .500 mark until 2001.

The following year in 1994, John Lynch Sr. contacted me again and offered me a talk show and the color analyst job for the San Diego

Chargers. They flew me out, wined and dined me, but I still wasn't quite ready to make the move. My daughter was still in grade school and things weren't properly aligned yet. I turned them down again. As it turned out, an awful tragedy saw the San Diego gang reach out to me one last time in 1996. Chet Forte, longtime director of ABC's *Monday Night Football* and a San Diego talk show host, died suddenly of a massive heart attack in May of that year. I was contacted by sportscaster Lee Hamilton and my future partner Steve Hartman, who both asked me to audition. I told Channel 10 I had "personal problems" that needed to be taken care of, and I went out west for four days. With the way social media is today, there would be no way I could get away with that now. After I worked some shows with Steve for a week, management at the station asked him who he wanted to replace Chet. Originally, he wanted Chris "Mad Dog" Russo (from *Mike and the Mad Dog* fame out of WFAN in New York), but Chris wanted to stay on the East Coast. I was Steve's next choice. I was back in Philadelphia attending Eagles training camp at Lehigh University, when I received a phone call telling me the job in San Diego was mine if I wanted it. At 50 years of age and having received two previous offers, I made the bold decision to move away from my lifelong home and start a new career in a sports market that was completely foreign to me.

After they met my so-called "demands" and offered me a three-year deal, I didn't turn them down this time.

I took the job.

Me and Mom. March 10, 1952.

With former Channel 6 news anchor Gunnar Back (left) and former Minnesota Senator and 38th Vice President of the United States, Hubert Humphrey. 1967.

Posing for a picture with Academy Award-winning actor and comedian Red Buttons.

With my cousin, Walter Artymovich, and WPVI Channel 6 sportscaster Joe Pellegrino.

With Eagles cornerback and future NFL head coach and analyst Herman Edwards on November 19, 1978. This photo was taken just moments after he recovered a fumble and scored the game-winning touchdown in the "Miracle at the Meadowlands" game against the New York Giants. Look it up!

With my Channel 10 colleague Ron Burke. 1992.

My Channel 10 colleagues and yours truly, during my Philadelphia Farewell Tour, 1996. To my right is WPVI Channel 6 sportscaster Gary Papa, who fought a valiant battle with cancer that claimed his life in 2009 at age 54.

With NFL legend Jerry Rice, who the Eagles should have picked in the 1985 NFL Draft.

*With Cowboys' Hall of Fame running back and
Philadelphia Eagles' nemesis Emmitt Smith.*

Me and the late, great Major League Baseball Hall of Fame catcher Gary Carter.

Me, my daughter, Ashleigh and her husband, Brandon South, with my grandchildren McKenzie and Mitchell.

With Corrine and my sister-in-law, Rosie Anescheck.

Posing for a pic with Corrine and her son, Victor DiMarco.

Spending time with Corrine and her daughter's family: Leslie Ann Boccio, son Anthony III, husband Anthony Boccio, daughters Gia (front), Liana (back), and their family dog, Molly.

CHAPTER 18

"Philly" Billy and the Loose Cannons

Despite the excitement of starting a new phase of my career, I was very apprehensive about leaving Philadelphia. I had a good job at Channel 10, but things were changing. The station was owned by CBS when I started there, but they flip-flopped with NBC in the summer of 1995 and changed networks. They were bringing in their own people and I didn't have a good feeling about it, so it was another reason for me to make the move.

As it turned out, I would not be the only one making a move to the West Coast. Another person I had to convince was my new wife, Corinne, who I married in October 1994. Right off the bat, she experienced the rigors of what my job entailed.

Corinne Werndl: "The day after we got married, I went with Bill to Florida because he had to spot a football game between Florida and Georgia. The next day, we had to get up at four in the morning to fly back to Philadelphia, so he could work the Eagles pre-game show! I knew what I was getting into when I married Billy, but that was a good lesson for me.

"Then we went to Hawaii for our honeymoon the following January. Bill wasn't expecting to work, but all of the sudden, I was sitting outside, there's this big bus, and I heard someone giving instructions to these guys who were on the bus. It was my husband's voice. Turns out that Mike Gottfried, who was one of the broadcasters at ESPN, had elected Bill as his special teams coach for the Hula Bowl. Billy then came over to me and started apologizing. He wasn't even supposed to do that, but Mike just put him to work. And of course, Billy can't say no, and that's one of his problems. He can't say no to anybody!

"Then in 1996, I had finally found my dream home in Chadds Ford, Pennsylvania. I loved it and was really happy. For two years, I decorated everything, and then Billy got the job in California. In the beginning, I had mixed emotions, because I had always wanted to see California. On the other hand, it was tough because I really missed my family, but I knew that was where he needed to go. Billy never stops. He's a machine. He's plugged in, and there's no way you're going to be able to unplug him!"

Although she visited me occasionally and completely supported my decision, my one regret was that I had to leave my daughter Ashleigh behind. I still have the letter she wrote me when I left for San Diego in my briefcase. My mother passed away in August 1994, so Ashleigh was my primary link to Philadelphia. Deep down inside, it really hurt that I couldn't take her with me. It was difficult for her, too, but I always talked to her on a regular basis and still do. We have a good relationship.

Ashleigh South (Bill's daughter): "My dad is my best friend. He still calls me every day without skipping a beat. I talk to him about everything. He just loves his grandkids. He spoils them to death. At the time my dad left for San Diego, I was only 11 and didn't fully understand things. But now, in retrospect, I realized he had the opportunity of a lifetime. That was his dream. I couldn't be mad at him for that. Not many people can get up, go to work every day and say they love to do what they do. I missed him and it was hard not having him around all the time, but he was following his dream and I was happy that he had that chance. When I was in high school, he came home for my cheerleading competitions and my prom. He got home on a Thursday and flew back to San Diego that Friday after I left for my prom. With the time changes from Pennsylvania to California, I thought he was crazy, but that's him. He made sure he was still there for all the important events. He knew how important those things were to me and he didn't want to miss them."

My working home for the first four and a half years in San Diego was *XTRA Sports 690 AM*. Luckily, that station had a blowtorch signal. You could hear it up and down the West Coast, which wasn't necessarily the best thing for me in the early going. It was rough at the start. My first day on the air was August 4, 1996. I was replacing a popular guy like Chet Forte and that was tough. But my co-host, Steve Hartman, who immediately gave me the moniker "Philly" Billy upon my arrival, couldn't have been more helpful. Steve would run certain topics by me before we got on the air, so I knew what was coming when we went live. Then I would offer my opinions on the subject and we would battle back and forth on the air about it. Steve was easy to work with. The two of us just had a certain type of chemistry.

What made the show so unique with Chet and Steve (and later with me and Steve) was our loyalty to our respective coasts. Chet, who was from New Jersey, had an East Coast bias, as do I. Steve, a California native and lifelong Lakers fan, has a West Coast bias. Steve went to college at UCLA, and we were able to get Sonny Vaccaro on our show several times. Sonny was a former sports marketing executive who signed Michael Jordan to his first sneaker deal with Nike. Sonny would come on and mention how legendary basketball coach John Wooden wouldn't have won all those championships if it weren't for Sam Gilbert, who "provided funds" for the UCLA basketball and football programs. In other words, Sam made sure that certain high school players were going to attend UCLA, and he did whatever it took to get those players. Of course, Steve would reluctantly agree. It was funny. One time, Joe Natoli, one of my good friends who

Me, my wife, Corrine, and my co-host/fellow "Loose Cannon" Steve Hartman with President Bill Clinton.

lives in Ohio, called the show and encouraged me to be on the lookout for a sophomore at St. Vincent–St. Mary High School in Akron by the name of LeBron James. I ran his name by Sonny the next time he came on the show, and he was floored that I knew about him!

After about nine months in San Diego, things started to come together. The fact that I was a color analyst for the Chargers helped increase my profile as well. I had some absolutely wonderful times working on those games. Bobby Ross was the Chargers head coach for some of my time there and was a just a quality guy through and through. I still keep in touch with Bobby to this day. Before I knew it, the 2.0 version of the Loose Cannons had the number-one rated sports talk radio show in Southern California. Here I was, a guy primarily known for his work behind the scenes over several decades in Philadelphia who was starting another phase of his career, and now I had this sudden notoriety. That was mind boggling!

One time in a Beverly Hills restaurant, I was eating with Steve and Ed Goran, a founding FOX Sports executive, when our waiter came to take our order. As soon as I spoke, he yelled with excitement "Philly" Billy?! Is that you?!" His name was Henry Finkelstein. I still remember his name. I couldn't believe he knew who I was. That was a great, great moment. People would recognize me in the supermarkets and in airports as well. One time, I was in El Paso, Texas at 12 am in the morning, and I asked a guy where I could find my luggage. The moment I spoke, he knew who I was! Unbelievable! You dream about fairy tales and dreams coming true, and San Diego was it for me.

In order for me to become more immersed in the San Diego area, I had to do my homework and find out more about the history of sports in the city. San Diego's first year of professional sports was in 1961, when the San Diego Chargers arrived from the AFL (they spent their first season in Los Angeles). Baseball didn't come to the city until the San Diego Padres played their first game in 1969. Although San Diego's sports history wasn't as long and distinguished or even celebrated like Philadelphia's, the city had produced some great high school athletes. Ted Williams, Marcus Allen, Brian Sipe and Junior Seau are just a few of the *Who's Who* that have hailed from San Diego. I was in awe. On the radio, Steve and I covered the

Chargers, the Padres and San Diego State basketball and football. When I got there, the school's basketball team was in really, really bad shape. During the 1998-99 season, they were 4-22. It took them a while, but once they got head coach Steve Fisher, they changed the culture of the program. We also covered some great golf tournaments as well, including the Bob Hope Classic and Torrey Pines. Remote broadcasts were always fun when it came time for those tournaments. Every year, Steve and I would go to the Super Bowl and the NCAA Tournament in March. It was a lot of fun.

The crowning achievement for San Diego sports while I was out there was the Padres' 1998 World Series run. That year, the team upset the Atlanta Braves in the NLCS and it was an unbelievable scene. The fans were waving their white rally towels and it was just wild. The Padres thought they had a chance to compete with the Yankees in the World Series, but in Game 1, Padres left-hander Mark Langston got squeezed on a pitch he threw to Yankees slugger Tino Martinez in the seventh inning of a tie game. What should have been strike three turned into ball three. Martinez then promptly hit a grand slam into the upper deck at Yankee

With Steve Hartman and boxing legend George Foreman.

Stadium, putting the game out of reach and completely altering the tone of the World Series. Unfortunately, the Padres never recovered, and the Yankees swept them in four games.

Padres skipper Bruce Bochy, who managed that 1998 team, was a lot of fun and one hell of a manager. One time, I wasn't happy with the Padres' starting lineup for a certain game. So Bruce, who knew I would always come down on the field after our radio show, stood at the top step of the dugout with a blank lineup card.

"If you're so smart, you fill out the lineup," Bruce said.

"You want me to?" I asked him.

Bruce just shook his head and started laughing. He was one of the most regular guys I've ever met in sports. I truly believe that the Padres could have won a World Series in that era, but the management of the team didn't do enough to give Bruce the proper weapons he needed to really compete with the big boys. The team wouldn't exceed their $70 million dollar payroll. In my opinion, all they needed to do was raise it to around $78-80 million, but they just wouldn't do it. I thought that particular group of players was *thisclose* to doing something special. After Bruce left the Padres, he went on to win several World Series titles with the San Francisco Giants. How many managers can sit in their office and say they've won three (and counting) World Series championships? In my opinion, Bruce should eventually be considered for the Baseball Hall of Fame.

I struck up some nice friendships with the Padres players over the years, including Tony Gwynn, who I will discuss later. I was in the parking lot prior to one of the 1998 World Series games at Qualcomm Stadium, when Mark Loretta, then a player on the Brewers and a future Padre, approached me expressing his desire to meet me. That always stuck with me, and I became very good friends with Mark. One of my favorite players on the Padres during this time was Phil Nevin. When I flew out to Seattle for the 2001 All-Star Game, I was getting on the plane and Phil recognized my voice when he was sitting in first class! Phil would get ticked off at me every now and then, but we always had a good relationship. Before he left the Padres, he thanked me for always having his back and gave me a signed bat. A lot of people came down on Phil during his time in San Diego, but he was a very talented player. I enjoyed him.

Bruce Bochy has won multiple championships with the San Francisco Giants, but he's still the same guy he was back when he managed the Padres.

I also can't say enough about former Padres closer Trevor Hoffman, the greatest closer in National League history. Back on Opening Day 2005, I remember Trevor gave up a game-winning three-run homer against the Colorado Rockies. The fans were angry, calling into our show wanting Trevor to retire, the whole deal. I objected to this, urging the callers to let the season play out. I also reminded them of all the work Trevor had done for the San Diego baseball community. So the Padres came back home, and when I said hello to Trevor, he jumped on me and refused to speak to me. Turns out, some third party delivered what I previously said about

Trevor in a rather convoluted twist, as if I was trying to run him out of town. My engineer managed to make me a tape of the broadcast and I put it in Trevor's locker. I went up to the press box right before the game and my cell phone rang. It was Trevor. He called me and apologized. That's the kind of guy Trevor Hoffman is. In a twist of fate, I had the pleasure of throwing out the first pitch at the game where he got his 500th career save!

Longtime Padres broadcaster Jerry Coleman was also terrific. They called him "The Colonel" because he was a Marine Corps pilot in World War II. Jerry also served in the Korean War prior to starting his Major League Baseball career. Jerry was the Associated Press Rookie of the Year in 1949 for the New York Yankees and the World Series MVP in 1950, when the Yankees swept the Phillies in four games. The Colonel was a very engaging and terrific guy. He talked about Joe DiMaggio and the presence he had in the Yankees locker room, as well as Yogi Berra and the Yankee tradition. Jerry always talked about how much it meant to wear the Yankees jersey, as well as the expectations of performing at a very high level to stay on the team. He also had a managing stint with the Padres in 1980, but the game had changed too much for him. By that time, the players were mostly dictating how things were run, as opposed to the manager taking charge back in the day when he played. Despite the lack of overall success the team had during his time broadcasting, Jerry loved the Padres and always had enthusiasm. He was so happy when the Padres went to the World Series in 1998 because the Fall Classic was such a part of his baseball pedigree with the Yankees. I'll never forget one of his famous slogans: *"You can hang a star on that baby!"* I really miss Jerry Coleman. He was just a prince of a man.

It wasn't all fun and games, however. A few months after I arrived in San Diego, Steve and I became the focus of a national story, and a case of mistaken identity on one of our broadcasts found me face to face with a very unhappy NFL Hall of Fame offensive lineman.

CHAPTER 19

A Dan Dierdorf Impersonation Gone Wrong

THE WEEK AFTER NFL Hall of Famer Dan Dierdorf played his final game in 1983, he went to work at CBS Radio for the NFL Playoffs. Dan's first game was an AFC Divisional Playoff matchup between the Miami Dolphins and the Seattle Seahawks. Jim Kelly (again, not to be confused with the Bills' Hall of Fame quarterback) and Dan were the broadcast team, and yours truly was the spotter. A week later, we worked the NFC Championship Game between the Washington Redskins and the San Francisco 49ers. During the time on the plane traveling to the games, I sat with Dan, talked football and got to know him real well. When all was said and done, he had a long and successful career on the football field as well as in the broadcast booth.

As cordial as my first meetings were with Dan, however, it was another incident involving the two of us in November, 1996 that garnered some pretty big national attention. In the process, it got me and my *XTRA 690* co-host Steve Hartman in a little bit of trouble.

Jack Evans, *XTRA 690*'s programming director, had a friend from Chicago who was an impersonator of Cubs iconic broadcaster Harry Caray. I was also working as the color analyst for the Chargers, who had a Monday Night Football game against the Detroit Lions later that evening. Dan was ABC's lead color analyst and would be working the game with Al Michaels. It was Jack's idea to bring in his impersonator friend and have him do a parody between Dierdorf and Michaels. Did I feel comfortable doing this? Not really, but when my program director says we have to put his friend on from Chicago, what are you gonna do? You're caught between a rock and a hard place, and the rock is your program director.

Steve was always the adventurous type, so he didn't mind. So we put this guy on the show and he was on the air for about 25 minutes. Whether he was supposed to be impersonating an intoxicated version of Dan Dierdorf or not, I don't know, but he sure sounded like it. During the parody, he accused Michaels of having halitosis and wearing a girdle, the whole deal. When the segment ended, callers dialed in and blasted Dierdorf, accusing him of being drunk on the air. Only thing was, we didn't bother to tell any of the listeners that it wasn't the real Dan Dierdorf. As I said, the guy was basically a Harry Caray impersonator. If you had any semblance of a brain, you wouldn't have connected Dan Dierdorf with this guy. They have stuff like this on Philadelphia sports talk radio shows all the time! But because we made such a big deal out of it, Dan got upset about it.

And I found out just how upset he was a short time later.

When the show was over, I left for the stadium to work the game and I was confronted by the real Dan Dierdorf in the broadcast booth! He wasn't happy with me at all! He knew who I was, and he was mad. I'm not sure he even heard the interview, but Kelly Carter from USA Today made a big deal out of everything. Allegedly, she was the one who approached Dan and asked him if he was drinking during the "interview." Let's be honest here. Dan Dierdorf is a 6'3" 275-pound former offensive tackle. I wasn't about to confront him or get into a tussle with him. He could kill me. We didn't come to blows or anything, as I tried to convince Dan it was a joke and we were just having some fun on the air. We didn't think it was offensive, but I think Dan got ticked off because we didn't tell the callers it wasn't him and we didn't have his back. After voicing his displeasure with me and letting me know how angry he was, Dan left the booth.

"Who does a Dan Dierdorf impersonation?" recalled my radio partner, Steve Hartman. "Because *XTRA 690* was the Chargers' flagship station, we called the impersonator about an hour before the pregame show and brought him on. So he came on the air, and we announced 'Joining us right now, getting ready for the big Monday Night Football game is Dan Dierdorf. Dan, how are you?' He starts doing his thing, and to me, it literally sounded like an inebriated Harry Caray, not Dan Dierdorf."

"We started asking him questions about Al Michaels and he went into the whole halitosis thing. It was so over the top goofy and obviously not Dan Dierdorf that we just sort of played along with it. At no point did we even think about telling the audience it wasn't actually him. It was just stupid. It wasn't even necessary to identify who the person was. So we finished the interview, and Billy went to the stadium to get ready for the game, and Dan Dierdorf popped his head in the Chargers' booth. He couldn't understand how we had somebody impersonate a drunken version of him on our radio show!"

"This was a huge national story. You have to understand how big our show was. We weren't just number one in San Diego, we had the number one-rated midday sports show in Los Angeles. By far. No one else was even close. Next thing you know, ABC was going to sue our radio station. But yeah, Dan Dierdorf was threatening Bill Werndl right there at the Chargers game. It was unbelievable. This was one of those stories where somebody else usually hears it about it, but then other people react to something they never even heard. There was no lawsuit, the whole thing completely blew over and nothing ever happened."

I don't think Steve or I would have had to pay any money if a lawsuit ever came about. We were told by the program director to put this guy on the radio. It wasn't our fault at all. Jack Evans came up with this cockamamie idea because we were doing the game and wanted to take viewership from the Monday Night Football crew. The controversy lasted for about a week and then it subsided. By now, we figured most people knew the interview was fake. Nonetheless, we apologized at the start of the show the next day.

I thought about having Dan on our show a few times after the incident, but I didn't think it was the right climate. One day, I'd like to talk to him, just to clear the air. I liked Dan. I was part of his first broadcast and he was very nice to me. I'm very proud to have seen the guy reach the heights he did. Dan did a hell of a job. At the end of the day, we have to take responsibility for our actions, and I feel bad things got misconstrued.

CHAPTER 20

Gene Mauch and the Lingering Pain from 1964

WITHOUT A DOUBT, manager Dick Williams was one of the greatest skippers in baseball history. Despite winning back-to-back titles with the Oakland A's in 1972-73, he was a very gruff guy who was tough to work with. Although his attitude and demeanor eventually wore thin on his players, it seemed some of his teams adopted his personality. At least for a little while. The players on those Oakland teams weren't exactly the type to get tea and crumpets together after playing nine innings, and does anybody remember the game-long brawl between the Williams-managed Padres and the Atlanta Braves back in the summer of 1984? Exactly. If you produced on the field, what happened in and out of the clubhouse didn't matter to him. An old school manager, Williams got a lot of his managerial training while playing under Paul Richards, a former player who was a manager and general manager of the Baltimore Orioles in the 1950s and early 1960s. Williams was a very interesting guy, and I once had the pleasure of interviewing him on my radio show. During my time with Dick, I asked him who he thought were some of the game's all-time greatest skippers.

One of Williams' answers was none other than Gene Mauch, the manager of the 1964 Philadelphia Phillies, who infamously blew a six and a half game lead with 12 games to play, losing the pennant to the St. Louis Cardinals. Williams insisted that if there was ever a clinic on managing, the one guy who should conduct that clinic was Mauch. As far as knowing the rules and how to play the game, Williams thought it was mind-boggling how Mauch was always one step ahead of everybody. Williams went on to say that although Mauch's teams never won the big one, he knew baseball inside out and upside down. The relationship between Mauch and his players could be a mixed one. Former Phillies second baseman Tony Taylor has credited Mauch with teaching him how to play the game of baseball, and despite all the issues Dick Allen had while playing for the Phillies, Mauch apparently wasn't one of them. On the flip side, there was apparently no love lost between Mauch and former Phillies pitcher/manager Dallas Green, who often discussed his relationship with Mauch in his book *The Mouth That Roared: My Six Outspoken Decades in Baseball.*

I was the sound technician at the press conference when Mauch got fired from the Phillies on a Saturday night in June, 1968. I also happened to interview him with Steve Hartman several years before he passed away in 2005. We had Mauch on the program before and always called him at his Palm Springs, California home. During one particular interview, I mentioned to Mauch how I used to watch him at Connie Mack Stadium when he managed the Phillies, and remembered him standing in the dugout watching the opposing team's infield practice. He would see who had the best or worst arm and who wasn't going for ground balls hard enough, just to get any kind of edge. Mauch also watched the opposing team's batting practice. He looked at all this stuff. Talk about a guy who got the most he could out of that Phillies team in 1964! As I've previously mentioned, that year is not a pleasant one to remember for fans of the club. Nonetheless, I was a professional with Mauch, and I fully went ahead with the interview with no problem whatsoever.

Gene was very succinct, direct and to the point. I remember asking him why he never sat down in the dugout during a game, which led to an interesting response.

"I'm not sitting down now. I'm doing this interview standing up in my kitchen," he said. "When you sit down, you're never as sharp as you should be."

It's been over 50 years since that 1964 Phillies debacle, and people in Philadelphia still remember it vividly. To this day, speculation remains as to why things unfolded for the Phillies the way they did. Were they just a bunch of overachievers whose luck ran out? Did they choke the pennant away? Were Phillies starting pitchers Jim Bunning and Chris Short burnt out? Nobody will ever really know the truth to those questions, but there's a possibility that there were other mitigating factors. I heard from some very good sources that back in the day that there were a lot of "greenies" and "red juice" in many major league clubhouses at the time. Red juice, which was very prominent, consisted of crushed amphetamines. At the end of the 1964 season, more and more national media were coming to Phillies games, and although Mauch thought the team would win anyway, he apparently insisted that the juice get disposed of, and the wheels came off soon after. Is it a coincidence? Who knows? What I do know is that I missed three days of school because I was so sick over the fact that the Phillies lost the pennant.

"They didn't run out of gas. Mauch killed their pitching by throwing Bunning and Short on two days' rest," insisted Stan Hochman. "Mauch didn't even wait for the losing streak to start. He pitched Bunning on two days rest against Houston in the middle of September, thinking he could pick up a quick, easy win. Of course, Bunning got beat, but they were still six and a half in front with 12 games to play. He didn't trust Art Mahaffey, he didn't use Ray Culp after the beginning of September. He went to Ed Roebuck, Bobby Shantz, Bobby Locke, and he just killed the pitching. Mauch once said Ferguson Jenkins wouldn't pitch inside and he had no guts. That tells you all you need to know about Mauch."

"First of all, the 1964 Phillies had no business being where they were in the first place," said Steve Hartman. "There was no doubt, at that point in time, that Jim Bunning was a better pitcher than Bob Gibson. Gibson's best days were still in his future. Man for man, however, the St. Louis Cardinals were a vastly superior team to the Phillies. Outside of Johnny Callison and Richie Allen, they didn't have much in their lineup. Of course, it was very easy for me to be the anti-Gene Mauch. When Mauch managed the Angels in the 1982 and 1986 ALCS, the guy just butchered those two series with his managing. The one thing everyone agreed about with Gene Mauch was that nobody knew the rules better. He knew every nook and cranny of every rule book. He knew rules that nine out of ten umpires had no clue about. He was a master. But obviously, a lot of managing has to do with handling your pitching staff, and he just blew it."

"He panicked in the last two weeks of that 1964 season. He had Jim Bunning and Chris Short, and kept throwing them out there hoping that somehow, someway, they could pull this thing out. But Mauch had no faith in any other pitcher, and the whole thing just blew up in his face. The same thing happened in 1982. The Angels won the first two games against the Milwaukee Brewers in a best of five series. They were one win away from going to the World Series. Instead of saving Tommy John on rest for a Game 5, he panicked, threw him in Game 4, and the Angels lost that game as well as Game 5. In 1986, Donnie Moore had a bum shoulder, and Mauch threw him out there to pitch. Gene Mauch knew baseball backwards and forwards. He had forgotten more about baseball than most people know. But ninety percent of managing is handling your pitching staff, and Mauch did not know how to do that. He just proved it time and time again and he would panic. He would ask more of guys than they were capable of doing. It happened in 1964, 1982 and 1986. In the biggest spotlights of his managerial career, he failed. Catastrophically."

When I told Bill White on that fishing trip just how much I hated him in 1964 for helping take the pennant away from the Phillies, he just chuckled, but I was seriously devastated. I listened to almost every game on the radio and watched every game on television during that stretch. I remember it like it was yesterday: Frank Robinson was at the plate for the Reds facing Phillies pitcher Art Mahaffey. Chico Ruiz was on third base for the Reds and stole home. The Phillies lost, 1-0, and that was the beginning of the downward spiral. It was seriously one of the most demoralizing times in my life.

It took the Phillies 16 years to finally exorcise those demons.

CHAPTER 21

How Sports Today Has Gone Soft

ON THE MORNING of the historic Monday night baseball game on ABC that never was, Bill White, Bob Gibson, and yours truly were eating breakfast over at the Marriott Hotel in St. Louis. After we sat down to eat, Bob brought up a certain incident that transpired between him and Bill a few years after Bill was traded to the Phillies and Bob was still pitching for the Cardinals.

"Hey Bill, remember when you came over to Philadelphia and I hit you on the elbow?" Bob asked.

"You're damn right I remember that," Bill shot back.

"You know why?" Bob inquired, as if he already knew the answer.

"Yeah," Bill acknowledged.

A few months earlier in May 1968, Bill beat Bob with a walk-off single at Connie Mack Stadium that won the game for the Phillies, 1-0.

Bob didn't forget that.

Several months later, Bill came to the plate with Bob on the mound in the second inning of a Cardinals-Phillies game in St. Louis. On the first pitch, Bob ran a slider on the outside part of the plate, which Bill fouled off. The next pitch was right on Bill's elbow. Bill went to first and had a few words for Bob along the way.

"What are you doing Bob?! We were teammates for years!" he yelled.

"We're not friends on the field!" Bob barked back at him.

Bob Gibson did not believe he had any friends on the baseball field. None. In his eyes, the opposing team was the enemy. He didn't care if it was his best friend in the world. Anyone else other than the person wearing the same jersey was an adversary, and that was that. After the game, the two went out to dinner.

Contrary to almost everything you see today, what happened between Bill and Bob was not uncommon back in the era which they played. One time early in his career, Bill was a rookie for the New York Giants and reached first base in a game against their main rival, the Brooklyn Dodgers. The Dodgers first baseman was Jackie Robinson, who didn't say one word to Bill when he reached first base. At all. Again, the feeling back then was that you were an opponent. Athletes had no time for the opposing team. They were out there to beat the other team's brains in. That was the mentality back then. And I don't care what you see on those old sports films of teams posing for pictures and talking before games. That was staged by the production company, who needed footage for their highlight reels. Remember Pete Rose's takeout slide of Mets shortstop Bud Harrelson in the 1973 NLCS? How about Graig Nettles vs. George Brett in the 1977 ALCS between the Yankees and Royals? You think it's crazy whenever two NBA teams go at it? They did that all the time back in the 60s! The bottom line was pure and simple: These players and teams didn't like each other! Only one player I can think of sticks out in my mind over the last decade or so who NEVER socialized with opposing players. That was Trevor Hoffman. That's it!

One time, Bill White told me a story about Maury Wills, the great Dodgers shortstop who stole a lot of bases during his major league career. 586 of them to be exact. Bill was playing first base for the Cardinals one game when Maury was taking a rather generous lead off of first base. The first pickoff attempt by the Cardinals pitcher landed in Bill's glove, and he tagged Maury on the back of the head. On the next throw, Bill tagged Maury a little harder. This time, it was on the shoulder. The next tag landed harder on Maury's back, and the next one even harder on Maury's back leg!

A baseball and a glove hitting you on the back of the leg hurts! Maury went in the clubhouse after the game and was black and blue from all those snap throws. He confirmed this story with me when I was in San Diego. Players don't do those kinds of things anymore! It's "Oh, I'm sorry. Did I tag you too hard?" That's what bothers me! It's all hearts and flowers. How many players in today's game slide hard into second base when trying to break up a double play? Back in the day, a player would go right through the shortstop or second baseman. You would just drill them! Old school players weren't vicious individuals. That's the way they learned the game, and that's the way they played the game! "Sad Sam" Jones was a tough right-handed major league pitcher for several teams during the 1950s and early 1960s. One day when he was pitching, Phillies second baseman Tony Taylor bunted for a base hit. Sam wasn't a very good fielding pitcher, and he fell off the mound while trying to field Tony's bunt. When Sam got up, he walked over to first base and warned Tony that he was going to pay next time he was up. That's the way they played back then. It was dog eat dog, not Huggy Bear and "What it is"! If I were Bill or Bob, I'd be appalled at what they see today. It is not the same game they learned.

The current game of baseball is an embarrassment. It really is. Honestly. I was fortunate enough to be around the old school players. Guys like Bill White and Pete Rose were throwbacks. They didn't make as much money as the players do now, but they played the game right! That's why it's so difficult for me to watch baseball and sports in general today, because I know how hard players like Bill and Pete played. They would do anything to get an edge. Anything. That's the way the game should be played, instead of this lovey-dovey stuff. I hate seeing first basemen talk to the opposing base runner who just got on base. Why should he have to talk to them? He just got on base! Infielders who help a guy up after a double play? Are you kidding me?! Come on! You're going to help a guy up that you're trying to beat? You're trying to take these guys down!

The same can be said for some of these "phantom" injuries that you see affecting today's players. Thirty years ago, we never heard of an oblique injury or pectoral injury! I need to go through my doctoral dictionary to figure out what half of these new injuries are. Players used to play through pain! Pete Rose played with a broken toe! You have some players who play the game the way it's supposed to be played in this era. Back when he played for the Phillies, second baseman Chase Utley reportedly played the majority of the 2008 season with a busted hip, but those guys are few and far between. The late former Yankee and Padres Hall of Fame broadcaster Jerry Coleman once told me an interesting story. One of the reasons his

Yankees teams from the late 1940s and 1950s had so much success was because they would make six to seven thousand dollars just making the postseason. They had offseason jobs, but these guys were driven to play! I don't begrudge a player for making the kind of money that they do, but come on: Play the game hard! Money has corrupted baseball and all the other sports. You're no longer getting an honest effort night in and night out.

Sometimes after the World Series runner-up loses, you'll see players from that team go into the locker room of the winning team to congratulate them. You'd never see me back there. No way. No how. I see players today around the batting cage or around the dugout waving to each other, shucking and jiving, hugging and kissing. It's appalling to me when I see players who just hit a double talking with the other team's second baseman. This is what I hate! Fifty dollar fines used to be handed out for players talking to opposing teams. They don't do that anymore!

Today's football players do the same thing, but that wasn't always the case. Former Pittsburgh Steelers defensive line coach George Perles once told me a story of a time when the Steelers were playing the Cincinnati Bengals back in the 1970s. Usually, a team takes one side of the football field during game day, while the other team takes the opposite side. Well, the Bengals took both sides of the field before the Steelers made their way out of the tunnel for that particular game. Somebody went into the Steelers locker room and informed George of what the Bengals were doing. All George had to do was summon "Mean Joe" Greene, L.C. Greenwood and Dwight Wright to make their presence known to the Bengals, who quickly began using just one side of the football field.

Basketball is probably the biggest culprit of them all in regards to fraternizing with opponents. When the San Antonio Spurs beat the Miami Heat in the 2014 NBA Finals, LeBron James was hugging Tim Duncan moments after the Heat lost the championship. Why?! You lost the championship! Why don't you go back into the locker room and figure out what went wrong and what your team did to lose?! Dr. J cried after the Lakers beat the Sixers in the 1982 NBA Finals. He wasn't hugging anybody. I don't wanna see that crap! I have a tough time with that stuff. He's your opponent who is trying to beat you, and you're trying to do the same. You're not a sore loser if you don't do those things. You're upset you lost a chance to get a ring. The plane ride back home from New Orleans after the Eagles lost Super Bowl XV was like riding in a funeral hearse!

Hockey is the only sport where you see none of that stuff. You might see an opponent in the tunnel before taking the ice, but the only real interaction of any kind between opposing players is during the shaking of hands after a playoff series. During the Broad Street Bullies era, the Philadelphia Flyers were ticked off whenever they lost a regular season game!

Players take winning and losing too graciously today, especially in championships. Why should a player be gracious when they're on the other end of a losing effort? Why should players be all smiles when they just got their asses handed to them? Winning defines everything in sports, or at least it should. I don't think things will ever go back to how they used to be in this aspect, and that's a real shame.

CHAPTER 22

Can Anybody Save Pete Rose from Himself?

THE FIRST OCCASION I spent some quality time with Pete Rose was just before his initial spring training with the Phillies in 1979. After 16 years with the Cincinnati Reds, Pete had just signed a new contract with Philadelphia the previous December. After the signing, I flew out to Ohio with Don Tollefson, a reporter from Channel 6, and we spent the day with Pete at his home. Pete was very engaging, and during our stay we really just talked about his love for all things sports. I remember him telling us how he had just come back from visiting legendary college football coach Woody Hayes. As much as Pete loved baseball, I think football was honestly his favorite sport. We really hit it off that day, and I developed a nice relationship with Pete over the course of his five seasons spent with the Phillies from 1979 to 1983. While Mike Schmidt might have been the 1980 National League MVP, there's no way that Phillies team could have won the World Series without Pete. Prior to his arrival in Philadelphia, the Phillies had won two National League pennants in their entire history. During Pete's time in Philadelphia, the franchise equaled that total! You can never take away what he did on the field for those Phillies teams.

One day in June, 1987, I travelled down to Baltimore with Bill White, who was broadcasting Yankees games at the time. During the drive, we talked about everything from business to family. Then, the conversation turned to baseball. I had recently heard some rather unflattering news behind the scenes that Pete was in a lot of trouble in regards to gambling. Being that Bill had played against Pete for years in the 1960s when he was with the Cardinals and Phillies, I felt compelled to share the news with him. Keep in mind that Bill was predominantly associated with the American League at that time due to his employment with the Yankees, so he had very little, if any, contact with Pete during these years. I told Bill that I thought Pete was in too deep, but I had no idea he was actually betting on baseball.

So let's fast forward two years later to 1989. Bill was the newly elected National League President and I called him to offer my congratulations. To this day, I can remember the words that came out of his mouth.

"How did you know?" Bill asked.

"Bill, it's on ESPN and all over the newspapers this morning," I replied, assuming he thought I was talking about his new position.

"No, how did you know about Pete Rose?" he asked back. "I have 12 volumes of evidence on my desk I have to sift through."

Some of the evidence Bill was referring to was the Dowd Report, the now-infamous document that described Pete's gambling infractions. The complete report, which is 225 pages long, was compiled by attorney John Dowd, who was serving as a special counsel to new Major League Baseball commissioner Bart Giamatti. As the investigation took place, I brought my camera crew and interviewed Dowd in Washington D.C. Dowd told me that, in order to corroborate the story and have something factual, you need three pieces of concrete evidence.

Then in May, 1989, I went to Montreal to cover the Flyers, who were playing in the Eastern Conference Finals against the Canadiens. For all you Flyers fans out there, that was the series where Canadiens defenseman Chris Chelios took down Flyers left winger Brian Propp with an absolute cheap shot. After the game, we flew back to Philadelphia, where Pete and the Cincinnati Reds were coming into town to play the Phillies in a weekend series. After I got word that the Reds were arriving in Philly on a Delta Airlines flight at 11:55 am, there was no way I was going back to the television station. I wasn't going to deal with that dog and pony show taking place at Veterans Stadium for those three games, either. I wanted to interview Pete immediately after the Reds landed.

Eventually, the Reds arrived in Philly, and I saw Pete walking through the concourse. Man, was he not happy to see me. Even though we had a good relationship, he was under such scrutiny from Major League Baseball. Sports Illustrated had recently written a pretty scathing story and Pete was feeling the heat. In essence, his life and career were going down the tubes. Pete went from being Mr. Congeniality with the media to downright surly over everything that was happening. And in all fairness, I probably would have reacted the same way. The hostile environment continued at the ballpark the next night. After the game, Pete got further upset with me, questioning why I would come at him the way I did the night before. I told him I was just doing my job, which was true. After that night, it would be a long time before Pete and I spoke again. If I had to cover a card show and Pete was there, he would motion for me to go away. He wanted no parts of me. This went on for 15 years. You know how the rest of Pete's story played out. By August, 1989, the amount of incriminating evidence against him was overwhelming, and Giamatti had no choice but to ban Pete from baseball for life.

While Pete's trials and tribulations came as a shock to most of the general public, those in the Philadelphia media who knew him best should have seen this coming a mile away. Back in the late 1970s and early 1980s, there used to be a phone outside the Phillies clubhouse. A number of reporters would periodically see Pete on that phone before games. I would sometimes sit in the clubhouse, and Pete would get very inquisitive and ask me lot of questions, usually pertaining to who I liked in some upcoming football or basketball games. It was no secret to anyone behind the scenes that Pete liked the "action" (i.e., gambling). He made no secret about it. Pete was often seen at Brandywine Raceway in Delaware and the race track at Garden State Park in South Jersey. Although betting on horses is legal, who provides "action" if you want to place a bet outside those confines? It's not the milkman or the postman; it's the illegal bookmakers. Coincidentally, around 1981 or 1982, that phone outside the Phillies clubhouse was removed. You didn't need to put two and two together to assume what was going on. For the record, I never actually heard any conversations Pete had on that phone and we didn't have evidence to suspect any wrongdoing. However, when I look back on all the things that eventually came to light regarding Pete, I think it's pretty apparent that a lot of us in Philadelphia (and I include myself in this) dropped the ball on arguably the biggest scandal to hit baseball since the Black Sox debacle of 1919.

On the day that Pete was banned, I interviewed former Governor of Pennsylvania Ed Rendell (who was Philadelphia's District Attorney during Pete's playing days with the Phillies) on whether he had any idea that Pete had been dealing with bookies. Ed didn't think this was the case, but I'll leave it up to you guys to determine whether to believe that or not. Maybe I'm wrong here, but if you're the former DA of the same city Pete played in for five years, wouldn't you know if there was any illegal activity going on in your city? It makes me wonder. That's all. While I never heard of Pete having any alleged mob or gambling associations during his time in Philadelphia, do you think he was calling Cincinnati every day to place bets on basketball and football? What would be more sensible?

Several years after Pete's ban, I ran into former Reds general manager Dick Wagner in Philadelphia during the 1993 World Series (the night the Phillies lost the legendary 15-14 rain-drenched game to the Toronto Blue Jays). Dick, who had become a top baseball aide since leaving the Reds, was the most hated man in Cincinnati back in 1978, when he allowed Pete to leave the Reds via free agency. After talking in depth with Dick, however, he told me that the Reds had no choice but to get Pete out of town due to his alleged gambling ties. Yes, Pete would have turned 38 at the start of the 1979 baseball season, but don't you think it's kind of funny that the Reds would sever ties with Cincinnati's favorite son after a season highlighted by a 44- game hitting streak and a career high 51 doubles?

Years later, after decades of not speaking with Pete, Mark Chlebowski, my on-air producer in San Diego, approached me in the radio station's conference room one afternoon following my show.

"Tomorrow, you'd better behave yourself," Mark said.

"Why?" I asked him.

"Because we have a 10-minute interview scheduled with Pete Rose," Mark replied. "You'd better be under control."

I was shocked.

"Does Pete know who I am?" I wondered.

"Oh yeah," Mark confirmed. "He knows. He listens every day."

It's true. Pete was living in Los Angeles at the time and would hear me rip him regularly about what happened with his gambling transgressions.

144

I had been very tough on Pete, so I can understand why Mark instructed me to conduct myself in a professional manner. At four o'clock the next day, we went to a special studio because we were off the air at the time. Shortly after we arrived, the phone rang and it was Pete. Steve Hartman introduced me and asked the first question. Then I followed:

"Pete, I'm not going to be a phony-baloney," I said to him. "You know I've ripped you quite frequently," which Pete acknowledged.

The interview, which was supposed to last 10 minutes, ended up lasting 34 minutes. Pete forgot Steve's name and kept going back to me. So a few months later, I flew out to Vegas with my wife for a boxing match. After we landed, she was shopping over at some of the outlets and called me on my cell phone to tell me Pete was signing autographs at one of the memorabilia stores. I made my way over there and got to within 15 feet of him.

"Remember me?!" I yelled at him.

"I don't have Alzheimer's, "Philly" Billy. Get your ass over here!" Pete yelled back as he got out of his seat. I sat down with him and it really broke the ice. We talked for quite a bit, I got my picture with him and asked for his phone number. Since that day, the two of us have had a very congenial relationship, just like we did back when he played for the Phillies.

I established a nice relationship with Pete Rose during our time in Philadelphia. After several years of estrangement, I managed to get reacquainted with baseball's all-time hit king after I arrived in San Diego.

Regardless of whatever our relationship was off the field, I always believed that Pete Rose should be enshrined in the Baseball Hall of Fame—for what he did on the field as a player. And despite the fact that I have been immensely hard on Pete over the years for what he did, his lifetime banishment from the game should never have happened in the first place, and I blame the offices of Major League Baseball for this. I'm not referring to Bill White on this matter, as he took over as National League President when the investigation was winding down. I'm talking about former commissioners Bowie Kuhn, and to a lesser extent, his successor, Peter Ueberroth. Dick Wagner was not exaggerating when he told me what he did that night at the World Series. Even as far back as 1975 and 1976, it was no secret Pete was betting on sports events.

In the summer of 2015, yours truly and my co-host Paul Jolovitz had John Dowd on our show to discuss Pete appearing at Major League Baseball's All-Star Game in Cincinnati on WCHE 1520 AM in West Chester. John, who disagreed with baseball's decision to let Pete participate in the on-field ceremonies prior to the game, confirmed that there was indeed a previous investigation into Pete's questionable activities involving the late former baseball commissioner Bowie Kuhn, who served as president from 1969 to 1984.[1]

According to Dowd, "Bowie Kuhn's got the secret, and he may have gone to his maker......but Bowie hired a lawyer in New York to investigate Pete's gambling and hanging out with hoodlums. And lo and behold, there's no file in the Major League Baseball office. I can tell you that for every investigation ever conducted in Major League Baseball, there's a file, because I've read them. And I've read all of them that involve gambling on baseball and on your own team, but that one's not there," John said. "So we went and talked to the guy, the lawyer, and unfortunately, he was laboring under a terrific alcohol issue, and so we couldn't get (him) to talk, and then Bowie Kuhn had fled town to Florida, you remember the cops were chasing him, so he went down to Florida to escape, so we could never get the truth from Bowie as to what happened back there. But from time to time, we've had people refer to that. Those instances. But beyond what I just told you, we were unable to get the information. But he's been a problem for a long time. I mean, he just didn't wake up one morning over his Cheerios and decide he was gonna bet on baseball. He's been doing it for a long time, and Ron Peters (Pete's confessed bookmaker) said he'd been betting on the Reds from '84, '85, and '86."

This is right along the lines of John's similar remarks from a 2007 interview, when he stated that Pete didn't always place bets with a bookie, most noticeably whenever pitchers Mario Soto and/or Bill Gullickson started.[2] What is Pete telling the gambling fraternity by doing this? Paul then asked John if he thought Pete had any redeeming qualities that could assist baseball in justifying a possible reinstatement. John then proceeded to drop a bombshell that had me almost fall out of my chair.

"Michael Bertolini (a former Rose associate) told us that he (Rose) not only ran bets, but he ran young girls for him down at spring training, ages 12 to 14. Isn't that lovely? So that's statutory rape every time you do that. So he's not the kind of person that I find pretty attractive. He's a street guy. Did I get along with him? Yes. If I had gotten him alone, do I think I could have brought him around? Yes. He knew we had him. When I played the tapes for him, and also showed him the betting slips and the fingerprints, he turned green and grey. I mean, I thought he was going to go over in that deposition I took home. He knew he was a goner, and then he chisels, you know? He gets his book, he defrauds the publisher a million bucks. I mean the guy only sold 40 thousand copies, so he lost a million, and then he says 'I'm gonna come clean, well he didn't come clean.'"

Ouch. As the father of a daughter, that hit me right in the gut. Right in the gut. If that's true, boy oh boy. This is really a sad commentary. Pete and I had our ups and downs, but that was the most jarring thing I've heard in all the times I interviewed John Dowd. I was flabbergasted by that. John is not out there trying to destroy anybody. He is a lawyer. He knows he will be held accountable for that in a court of law if he's out there making outland-ish or nefarious statements. John made those statements to John McHale, who was assigned by Manfred to review John's report and the investigation.

Any speculation on Pete's future in Major League Baseball was put to rest in December 2015, when Commissioner of Baseball Rob Manfred upheld Pete's ban.

"Mr. Rose has not presented credible evidence of a reconfigured life either by an honest acceptance by him of his wrongdoing, so clearly established by the Dowd Report, or by a rigorous, self-aware and sustained program of avoidance by him of all the circumstances that led to his permanent ineligibility in 1989,"[3] said Manfred in a statement regarding his decision.

While many held out hope that Manfred would let Pete back in the game he once claimed he'd go through hell in a gasoline suit to play, it was always a long shot. The odds are stacked too high against him and the damage has been done. If Pete somehow ever gets inducted, which is actually a separate issue than reinstatement, it has to be put on his plaque that he was banned for life for gambling on baseball, because he jeopardized the integrity of the game by committing its ultimate cardinal sin. That being said, the moment Bowie Kuhn got wind of Pete's off-the-field actions, they should have called Pete into their offices, adamantly insisted that these activities had to stop, and forced him to clean up his act. If they would have done this, maybe there was a good possibility they could have nipped Pete's problem in the bud. We'll never know for sure. What I do know is that they let it fester until they had a sticky wicket on their hands. Nobody did a damn thing in regards to Pete Rose's wrongdoings until there was enough evidence to bury him.

Why is that? Well, think about it for a minute. In retrospect, it's probably fair to say that baseball needed Pete as much as Pete needed baseball during that time. Pete was not only a great superstar, he was a great white superstar, who in the words of Phillies chairman Bill Giles, put "fannies in the seats." Much like boxing's need for a great white hope, baseball needed a racial alternative to complement the likes of Willie Mays, Hank Aaron, Ernie Banks and Roberto Clemente. Because Pete was a great player who happened to be chasing Ty Cobb's all-time hit record, he was making money for the game, so baseball looked the other way in regards to anything else he might have been involved with. However, after his playing days ended and he was primarily a manager, it didn't matter anymore. Fans will always go to games to see a player break a record, but how many times have you ever heard somebody say "Gee, I can't wait to go to the game tonight and watch Tony LaRussa manage?"

Pete's scandal wouldn't be the last time baseball temporarily turned a blind eye to cash in on a quick buck. Back in the summer of 1998, the sport wholeheartedly embraced Mark McGwire and Sammy Sosa during their historic home run chase. McGwire and Sosa's epic march towards Major League Baseball's single season home run record was the perfect shot in the arm for the sport, which hadn't fully recovered from the disastrous strike of 1994 that cancelled the World Series. With their Ruthian-like blasts, the two sluggers brought excitement back to the game and made baseball fun again. Who didn't turn on the television or watch Sportscenter every night when this was going on? Everybody did! And baseball knew this! However, when talk of steroid use among players really started gaining traction, McGwire and Sosa became sitting ducks, and Major League Baseball Commissioner Bud Selig testified in front of Congress in 2005 and looked like a blithering idiot. He was totally unprepared and had no answers. Instead of Selig going to the executive director of the Major League Baseball Players Association, Donald Fehr, and finding a way to handle the problem in-house, the Mitchell Report scared baseball, and they feared that the Feds would once again get involved. There were no rules when these guys allegedly first started taking steroids, but McGwire, Sosa, Barry Bonds, Roger Clemens and all of the other players involved were made scapegoats. Some have argued that Pete's gambling had less of an effect than the games played during the steroid era. So here's the million dollar question: Do you let Bonds, Clemens, McGwire and several other players into the Hall of Fame who've been associated with steroids if you do or don't let Pete in? Keep in mind that Hall of Fame voters also elected Gaylord Perry into the Hall of Fame. The same Gaylord Perry who was caught throwing a spitball! But are contradictions in every argument, I guess, and no particular scenario is exactly like the other.

Not only did Pete's gambling scandal alienate many of his fans, but his actions affected former teammates as well. While Hall of Famers Joe Morgan and Mike Schmidt have lobbied for Pete's reinstatement over the years, Hall of Fame catcher and former Reds teammate Johnny Bench hasn't always echoed their sentiments. Over the years, Johnny has openly displayed some deep-rooted animosity towards Pete, typically referencing

Rule 21(d) of the Major League Baseball rulebook whenever he is asked about Pete's possible Hall of Fame chances. The rule, which can be found in every baseball clubhouse, declares that anybody associated with baseball must be made permanently ineligible if they bet on the sport.

Is Johnny right regarding these sentiments? To a certain extent, yes, but have always been conflicting reports as to how well Johnny and Pete actually get along. On the other side of the coin, Johnny was not the nicest person to deal with in the media and was very standoffish. During the heyday of the Big Red Machine, it was perceived by many that Johnny always thought Pete got too much credit and publicity, but Pete was such a gregarious guy. Further complicating matters in their relationship was Pete's gambling scandal, which cast a big shadow over Johnny's Hall of Fame induction in 1989. There was a *Pete Rose Way* street sign in Cincinnati long before there was a *Johnny Bench Way*. Don't think that didn't stay in Johnny's craw. Then again, Johnny, just like every one of Pete's teammates, could have known Pete was betting with bookmakers. They can lie all they want as to whether they did or didn't know, but if they did, they should have pulled Pete aside, grabbed him by the throat, told him to stop doing what he was doing, and tried to get him help. Now whether they tried this or not, I'm not sure. However, Pete is a grown man, was responsible for his own actions, and ultimately fell prey to these pitfalls.

Be that as it may, I often wonder what would have happened if Giamatti hadn't died of a heart attack a little more than a week after he issued Pete his verdict. Giamatti was a very intelligent man. Do you think he really wanted to banish baseball's all-time hit king from the sport, along with the black marks and scars that would come with it? No way. Giamatti, along with Bill White, stepped into a towering inferno of a mess with Pete's case. Unlike Fay Vincent or Bud Selig, who don't understand baseball and seem to carry grudges against Pete, Giamatti was a fair and unbiased commissioner. If you recall, Giamatti was going to allow Pete to apply for reinstatement one year after he was banned. To be fair, however, it was under the condition that Pete reconfigure his life. According to Manfred and John Dowd, he has not. What do you think went through Manfred's mind when he had learned that Pete still bets on baseball? Even though it is supposedly by legal means, it probably made his decision a lot easier in regards to keeping Pete's ban in place.

Whether it involves an athlete, referee, or just a regular fan, gambling and sports have been synonymous with each other for practically a century. The scenario surrounding Pete's 1989 ban is not unlike what happened with former Green Bay Packers halfback Paul Hornung, who was suspended from the NFL in 1963 for one year (along with Detroit Lions defensive tackle Alex Karras) by NFL Commissioner Pete Rozelle for betting on professional football games. Hornung, the 1961 NFL MVP, immediately came clean, showed remorse for his actions, and was back on the field the next season. While Pete is not a guy who is going to finesse you, he says he wants a second chance and I truly believe that. But the question is whether he's done enough to grant that chance. I also think Pete should have been honest about his wrongdoings from the start like Hornung was. Hornung's admission most likely made it easier for him to be inducted into the Pro Football Hall of Fame in 1986. Would earlier admission of Pete's actions have granted him clemency or a spot in the Hall? I can't answer that, but he probably would have had a better chance than he does now. While John Dowd claims that influential people were ready in multiple ways to assist Pete in tackling his gambling addiction, by this time the mob had a mortgage on Pete.

"The rule doesn't say, you bet for or against, and my answer to Pete is, if you think because you bet for your team it was ok, why didn't you tell everyone?" John Dowd asked us on our show. "You know. Come on Pete. You can't have it three ways. You can't have it two ways. The rule says you wager on a game in which you participate. It doesn't matter about the outcome. In addition, it's very important for people to understand that, when (I) bet on a game that I'm participating in, I have put my own financial interest ahead of the interest of the team, and my obligation under the major league contract that I signed. So, you know, (there's) two strikes against me as soon as I call in that bet."

Commissioner Rozelle was actually forced to tackle another off-the-field incident several years after Hornung's and Karras' suspensions. This time, it involved New York Jets quarterback Joe Namath, who led the Jets to a Super Bowl III victory over the Baltimore Colts in January, 1969. Later that year, Rozelle had to inform Broadway Joe that bookies and gamblers were frequenting his New York saloon, Bachelors III. There was never evidence of Namath doing anything illegal, but instead of ending his association with the bar, a tearful Namath defiantly retired from football at a press conference. Although Namath eventually came out of retirement and ended his association with the bar, there were reportedly plans to raid Bachelors III prior to his retirement announcement. Namath had just won Super Bowl III and was the toast of the sports world. Can you imagine the backlash if his bar had been raided?!

Much like football and baseball, the NBA has faced several challenges over the years that could have affected the integrity of their sport. Personally, I feel the league learned what not to do by watching the way baseball handled Pete's gambling issues and subsequent banishment. I was glad to see the league levy fines against the Sixers' Charles Barkley and the New York Knicks' Mark Jackson for openly making bets during a game back in 1990. This isn't a game of HORSE or the WWE! While I was adamant in my insistence that Barkley and Jackson should have been suspended the rest of that season, I was still glad to see the NBA take some sort of action in regards to the matter. Indeed, whether it was the Phoenix Suns' drug scandal of the 1980s, the "The Malice at the Palace" involving the Pacers and Pistons, or the allegations that former referee Tim Donaghy bet on games he officiated, there always seems to be a dark cloud hovering over the NBA.

While the aforementioned issues have certainly left a lasting impact on the league, there's also been speculation regarding the alleged gambling habits of one of the sport's major icons.

I'm referring to "His Airness" himself: Michael Jordan.

Even if you're the most moderately knowledgeable sports fan, doesn't it arouse suspicion that the greatest basketball player of his era, who had just won his third consecutive NBA title with the Chicago Bulls, suddenly decided to retire from the game to go play minor league baseball? You don't find that strange? That's like the greatest writer in the world suddenly wanting to become a plumber. And what baseball team did Jordan sign a minor league contract with? The Chicago White Sox, who were coincidentally owned by Bulls owner Jerry Reinsdorf.

Jordan initially walked away from basketball in October 1993, several months after his father had been found shot to death in a South Carolina swamp. There was talk that Jordan's father had always wanted him to play baseball and maybe that factored into his decision to step away from basketball. Who knows? Maybe I'm looking too much into things. Maybe Jordan was tired of basketball and simply wanted to try another sport, but I'm not so sure of that. Several months prior to his retirement announcement, speculation had arisen that Jordan was developing some intense gambling habits. During the 1993 Eastern Conference Finals against the Knicks, Jordan was apparently seen gambling in Atlantic City between games. Richard Esquinas, a San Diego businessman and former golfing buddy of Jordan's, discussed his and Jordan's gambling wages in his book, *Michael & Me: Our Gambling Addiction. . .My Cry For Help!* Now I've been around the block quite a few times, and when there's smoke, there's usually fire.

While Pete Rose is certainly considered one of baseball's all-time greats, Michael Jordan is considered by many to be *the* greatest player in NBA history. If he was involved in issues that required a potential cover-up comparable to Watergate, the league could ill afford to let this story get out to the general public. Is it a stretch to say that former NBA Commissioner David Stern could have encouraged Jordan to walk away from the game for a little bit, due to some incriminating evidence that the league offices possibly had against him? Think about it. Just four years earlier, baseball lost one of its most iconic figures in a shocking scandal. Can you imagine if a similar scenario reared its ugly head again in another sport? The impact of a possible Michael Jordan ban would have rocked the league beyond repair.

We may never know the actual reasons why Michael Jordan left basketball, or if anything transpired behind the scenes leading to his brief departure from the sport. Much like Pete Rose, maybe we didn't do our due diligence in the media with Jordan, either. On the other hand, maybe we wouldn't have liked what we uncovered. If there was a hidden subplot to Michael Jordan's story, the NBA went to great lengths to make sure he wasn't hung out to dry.

It makes you wonder why Major League Baseball didn't do the same for Pete, before it was too late and everything came crashing down. I realize at times I sound like a Pete apologist, and I'm really trying not to be. Because I'm in the business of analyzing sports, it's my job to present both sides of the coin here. However, at times, it's easier said than done. Without question, what Pete did in regards to betting on baseball was wrong. Absolutely wrong. But even though Pete portrays himself in a less than favorable light most of the time, he has done some very nice things for me, as well as other people, too. Several years back, there was a particular bad stretch of California wildfires and a lot of people lost everything. I asked Pete if he'd go to dinner with two listeners who spent $5,000 for the fire relief fund at the radio station. Pete did not ask for a dime, and went to dinner with the listeners. Then there was the time when he spoke to my Widener University class over the telephone and fielded questions from many enthusiastic Philly sports fans, who thanked him for helping the Phillies win their first World Series title ever in 1980. I think Pete does have a good heart, but he just can't seem to channel that in the right direction. If he could do that, he would be an American hero.

Unfortunately, Pete's other side always seems to rear its ugly head. He gets himself into more messes than anybody I've ever met in my life. He's just so self-destructive, and every time there's a glimmer of hope and it looks like his luck is about to change, he somehow ruins it for himself. John Dowd's claim about those young girls was the shocker of all shockers. I really hope that's not true. But like I said, why would John put himself out there and say that? And why hasn't Pete sued him for defamation of character? People can get mad at Commissioner Manfred all they want in regards to his decision, but you have to ask yourself whether Pete has truly attempted to reconfigure his life since 1989. It's difficult to argue that he really has. Ultimately, you have to help yourself, and Pete wasn't willing to do that. He's only kidding himself when he downplayed the notion that his gambling was less severe because he bet on the Reds to win. And why in God's name would you tell the commissioner of baseball that you still bet on the game, when he's the man that could reinstate you? Come on, Pete! You've been trying to get back into the game for more than a quarter of a century! I'm not saying Pete should have lied. I'm saying that he should have previously cut ties with each and every one of those undesirables that enabled him and might still enable him. Then, none of that would have mattered. He's in his seventies now. If Pete hasn't learned what to do and what not to do by this stage of his life, I don't think he ever will.

And because of this, there will probably never be a Pete Rose plaque in the Hall of Fame.

At least in his lifetime.

CHAPTER 23

If I Was the Czar of Sports Security...

Back in the day, I saw the people Pete Rose was hanging around with, and I had questions about those people. Real questions. I asked myself "How does baseball allow these guys to come into the clubhouse? They don't know what's going on? They had no idea what was happening behind the scenes?"

Whether it applies to real life or sports, when scandals and wrongdoings are swept under the rug, the real truth usually comes out. Look at Wall Street, the banking industry and the housing industry several years back. What happened? Boom! Everything went right into the dumpster and our economy crashed, because the powers that be were hiding things that eventually came to the surface. As much as we're led to believe that the athletes who we idolize walk on water, sports are not exempt from this, either. Too often, sports franchises are more worried about feathering their own nest than righting a wrong and getting to the bottom of a problem that could potentially damage the integrity of their sport. There's always an outrage whenever an athlete gets in trouble. 'How does this happen?!' Ever hear that one before?

Yes, I think it's fair to say that sports in general is all over the map with its overall lack of accountability. There's no consistency anywhere! And on several occasions, they don't do anything about the serious problems they uncover! For example, you don't think the Dallas Cowboys knew what was going on in the "White House" back in the 1990s, where several self-employed "models" would "entertain" Cowboys players? They didn't care! The Cowboys won three Super Bowls during that time

Look what transpired in the NFL with incidents involving Ray Rice, Adrian Peterson, Aaron Hernandez, Greg Hardy and several other players too numerous to mention. If you're NFL Commissioner Roger Goodell, you have to face the public, appear front and center and deal with these issues very harshly. It's not every player. It's not even 90 percent of the players, but a sizable amount of them are stepping out of bounds. Why would Goodell go underground for a couple of weeks after the Ray Rice debacle the way he did? You've got to be kidding me! If I were Goodell, I'm sending security agents down to the Revel Casino the day after the Rice elevator incident, and I would make sure they got a detailed portfolio of information regarding what happened in that elevator upon their return to the league offices. I'm surprised there wasn't even more of an outcry over this when it happened. The only reason the NFL got more conscious of public perception is because sponsors were thinking of backing out and cutting ties with the league. Once again, the almighty dollar rules all.

Goodell had so much egg on his face over the last half of 2014 and 2015 (Deflategate, anyone?) that the NFL had no choice but to put their best foot forward. As a result, changes were made that were supposed to revise and strengthen the Personal Conduct Policy for all NFL employees. There is also a new League Conduct Committee to ensure that respect and appropriate behavior are the norm and not the rule. Apparently, a disciplinary officer will eventually oversee investigatory procedures and determine appropriate disciplinary actions for off-field misconduct. In addition, there are now heavier fines and suspensions for egregious behavior, independent investigative procedures, and clinical evaluations for any NFL employee violating this policy. From the looks of it, there seems to be quite a few loopholes in this policy, and it could lead to mistrust among the players. Let's just say the NFL wants to get rid of a certain player for reasons detrimental to the game. Even though the revisions to the policy seem to cover a lot of scenarios, they could still easily set up a player to have him take a fall if they wanted. Then, just when you thought the NFL was turning the corner, NFL Football Operations chief Troy Vincent flat out admitted that he didn't even look at the report released by former FBI director Robert Mueller, which detailed his four-month investigation into the NFL's handling of the Rice situation. In the report, Mueller confirmed what we all knew: that the NFL should have investigated the incident more thoroughly. Yes, the crime had already been committed, but wouldn't you think it would be the least bit advantageous on the part of Vincent and the NFL to read over an official report stating where they went wrong, so they can take the necessary steps to prevent another incident like this from happening again?

To be fair, football isn't the only sport that's had to deal with their share of issues. There are probably several more issues in sports that we could discuss here, as we've already touched on baseball's steroid era, and how the league turned its back on the players who were generating interest in the game again after the strike. As I mentioned in the previous chapter, a very serious drug problem plagued the NBA back in the 70s and early 80's. The public was so turned off by the league that the biggest games of their season were usually broadcast on a tape-delayed basis, including Game 6 of the 1980 NBA Finals between the Sixers and Lakers! Magic Johnson scored 42 points in arguably the greatest game he ever played, and a lot of people probably didn't even see it! Now fast forward to 2014 with the whole debacle involving now-former Los Angeles Clippers owner Donald Sterling. Do you mean to tell me it took some secret recording that was apparently "leaked" to get him thrown out of basketball?!

Nevertheless, all of the aforementioned incidents prove that, in general, sports should be significantly more proactive in cracking down on individuals and league issues than they currently are. In the process, those who choose to turn a blind eye contribute in damaging the integrity of anything associated with the four major professional sports leagues. And if integrity is questioned, you might as well run things like the WWE in the sense that you already know what an outcome is going to be. To a certain extent, you have to include colleges in this scenario as well, although I think certain teams are allowed to slide, while other universities get burned. They pick and choose. I read how one college suspended a basketball player for being given $150 to fly home for his grandmother's funeral. How many times have you heard of a university getting penalized for a "recruiting violation" or a player getting into trouble for "using a cell phone"? You don't think every university does these things? I'm not saying it's right, but it kind of makes a $150 airplane ticket not seem like that big of a deal. On the other side of the coin, you have the Penn State child sex abuse scandal and the alleged actions of certain school officials, in regards to whether they knew these transgressions were happening.

I will tell you this: If I was the czar of sports security, I'd most definitely enforce rules that had tougher implications. Most athletes associated with sports today are extremely well compensated! These guys aren't making $50,000 a year anymore while needing to work part-time jobs in the off-season. Owners now have big investments in the majority of these individuals. If I have that big of an investment, I have to make sure my superstars aren't associating with a bunch of lowlifes and bad apples, just like baseball should have done with Pete Rose. Overall, sports teams do not do a good enough job of investigating non-athletes who fraternize with their players. I would also find out who has access to these players, who they hang around with, and why. Whether they're friends, media members, or whomever, you should have a dossier of everybody who comes into contact with these athletes. Then, all these scandals and problems would almost surely be drastically reduced. While security is tighter now than it used to be, it still needs to get a lot tougher. Even more difficult access to these players is needed, because some of these non-athletes infiltrate the ranks and use it to their own benefits. If you're an owner making millions of dollars in one or more of the four major sports, you mean to tell me you can't put a couple million into hiring former FBI guys or police chiefs to follow athletes around for a spot check here and there? Is it an invasion of privacy to take a picture of somebody on a cell phone who isn't in the confines of their own home?

I've seen it up close and personal for decades. The players change but the undesirables are always there in some form. They love to be around athletes, rub elbows with them or have some kind of connection with them. There are a lot of sports groupies out there who want to be around people who are front and center. Just look at Major League Baseball's Pittsburgh Drug Trials, which took place in 1985. Curtis Strong, one of the six men convicted on 11 counts of selling cocaine to players dispersed throughout the major leagues, received a 12-year prison sentence (which was later reduced to four). Strong just so happened to be a former Philadelphia

Phillies clubhouse caterer! Are you kidding me?! Nobody in the Phillies organization found out more about this guy before giving him clubhouse access?!

I understand how some people might think I'm a radical when talking like this. Maybe I am, but maybe it would eradicate some of these problems. If you think it sounds a lot like Big Brother, well, maybe we need Big Brother in this regard. At the end of the day, sports needs to be held more accountable for players, general managers, coaches, owners, and anybody affiliated with their respective businesses. The mushroom cloud caused by any scandal that could damage the overall reputation of sports will only get bigger and bigger. Yes, people should be responsible for their own actions, but you can't continue to keep on having another embarrassing situation for any sport. And whether it's an incident involving Greg Hardy, Ray Rice, Adrian Peterson or anybody in between, all of these situations are embarrassing.

CHAPTER 24

Ted Williams, Tony Gwynn and the San Diego Connection

HERE'S A TRIVIA question for you: Do you know the ballpark where Ted Williams accomplished the goal of being baseball's last .400 hitter?

The answer is Shibe Park, later known as Connie Mack Stadium, the former home of the Philadelphia Athletics of the American League and the Philadelphia Phillies of the National League.

In September 1941, Williams was hitting .400 on the nose when the Boston Red Sox arrived in Philadelphia to face the Athletics for the final three games of the baseball season. After getting only one hit in five plate appearances in a Saturday game, Williams' batting average stood at .39955 as he entered the season-finale doubleheader that Sunday. Williams proceeded to go 6 for 8 in those two games to cap off one of the most historic batting seasons in baseball history. As of this writing, no player in the major leagues has hit over .400 since. Tony Gwynn of the San Diego Padres hit .394 in the strike-shortened 1994 season, while Kansas City Royals Hall of Famer George Brett came closest to reaching the mark over a full season when he hit .390 in 1980. I had the pleasure of watching Brett in the 1980 World Series, when the Royals came to Philadelphia to play the Phillies.

In 1970, Connie Mack Stadium was about to be demolished, as the Phillies were moving into Veterans Stadium for the 1971 season. The final game of the 1970 Phillies season wasn't going to be televised (that would never happen now!), so Channel 6 decided to have a special that commemorated the last televised game at the stadium. I was in charge of locating and interviewing athletes who celebrated some of their greatest moments playing at Connie Mack, so I attempted to contact Ted Williams, who had since retired and was managing the Washington Senators. I spoke to his secretary and she took down my information. I was thinking the entire time that my message would probably wind up in a grey waste can, and Williams would never even see it or bother to call me back.

The next day, however, somebody in the Channel 6 newsroom informed me that a Mr. Williams was on the line waiting to speak with me. I couldn't believe it. Ted Williams called me back! When I got on the phone with him, I instantly recognized who was on the other end of the line.

"Kid, I've got 10 minutes," Williams said in his familiar, booming voice.

"You got it, Mr. Williams," I told him. It was obvious after talking with Williams for only a little while that his recall was tremendous.

"Connie Mack Stadium was a great place to hit, let me tell 'ya. I can remember the counts, the pitches, the pitcher and the stadiums I hit my home runs in. Every one of them," he said.

When I asked him about the famous "Ted Williams shift," when infielders would move to the right side of the field whenever he came to bat, Ted didn't pull any punches.

"If I wanted to hit to left field I could have. I just didn't want to," he said during our conversation.

This appears to be true. "Irish" Mike Ryan, a former Phillies catcher and coach, once recalled a story to me about a time during spring training when somebody challenged Ted to hit the ball to left field. Whoever challenged Ted was so confident he couldn't do it, and they put some hotshot youngster out there to try and prove it. Although he was no longer an active player, this was the worst thing you could do to Ted Williams, who promptly entered the batting cage and sprayed every pitch down the left field line like it was nothing.

On the afternoon I spoke with him, Ted told me story after story. Next thing you know, 45 minutes had passed and he was still going. He talked and talked and talked. He remembered the time he shattered one of the stadium speakers at Connie Mack Stadium. His memory was like a steel trap. It was incredible to talk to him.

Years later, when I was working in San Diego, I saw Ted at a restaurant with a friend of mine named Bob Breitbart. Bob was a former high school classmate of Ted's and I often sat in his luxury box at Chargers games, so I took it upon myself to say hello to him and reintroduce myself to Ted. I didn't think he would remember our conversation, but Ted claimed that he did. I don't know if he was throwing the bull or not, but the very next day, we had Ted on our show. He was a blast. It was amazing just to be in his presence.

Another thing I admired about Ted was his respect for Negro Leaguers. He used his Hall of Fame induction ceremony in 1966 as a platform to acknowledge the fact that these players should have been honored and weren't receiving their due diligence. Bill White and Ted would go fishing together, and Bill has often spoken of his honor and integrity. He had the utmost respect for Ted. You can talk about Ty Cobb, Tris Speaker and Rogers Hornsby, but arguably the greatest hitter of all-time was Teddy Ballgame. He hit for average and power. People sometimes questioned Ted because he was such a stickler about the strike zone, but he was one of the greatest players of all-time. I know he was tough with the media in Boston, but they were really tough on him as well. The courtesy of this great player, who had the negativity he did towards the media, to return the call of an unknown associate producer and spend 45 minutes on the phone with him was just an honor, and definitely a moment I'll never be able to relive. From my standpoint, you can't say enough great things about Ted Williams. He was more than just a baseball player. Interviewing him and having him on my show all those years later were some of the greatest highlights of my career.

Williams was very instrumental in the career of another fellow Californian: San Diego Padres Hall of Famer Tony Gwynn. Tony happened to be from Long Beach, and Ted was from San Diego. My first meeting with Tony took place at the Major League Baseball All-Star Game in Philadelphia during the summer of 1996. It was quite a memorable experience. Although he was voted into the game, Tony showed up in a cast and on crutches after suffering a heel injury. I happened to be in the National League locker room before the game, and Tony came over and approached me.

"Hey, when are you coming out to San Diego?" Tony asked. I had no idea that Tony Gwynn even knew who I was. Keep in mind the internet was in its primary stages back then, so I assumed he heard me on *XTRA Sports 690* out in San Diego, when I would periodically call into their football show.

"Two weeks," I told him.

"That's great! It's great that you're coming out here!" Tony said with his great, big smile.

Prior to that encounter, I had never met Tony Gwynn in my life, but he took a liking to me and we developed a very nice relationship. Talk about guys who took their trade seriously. Tony was the first in a very long line of players who used video to critique their hitting performances. The Padres staff would load so much equipment for road trips it was out of control. Tony spent hours in his room on the road and in the Padres clubhouse, trying to find flaws in his swing. If the 1994 season would have lasted 162 games, I believe Tony would have hit .400 (he finished at .394).

It's a shame Tony was never able to bring a championship to San Diego. The two times the Padres made it to the World Series in his career, they faced off against two of the greatest baseball teams of the last half century: the 1984 Tigers and the 1998 Yankees. I was there for the 1998 World Series at Qualcomm Stadium (formerly Jack Murphy Stadium). The noise there was just deafening and the fans were going crazy with their white rally towels. Tony hit .500 in the series, but the Yankees just had more talent and swept the Padres in four games. If you're ever going to compare Cobb, Speaker and Hornsby, you also have to include Tony Gwynn in that conversation. Tony hit over .300 for 19 straight seasons! If you needed a big hit, he could get it. If the Padres needed a single, he got it. A double or a home run? Consider it done.

The first time I saw Ted and Tony together was at a banquet in San Diego. It was a tremendous dinner, and the dialogue between the two of them was priceless. Ted was talking about how great of a player Tony was, and vice versa. The two had such a tremendous respect for each other. Ted loved Tony Gwynn. If you can recall the 1999 All-Star Game in Boston, it was Tony who got Ted off the golf cart he was riding and guided him towards home plate to throw the game's ceremonial first pitch. Even though Tony predominantly hit for average in his career, Ted encouraged him to try to hit more home runs. Tony was basically a singles hitter, not possessing the power of Ted or a player like Stan Musial. However, after having conversations with Ted, Tony started to hit for more power, even hitting a career high 17 home runs and 119 RBIs in 1997. And if that wasn't enough, Tony hit .372 that year, which was the highest full-season batting average of his career! Tony was a master at the art of hitting, the strike zone, everything. For the people who accused Tony as a guy who was only worried about stats, let me tell you something: Tony Gwynn was a pro's pro and just an absolute, consummate professional who loved the game of baseball. He played on some of the worst Padres teams of all-time, yet he always took his trade seriously. Tony was *the* hitting machine.

Even though Tony continued to produce in the later stages of his career, Steve Hartman, my radio co-host at *XTRA 690* in San Diego, thought Tony had the potential to be even better.

"Tony was so beloved in San Diego, but his weight continued to sky-rocket out of control, and he was missing more and more games because of his injuries," Steve recalled. "I emphasized that if he took care of himself, forget 3,000 hits, he would have had 4,000 hits! He would have been a serious challenger to Pete Rose's all-time hit record."

Speaking of Pete Rose, he was a tremendous fan of Tony. In fact, Tony got his first hit against the Phillies in 1982 at Jack Murphy Stadium in San Diego. Pete, who happened to be backing up the play near second base, walked up to Tony after he got the hit, and said 'Congratulations, kid. Don't catch me in one night.'

I remember going to Tony's Hall of Fame dinner in Cooperstown, New York that former Padres owner John Moores threw for him. Even though Tony was a first ballot Hall of Famer, he wasn't the first Padre to be inducted into the Baseball Hall of Fame, and that bothers me to this day. That distinction goes to Dave Winfield, who left San Diego and decided to go elsewhere when the Yankees offered him a lot of money. Yes, I realize that he later returned to the club in an advisory role, but you don't think of Dave Winfield being synonymous with the San Diego Padres.

Whether you're in Philadelphia, Chicago, Milwaukee or Houston, you can ask any baseball fan and they will all agree that Tony Gwynn is Mr. Padre! It says so right on his statue outside of Petco Park. He deserved to be the first Padre in the Hall. No questions asked! None whatsoever. We look at athletes today and practically view them as mercenaries. Tony had opportunities to leave the Padres many times, but he turned down a lot of money because he absolutely loved the city of San Diego. He went to college there, played baseball and basketball there, and was drafted by the Padres and the NBA's San Diego Clippers (who are now the Los Angeles Clippers)!

After he retired, Tony never forgot the people he liked. I had stayed in touch with Tony's agent, John Boggs, and John told me that Tony wanted to be a guest on my show at *WCHE* in Pennsylvania. His son, Tony Jr., signed with the Phillies in 2014, and everything would have come full circle. However, I learned from John that Tony was battling some severe health issues at that point, and wasn't really feeling up to talking with anybody. Sadly, I never got the opportunity to speak with Tony again. Several months later, he passed away at just 54 years of age. Tony was a tremendous individual, genuine human being and a great man. I'll never forget how one of the greatest hitters of all-time acknowledged some television producer he didn't even know and welcomed him to his city with open arms. It made me feel like a million bucks. Tony Gwynn is sorely missed.

CHAPTER 25

Mike Piazza Should Not Be a Fourth Ballot Hall of Famer!

MIKE PIAZZA'S BASEBALL journey started at a very young age in the city of Phoenixville, Pennsylvania. Mike's dad, Vince Piazza, was a very successful businessman in the Philadelphia area who was friends with legendary Dodgers manager Tommy Lasorda. Lasorda was the godfather of Vince's youngest son (and Mike's youngest brother) Tommy. When Lasorda and the Dodgers would come into Philadelphia during the baseball season to play the Phillies, Mike was the team's bat boy. Lasorda's relationship with the Piazza family was so strong that he was very insistent on the Dodgers drafting him![1] Looking back, can you believe that?! You had to practically encourage any baseball team to take Mike Piazza!

I knew Vince, and after the Dodgers drafted Mike in the 62nd round of the 1988 Major League Baseball Draft, I kept encouraging him to let me do a story on Mike. After some initial reluctance, Vince called me at Channel 10 and finally gave me the go-ahead to do a segment. Shortly after our conversation, I went up to Vince's house in Phoenixville, Pennsylvania on a cold January day for the story. Vince had built an indoor batting cage for Mike in the basement of his house. Mike, who was in either Double-A or Triple-A at the time, was swinging away in the batting cage and getting the bat through the zone very quickly. Bang! Bang! Bang! Mike kept hitting line drive after line drive. Just smacking the hell out of that ball. I remember thinking he had tremendous bat speed.

"So what do you think? Do you think he has a chance?" Vince asked me about the possibility of his son playing pro ball.

"Look Vince, I'm not a hitting instructor, but based on what I saw, you never know," I responded. "He really swings the bat very effectively."

Vince then mentioned how Lasorda brought Ted Williams over to his house the week before, and that Ted was really impressed with Mike's swing. In fact, Lasorda and Williams both came away saying Mike was going to be a player in the major leagues. They didn't say he was going to be an All-Star or potential Hall of Famer, but nonetheless a major league player. Now Tommy and Ted were two experts. Ted, who had apparently known Mike for years dating back to when Mike was a youngster, knew hitting as well as anybody in the game of baseball.

So I finished the story and ran it with Al Meltzer on Channel 10's 5:30 pm news broadcast. The piece ran about two and a half to three minutes. After the piece was over, Steve Doerr, the station's news director, saw the story and called me in his office.

"Why are you doing a story on this pizza pie guy?" Steve asked me.

"His name is Mike Piazza," I shot back in a rather bold and brash manner. "Let me tell you something, Steve. You're gonna be hearing about this guy someday in the major leagues," I told him. "I'll go as far as to say he'll be an All-Star."

Now I don't profess to be a genius, but I was right. After spending a month in the big leagues as a September call up in 1992, Mike won the Dodgers starting catcher's job the next year and won the 1993 National League Rookie of the Year Award, hitting .318 with 35 home runs and 112 RBIs. The Dodgers lost 99 games in 1992, and Mike was an instant difference maker on that team. On the last day of the 1993 season, Mike hit two home runs with four RBIs as the Dodgers beat the hated San Francisco Giants and prevented them from making the playoffs. In the process, the win secured a .500 season for the Dodgers, which marked an 18-game improvement from the previous season. Fast forward to 1996, when the Major League Baseball All-Star game came to Philadelphia. Mike had two hits and two RBIs, including a gigantic home run off Cleveland Indians pitcher Charles Nagy in the second inning. This just further reminded me that Mike Piazza was something special, and the first time I saw Steve Doerr after that game, I reminded him of how great that "Pizza Pie Guy" was doing.

After my move to San Diego, I got to see Mike play more frequently, as the Dodgers were in the same division as the Padres. Steve Hartman and I used to argue back and forth on the air about Mike all the time. Steve didn't think Mike was a good defensive catcher. 'Was Yogi Berra a great defensive catcher?' I'd fire back at him. Mike could hit a ball 900 feet, and Steve would brush it off and say the ball just made it over the wall. It was great give and take. The Philadelphia guy protecting the other Philadelphia guy. One time I was at Qualcomm Stadium with Steve when the Dodgers came into town for a three-game series against the Padres. As we made our way into the Dodgers clubhouse, Mike, who knew me from back home, came in and greeted me warmly. I then expressed my interest to Mike in possibly interviewing him.

"Bill, I'll do it for you, but not for him," as he pointed to Steve. After dodging a bullet, Mike gave us a great twenty minute interview.

I didn't see Mike as much after my first year or so in San Diego, because the Dodgers traded him to the Florida Marlins early in the 1998 baseball season. Then about a week after his trade to the Marlins, the team shipped him off to the New York Mets. Mike apparently wanted a six-year, $60 million contract extension, but the Dodgers said no way. Right around this time, the Dodgers were being sold by the O'Malley family. The team dragged their feet and later offered Mike a six-year, $80 million contract, but Mike refused it.[2] Collectively, Mike ended up playing for three teams in 1998. Eventually, the Mets signed him to a contract worth $91 million over seven years. Here was Mike, a great looking guy and home run hitter playing in New York. That was pretty great. He had some remarkably productive years with the Mets, almost winning a World Series in 2000, when the team played the Yankees in the Subway Series.

By 2006, Mike's career was winding down and he returned to the West Coast, signing a one-year deal with the Padres. His father Vince told me he was going to sign with the team prior to the deal officially happening. I probably cost Mike a couple million dollars, because it came down to the Phillies and Padres, and I leaked the story and it got out of the bag. One night, I had to fly out to Vegas to cover some fights, and I decided to stop by and see Pete Rose, who was in town signing autographs during my stay. There were several Padres players who were favorites of mine who I wanted to get Pete's autograph for. I can't remember the players, but one of them was Mike. Now remember, Pete played with Johnny Bench, and after he signed an inscription for Mike, I took a look at it. The inscription read "To the greatest offensive catcher in baseball history." As I previously discussed, Pete and Johnny always had an uneasy relationship, so I'm not sure whether Pete wrote that on purpose or not. You make the call. If Mike and I were ever in private or in the Padres locker room, I would ask him if he could back Pete whenever he got inducted into the Hall of Fame. Mike would kind of just look at me with a wry smile. He was apprehensive about doing that, because his playing career wasn't over.

Despite what happened with Mike in Los Angeles, there are Dodgers fans who still love him. One time after a Padres Sunday afternoon game, Mike called me and we went out to a local restaurant that my friend, Paolo Pastorelli, helps run for a friend of his. Mike walked through the doors and Paolo was just dumbfounded. He almost had a heart attack. Paolo waited on him and couldn't do enough for him. He even took care of our check! I convinced Mike how much Paolo liked and admired him as a player, but contrary to most athletes, Mike never liked to be given anything for nothing. He's a low-key, quiet guy, and he probably figured he was making so much money that it wasn't really necessary. He was very uncomfortable with it. Several athletes usually frequent that restaurant, but to this day, Paolo still says that Mike was the most genuine athlete he had ever met.

Unfortunately, my radio co-host, a lifelong Dodgers fan, didn't share the same sentiments regarding Mike that Paolo did.

"I was never a Mike Piazza fan. And this was before I knew he was a big steroid guy, which he was," insists Steve Hartman. "There's no doubt. A 62nd-round draft pick becomes the greatest power-hitting catcher of the steroid era? Guys don't just drop that low in the draft who can hit 450-foot opposite field home runs. A telltale sign of steroid use is power to the opposite field.

"We were out in San Diego in 1998, where we had Ken Caminiti, Greg Vaughn, Kevin Brown, just about everybody but Tony Gwynn 'roiding up, pounding the ball out of the park, and everyone was excited. We had

60-70 home runs from different players in one season. It was great. It just completely destroyed the baseball record books, but it is what it is. At that time, we weren't thinking anything of it, because there hadn't been any law in baseball against using any kind of performance enhancing drugs. No, Piazza never tested positive for any PEDs, but keep in mind Lance Armstrong was also tested a million times. Not once did he test positive. Marion Jones, who was an Olympic athlete subjected to the most stringent testing around, never tested positive. Barry Bonds and Roger Clemens never tested positive, either. None of those guys did. You could use that stuff blindly and no one is ever going to stop you, unless you're stupid like Manny Ramirez, who got off his cycle and overused his injections.

"The process of using any kind of PED is so sophisticated, all you have to do is deny it and make people prove it. There is no proving it, expect the fact that everyone was doing it. I've said this about Mark McGwire, I said it about Sammy Sosa and everybody else. Baseball did nothing to stop these guys. The fact is, the use of performance enhancing drugs was not against the rules of baseball at the time. So if it was available to those guys, why not? I don't blame them for using it. If I had a Hall of Fame vote, all those guys would be in the Hall of Fame.

"When Piazza was traded by the Dodgers, you have to understand the backstory there. He demanded to be the highest paid player in baseball. He was basically holding the Dodgers hostage. Now what made the deal weird was that Fred Claire, then the general manager of the Dodgers, didn't make the trade. The trade was made by FOX, who had taken over the Dodgers from the O'Malley family. They made the trade without Fred Claire even knowing. My attitude towards Piazza was that he was a "me" guy first. The Dodgers hadn't won any playoff series. They hadn't done anything. Hey, it's great to have a catcher who hits .350 with 35 home runs, but if it doesn't translate into trips to the World Series, forget it.

"The complaints about Piazza's defense were overplayed. He wasn't Pudge Rodriguez, but his offense offset any defensive deficiencies he may have had. However, the guy wanted to be the highest paid player, but he wasn't the best player in baseball. Billy was shameless in his love for Piazza. It wasn't a personal thing with me. I just looked at the big picture.

Piazza refused to play unless he was going to be the highest paid player in baseball, and that's why the Dodgers dumped him. Right before the trade, Piazza then turned down a deal by the Dodgers that, honestly, would have made him the highest paid player in baseball. That was the kicker, when they actually made the offer. Now, how legit that offer was, I don't know. But when it leaked out that the Dodgers had actually offered him that money and he turned that down, my attitude was 'See you later.'"

I have to disagree with Steve regarding his initial comments. Maybe I'm lying to myself because I'm loyal to a fault, and maybe people will argue and disagree with me, but I will not believe Mike Piazza abused steroids. Apparently, the baseball writers agree with me. In January 2016, Mike, in his fourth year in the ballot, was finally inducted into the Baseball Hall of Fame. Frankly, I'm really disappointed that it took so long. If you're a writer, how do you decide that Mike Piazza doesn't deserve to be enshrined in the Hall with his numbers? He's never been implicated in any investigations involving steroids. None! He never tested positive or was never even linked to anything! His career numbers haven't magically changed since his retirement. Suddenly, he's Hall of Fame worthy now? It's very, very unfair. Again, Mike did not test positive, so why do people rip him every chance they get?! Because it was the steroid era, that's why. We can talk about testing until the cows come home. Unfortunately, every player from that era, whether it's Mike Piazza or Jeff Bagwell, will be under suspicion. Whether it's fair or not, there will be a cloud looming over anybody who gets inducted, including Ken Griffey, Jr. Like I said, I just can't get over why Mike was good enough to get called to the Hall in 2016, but not the first three times he was on the ballot.

Throughout the course of baseball history, we've had several eras. We had the dead-ball era, the live-ball era, and an era where there wasn't one African-American player involved in baseball until 1947! Ty Cobb sharpened his spikes high. Babe Ruth became baseball's greatest home run hitter. Was he taking something?! We don't know! We don't know a damn thing! Was that home run record a true record Babe Ruth had? Or was it an all-white record? Then you had the amphetamine era, which started in the 1950s and lasted until they were banned. We had an era where the pitcher's mound was lowered from 15 to 10 inches in 1969, the year after Bob Gibson's ERA was a microscopic 1.12, and Detroit Tigers pitcher Denny McLain won 31 games (they didn't call it the Year of the Pitcher for nothing).

Then there was the steroid era. What's even more embarrassing is that Major League Baseball profited from all of the players accused of taking steroids. Bud Selig allowed the World Series to be canceled in the wake of the 1994 baseball strike. Baseball needed Mark McGwire and Sammy Sosa's home run chase. They needed the long ball back in the game. If they didn't have the long ball, there would have been nine people in the stands. They needed to do something. Selig and all the other owners knew what was going on. If they were so concerned about it, they could have brought in executive director of the Major League Baseball Players Association, Donald Fehr, and really taken a strong stance on the problem. They didn't do a damn thing, because they were making millions and millions of dollars. You can rip the players all you want for signing these big money contracts, but what about the money the owners made during that time? Are they spending it on steroid education? No. They lined their pockets just like the players did! Any era of Major League Baseball can be called into question. How do we know today, after the crackdown on performance enhancing drug use by Major League Baseball, that players aren't taking any drugs of any kind? There's always a new chemist in town or a new drug to use.

Mike kind of went underground for a bit when he retired after the 2007 season. Personally, I think he was a little upset about being denied entry into the Hall of Fame during his first few years on the ballot, but Mike would never say that publicly. He's not a self-promoter. Maybe that's why I got along with him. He was a gifted athlete and just let his actions speak for themselves. This man is being dealt a severe injustice. I'm all out of answers. What Mike did on the baseball field, especially as an offensive catcher, will never be duplicated. Who would you rather have on your team? Pudge Rodriguez or Mike Piazza? I'd rather have Mike Piazza. Mike is one of those guys that you still want to see swing the bat when it's the eighth inning and your team is down nine runs. Pudge may have been great defensively, but some Major League Baseball coaches as well as players told me on more than one occasion that he always called for his pitchers to throw a fastball, so when base runners were attempting to steal, he'd get a better shot at throwing them out. Mike was your ideal number three or four-hole hitter with tremendous opposite field power! He never even struck out 100 times in a season! Hank Aaron, Joe DiMaggio, Yogi Berra, Stan Musial, Al Kaline, Ted Williams, Billy Williams, and Johnny Mize are just some of the others in that group. Not even Willie Mays and Frank Robinson are on that list! All of those players are Hall of Famers!

Pete Rose was right, and it's well-documented: Mike Piazza is the greatest offensive catcher ever to play the game.

And now, he's finally an official member of the Baseball Hall of Fame.

Case closed.

CHAPTER 26

Adventures in Spotting and the Shortest Trip Ever Taken to Japan

As you might have noticed, I really love being around football. I was attending Philadelphia Eagles games when football wasn't the number one sport in the country. That's how long ago that was!

Back in 1971, the first year of Veterans Stadium, I was approached by Jim Gallagher, the long-time Eagles public relations director, and a great man. The Eagles were playing the New Orleans Saints in a preseason game, and former Eagles offensive tackle Al Wistert and Packers Hall of Fame fullback Jim Taylor were working the radio broadcast and needed a spotter.

For those of you unfamiliar with what spotters do, they sit next to the broadcasters and relay the names and numbers of the players, as well as who makes the tackles, who recovers a fumble, who puts pressure on the quarterback, who deflects the ball, the whole deal. This is done through a series of hand signals you relay to the broadcasters while the game is being played. The alleged father of spotting football games was a guy named Bill Friel. Bill, a Norristown Pennsylvania native, played legion ball with Tommy Lasorda. Bill worked with well-known broadcasters Chris Schenkel and Chuck Thompson, and spotted the 1958 National Football League Championship Game at Yankee Stadium between the Baltimore Colts and the New York Giants. That game is known by many as "The Greatest Game Ever Played." Needless to say, spotting is not an easy job. You've got to be on top of things, and I was nervous, nervous, nervous! I told Jim I had never spotted before, but he had confidence in me that I would do a good job. Maybe they were just being nice to me, but after the game, Wistert reiterated Jim's initial thoughts and complimented me on the job I had done.

With my dad (left) and Bill Friel, who got me into spotting. July 1970.

Right around that same time, I had built up a friendship with Eagles play-by-play man Charlie Swift. Charlie saw me around different sporting events in the area and kind of took a liking to me. He told me he had a job for me on the weekends at WIP (which was primarily a music station at the time, except on the weekends) if I was interested. I would be in charge of Dial-A-Sports, where I would update the sports scores for the listeners. Eventually, I got to know Charlie very well, and in 1972, he asked me to be his spotter for the Philadelphia Eagles. At the time, I only had one preseason game under my belt. The Eagles had guys who were much more qualified to do that job at the time than I was, and I told Charlie that. It didn't matter to him. "You've got to be ready to spot games. Next year, you're my spotter," Charlie kept saying to me.

The first game I ever worked with Charlie and former Eagles fullback and color analyst Al Pollard was an intrasquad scrimmage with the Eagles at Widener University. The first radio broadcast I ever spotted for WIP was an exhibition game in Jacksonville, Florida between the Eagles and the Buffalo Bills. The star running back for the Bills at the time was none other than O.J. Simpson, who only played about a quarter and a half and then came out of the game.

When I was spotting, I always kept stats for the Eagles and broke down all the numbers afterwards. I went through the play-by-play of each game, and one time I stumbled across the fact that Eagles wide receiver Harold Carmichael had caught passes in 56 consecutive games. I alerted the Eagles and we updated those numbers every week. The number later reached 127 and was an NFL record at the time. The late Jim Barniak, a Philadelphia-based sportscaster and writer, wrote a very nice article about me discovering the streak in the *Philadelphia Bulletin*, which I was very grateful for. Another writer by the name of Gene Gomolka from the *Delaware County Daily Times* did a nice piece on me as well. Those writings got me some publicity in Delaware County and raised my profile a bit. It was nice.

I spotted Eagles games with Charlie from 1973 until December 1977, when something horrible happened. I was at home and my phone rang at 4:30 am in the morning. It was Tim Early, a friend of Charlie's.

"Bill, I don't want you to hear this on the radio or read it in the newspaper. I have really, really bad news for you. Charlie Swift committed suicide. He shot himself," Tim said.

I was just devastated. Charlie had me as his special guest on his radio show with Eagles linebacker Bill Bergey the previous Monday. Two days later, Charlie asked me to keep stats for him while he did play-by-play for a rematch of the 1977 NBA Finals between the Sixers and the Portland Trail Blazers on PRISM, a local Philadelphia cable network. Charlie gave me opportunities to work in Philadelphia sports and treated me tremendously. He was a very meticulous worker who expected everybody to do a good job and work hard. Charlie wasn't the easiest guy to deal with, but I had a good rapport with him. There were no signs of Charlie being unhappy, whatsoever. I had no idea that Charlie could and would do such a thing. I just couldn't believe it. It was like losing a family member. Packers Hall of Fame cornerback Herb Adderley joined the broadcast team for the season's final two games, while Merrill Reese, then the Eagles color analyst, handled play-by-play duties and became the official voice of the team the following year. It's a position Merrill still holds to this day, almost 40 years later. After the season ended, Merrill asked me to stay on as a spotter, which I really appreciated.

Merrill Reese: "Bill is a meticulous spotter. He understands the game and he follows plays very, very well. I depend on the spotter to tell me more of what is happening away from the ball. He has to stick with the basics to show me the ball carrier and who made the tackle, but for the most part, all he's doing there is seconding the motion, because I pick that up with very little difficulty on my own. But every now and then, there's a pile up or a tough angle to see something at, so it's nice to have a second pair of eyes. But where I really use a spotter is during situations when he'll tell me who threw the block that opened the hole for the running back, who was the guy who put the pressure on the passer, all the stuff away from the actual ball, and that's where Billy is exceptional. He goes out and gets that stuff, comes back, and with hand signals, reconstructs the play."

I spotted Eagles games for Merrill for the next five seasons, but the way I ended things with him was something I did not handle well, and it's something I regret. I was still with the Eagles when I got an opportunity to work on the network level after the 1982 season. Although Jim "Sports" Kelly left Channel 10 for CBS radio and TV, I had stayed in touch with him. Knowing I was a spotter for the Eagles, Jim called me and asked if I wanted to be his spotter for Monday Night Football broadcasts on CBS radio. Hindsight is always 20/20, but basically, I panicked. I should have gone to Merrill early on to let him know what was happening. It was a chance to make more money and move up the ladder, so I left the Eagles, Merrill, and WIP to work with Jim. It was tough for Merrill, because he found someone who could do a competent job spotting for him. If I were Merrill, I would be really ticked off to this day, but he has never held it against me and I give him a lot of credit for that. I owe a lot to Merrill. He's been a true friend for a long, long time. In the end, however, I have to take full responsibility for my actions, because I did not exit the Eagles broadcasts the way I should have.

*Me and Eagles play-by-play announcer Merrill Reese: a
great colleague and an even better friend.*

A few years later, Jim got an opportunity to work college football games
for ESPN, which at the time was still considered a fledgling network. We
worked all the PCAA (Pacific Coast Athletic Association) games on the
West Coast on Thursday nights. I remember one game we worked at
the home stadium of the now-defunct Long Beach State football team's
home stadium, when they played San Jose State. The school had all the
fans sit on one side of the field, because they wanted it to look like a packed
house! The other side was roped off! I would slip out on Thursday morn-
ings to fly out to the West Coast, do the games, and then fly back to work
at Channel 10. Needless to say, the station was not happy about this. Even
though I had my weekends off and those particular games were easier, I
was always wheeling and dealing to make this happen.

Unfortunately, the one deal I couldn't broker was the time I missed
the Holiday Bowl in 1988, which featured Oklahoma State running back

Barry Sanders against the Wyoming Cowboys. In that game, Sanders tore it up, finishing the game with 222 rushing yards and five touchdowns. I was in Chicago with Channel 10, covering what would become the infamous "Fog Bowl" playoff game between the Eagles and the Chicago Bears. I tried to convince Al Meltzer that I could fly out to San Diego to work that game and then grab the red eye back to Chicago, but Big Al wasn't having it. Even though I was disappointed, I would have never given Al a hard time about it. In fact, Al's probably one of the few people I haven't given a hard time to over the course of my near-50 year career! I'll be the first to admit, I'm not exactly what you would call a summer breeze. If something didn't go the way I felt it needed to when I was at the news station, you'd better believe I would raise holy hell about it. If a camera crew had to go into Philly for a water main break instead of covering the Flyers or Sixers game, somebody would get reamed out royally. Over the years, Al probably saved me from getting fired close to 80 times. I really have to give him credit for sticking with me.

I know this sounds ridiculous coming from somebody in 2015, but when ESPN started in 1979, there was a lot of skepticism as to whether it would ever make it. The network had the money and the resources, but a lot of people questioned whether an all-sports network would ever get off the ground. Well, luckily for me, it did, and it led to one of the biggest jobs I've ever had in professional sports. I didn't know it at the time, but I would be a part of the ESPN family on and off over the span of 25 years.

During my time working with Jim, I also developed a relationship with the great Super Bowl winning coach Hank Stram, a guy who I really miss. I remember one particular time when Hank was working an NFL preseason game featuring the Tampa Bay Buccaneers and Jim flew me out to be a spotter. Hank, wearing some kind of robe, spotted me and wanted to get something to eat. I had actually forgotten my wallet, and Hank always "forgot" his wallet.

Nonetheless, we walked into this restaurant called the Bay Harbor Inn. As we walked into the place, we bumped into none other than NFL Hall of Fame coach Paul Brown. Next thing you know, it's Paul Brown, Hank Stram, and Bill Werndl. Two eventual Hall of Fame coaches (Hank hadn't been inducted yet) and me. Paul and Hank are going back and forth discussing players, and I'm just sitting back enjoying every minute of it. We must've sat there for an hour and a half before leaving. As we got up to leave, I remember looking at Paul, who was wearing a seersucker suit and horn-rimmed glasses, and asking him a question:

"Mr. Brown, what is your philosophy on players?"

He pushed down his glasses and replied, "Young man, they will be tolerated until they can be replaced."

It was always great to work with NFL Hall of Fame
coach Hank Stram in the broadcast booth.

In between stints at ESPN, I briefly worked one year with Mel Proctor and Paul Hornung for TBS, who had a college football package at the time. I also worked with Fred Gaudelli, who is now the coordinating producer for Sunday Night Football on NBC, and current Washington Nationals broadcaster Bob Carpenter (not to be confused with the former Phillies owner). A short time after, I met Ron Franklin, who was hired by ESPN. Ron was a broadcasting legend, having done play-by-play for the NFL's Houston Oilers, as well as basketball and football play-by-play for the University of Texas. From 1987 to 1995, I worked every game with Ron, except the day that my father passed away on October 1, 1993.

I had a two-year sabbatical from ESPN in 1996 and 1997 after I got the San Diego Chargers color analyst job. However, after *XTRA Sports 690* lost the contract to carry the team's games, I ended up rejoining Ron in the booth for Saturday night games and occasional Thursday night games. Ron and I were also on board for the introduction of Tuesday Night Football. I spotted Marshall University's now-infamous upset victory over Ben Roethlisberger and Miami University (Ohio). It was a very controversial ending, as Miami of Ohio defensive coordinator Jon Wauford reportedly assaulted a Marshall fan and got arrested. After the game, I was in the press box, and the Miami assistant coaches were so angry how the game ended that they took a big dolly and rammed it into the wall of the coach's box, leaving a big indentation. As they were ramming the dolly, I alerted the cameraman to get the shot. They saw him taping them and started screaming. It was great stuff.

I worked the BCS National Championship Game from its inception, including the 1999 Fiesta Bowl, when Tennessee beat Florida State. There was also the Ohio State vs. Miami Hurricanes game in the 2003 Fiesta Bowl, when a late flag was thrown in the end zone, enabling Ohio State to come back and beat Miami. I worked radio with Ron during the 2006 Rose Bowl featuring USC against Texas, which was one of the greatest games ever played in college football history. I was there for the "Hook and Ladder" game, when little Boise State knocked off Oklahoma in the 2007 Fiesta Bowl, and I also spotted Tennessee's six-overtime victory against Arkansas in 2009.

Ron and I had a great, great run. I enjoyed working with him and we had an awesome time. In my dealings with him, Ron was always the consummate pro. He knew the game and took his job very seriously. Unfortunately, Ron was involved in several unfortunate incidents, which ultimately led to his firing by ESPN in 2011. It was a shame the way things ended with Ron, and it ripped my heart out a little bit when he left. I still stay in touch with Ron. He was one of the greatest broadcasters I ever worked with. After Ron was dismissed, I called my "Godfather," Fred Gaudelli, and he hooked me up with horse racing analyst Randy Moss (not to be confused with the former NFL wide receiver). Randy also covered football, and I ended up working five to six games a year with him, spotting games for the Ivy League: Princeton, Harvard, the whole deal. I've become immersed in academia in my older years!

I figured out one day that I've spotted roughly over 900 games in my career. When I said I never missed a game, I wasn't lying. One time, I worked a college game on Saturday, then drove eight and a half hours from Iowa City to Minneapolis to spot an NFL game at 12:00 pm. And if you think that's crazy, it's nothing compared to the most infamous spotting gig of my long and storied career.

In the summer of 1993, I received a call from Fred Gaudelli, who at that time was at ESPN. Fred informed me that broadcasters Mike Patrick and Joe Theismann were doing an exhibition game in Tokyo, Japan between the Eagles and the New Orleans Saints. Fred needed a spotter and asked me if I could fly out there to work the game, which was to be played Sunday morning in Japan, but was going to be broadcast at 10 pm on Saturday night in America (there's a 14-hour time difference in Japan). Fred then asked me if I could leave Wednesday from Philadelphia. I told him I could leave Friday, so that's what I did.

I flew out of Philadelphia to Detroit at 8 am in the morning and arrived in Detroit around 9:15 am. Then I went to the overseas terminal at the Detroit airport for what was supposed to be an 11:00 am flight to Tokyo. The flight was delayed and wasn't going to leave until the middle of the afternoon. Keep in mind I flew commercial. There was no Learjet. The flight eventually took off, and I finally arrived in Tokyo at 7 pm

(Tokyo time). Now if you've ever been to Tokyo, you know that the distance from their airport to any "local" destination is very inconvenient, especially after a long international flight. It isn't like the Philadelphia International Airport, where it's about a 40-minute drive from downtown or out in the regions of Chester County or Bucks County. The Tokyo airport is two hours away from downtown Tokyo, almost as if you drove from Philadelphia to Washington, D.C. When I landed, I had to hop on a bus, which had lace on the back of each seat and was very clean. I arrived at the hotel where the Eagles and Saints were both staying at around 9:30 pm that night. After I checked in, I started walking down the hallway with my carry-on bag when I bumped into Saints coach Jim Mora, who I knew from his days of coaching the Philadelphia Stars.

"Hey Bill. I didn't see you all week! How long will you be in Japan?" Jim asked.

"I just got here, Jim. I'm doing the game tomorrow," I told him.

"So I guess you're going to stay a couple days to recover?" he assumed.

"Nope," I said. "I'm on the Eagles' charter back to Philadelphia."

Now Jim knows that I'm a bit goofier than your average bear, but he was in shock. He couldn't believe what I was doing.

If you're keeping score at home, I was in the air for 27 and a half hours. I was on the ground for 19 hours.

When I arrived back in Philadelphia on Sunday at 6 pm Eastern Standard Time, I wasn't finished. I had a camera crew waiting for me, and I interviewed Eagles players as they came off the plane. I used the footage later that evening for our sports broadcast. When I returned to Eagles training camp that week at Lehigh University in Bethlehem, Pennsylvania, somebody asked me if I got jet lag from the trip. Let me tell you something, I went through so many time zones, my head was spinning. I didn't have a chance to get jet lag!

While my time in Japan was limited, I was there long enough to check out the Tokyo Dome (where the game was played), and it gave me fodder for the Eagles' pre and postgame show, which I was then hosting on WYSP. During one broadcast, I ripped Veterans Stadium for its Astro Turf and how decrepit the stadium was getting. The guest on the show happened to be Philadelphia Mayor Ed Rendell, and I had some points I wanted to express to him.

"Mayor, this is the worst stadium in the country," I declared.

"How do you make a statement like that?" Mayor Rendell responded.

"Mayor, I'm going to reverse that statement and take it back. It's the worst stadium in the world," I told him.

"What do you mean?" he snapped back.

"I did a game in Japan, and their stadium is a lot better than this one!" I replied.

While I've been extremely fortunate to cover some legendary games over my 40-plus years in spotting, I've been just as fortunate to have had the chance to work with such great and talented announcers over the years. I've worked with Lindsey Nelson, who was my idol as a broadcaster. Working with him was a dream come true. I've also spotted games with Jack Buck, Skip Carey, Kevin Harlan, Jerry Glanville, Marv Albert and too many others to remember. And the best part of all this is that I'm not done. I'm not ready to put the canvas over me. In addition to the Ivy League games I spot with Randy Moss, I still spot Eagles preseason games with Scott Graham on the Eagles Television Network. And I'm happy to say that after a 32-year absence, I rejoined Merrill Reese in the Eagles' broadcast booth, spotting home games and several road games during the 2014 and 2015 seasons. Merrill could have gotten anybody else, but he was kind enough to have me back. I was so honored. It was like old times, and it just goes to show you that you really can go home again. In that regard, I truly have come full circle.

I'm not hanging up my chart to sit on the sidelines. I'll be spotting games until the day they tell me I can't do it anymore.

CHAPTER 27

The Tragic Fall of Ryan Leaf

THE STORY OF former San Diego Chargers quarterback Ryan Leaf is really a sad tale.

Leaf was selected as the second player overall in the 1998 NFL Draft, which was also the same year quarterback Peyton Manning was drafted. I had a lot of contacts within the NFL, so I talked to a number of teams about both Manning and Leaf. At the time, there wasn't this overwhelming consensus that Manning was "The Guy." There were teams who actually thought Ryan Leaf could be "The Guy." They might not say that now, but when I talked to several NFL general managers and personnel, they told me it was a toss-up. There were differing views on both Manning and Leaf. I saw Leaf in person at the Rose Bowl when he was a sophomore at Washington State, and I was impressed with him. I thought he did a very good job. At the time, the Chargers were in desperate need of a quarterback after the retirement of Stan Humphries, who had taken a tremendous beating on the football field while suffering multiple concussions.

With the first pick in the draft, Indianapolis Colts general manager Bill Polian decided that he was very confident in Peyton Manning, and wanted to roll the dice on him. Manning might not have been as athletic as Leaf, but he was more cerebral. After all, his dad was Archie Manning, who played quarterback in the NFL for over a decade, mostly with the New Orleans Saints. The Manning family made sure Peyton had his feet on the ground. The Colts' selection of Manning left the Chargers to take Leaf with the number two pick.

Looking back, I think both Polian and Chargers general manager Bobby Beathard did their due diligence in selecting their picks, but the problem with Leaf was that he was extremely immature. There was once a rumor that he skipped a meeting with Colts coach Jim Mora because he reportedly didn't want to be drafted by the team. I can't confirm if that's true or not, but right off the bat, Leaf made mistakes. He skipped a mandatory rookie symposium after being drafted, and the Chargers fined him $10,000. The symposium tries to steer rookies on the right path. Looking back, he probably could have used that. Shortly after, during Chargers training camp, linebacker Junior Seau managed to snag Leaf's credit card and used it to pay for several teammates' dinners. Leaf apparently went to Chargers' management and complained about it. The next day at practice, Seau laid a pretty lethal hit on Leaf. Coincidence?

Then about midway through Leaf's rookie year, I was at the Las Vegas Bowl working for ESPN, when I was approached by an NFL general manager and his personnel guy - both of whom will remain unnamed. They asked me for two passes so they could stand up on the roof at the Vegas Bowl and evaluate certain players. I called my producer and he arranged this with no problem. At halftime, the three of us were talking, and the general manager informed me of something very interesting regarding Leaf.

"Do you know where your quarterback is every Tuesday?" he asked me.

"No," I said. "Where is he?"

"He's in Vegas. He leaves on Monday night, and he flies to Vegas and is there all day Tuesday. Sometimes he's back Tuesday night or early Wednesday morning, and he's not always in the right frame of mind when he shows up," he continued.

'Uh oh,' I thought to myself. Whether it was true or not, and I had no reason to believe it wasn't, this was a red flag and it was not good. While some might think this kind of news is a shock jock's dream, I never went on the air with this story. Although I've never shied away from controversy, I had to be very careful because I could be held liable if this wasn't true. I just put it in the back of my mind, but it was right around that point when things just spiraled out of control with Ryan Leaf.

Meanwhile, Peyton Manning would be at the Colts complex on his off days in Indianapolis at 6:30 am in the morning. They would have to chase him out of there! Leaf did not take the game of football seriously enough and clearly never had the same work ethic Manning did. Your quarterback has to be one of the leaders of your football team. He doesn't have to be the most talented guy in the world, but he has to be able to lead, and Leaf was not respected by his teammates in that Chargers locker room. Although the media isn't as tough in San Diego as it is in New York, Philadelphia, Chicago or Boston, the relationship between Leaf and the local media was rocky at best. Most of the time, he always blamed us or his teammates for his poor play. It was never his fault. I remember one particular ugly incident between Leaf and San Diego Union Tribune reporter Jay Posner. In Jay's defense, the incident was totally unprovoked. Junior Seau had to jump into the middle of it, and it was just a mess. Then just minutes into the first workout of training camp in Leaf's second season, he suffered a season-ending shoulder injury. Later on in camp, I saw Leaf accost a fan. He just started screaming and hollering, carrying on and going ballistic. Then several months into the season, Leaf got into a shouting match with Bobby Beathard and got suspended. It just never ended with this guy.

In hindsight, you're probably wondering what the Chargers were thinking when they drafted Ryan Leaf. Well, Manning and Leaf were the only two quarterbacks in that draft. The Chargers felt that any warts Leaf had were outweighed by the good he would do on the field. There are lots of guys who come out of the NFL Draft who have baggage who were able to reconstruct their career, but Leaf wasn't able to overcome the distractions he had. If you're a guy who is committed to being one of the best, as Manning has proven over and over again, you've got to be dedicated. All the great NFL quarterbacks have religiously looked at tape and film. Leaf didn't. He went golfing instead.

Steve Hartman and I had Leaf on our show a couple times. We weren't bosom buddies with him and he wasn't exactly a captivating interview, but he'd come on periodically and we had a decent relationship. As I mentioned before, I was impressed with Leaf's talent, and so was my co-host.

"Let's go back to draft day. There was all this talk about who was the better quarterback: Peyton Manning or Ryan Leaf?" recalled Steve. "While most people felt in the short term that Manning was going to be a better draft choice because he started all four years in college and had more experience, it was believed that Ryan Leaf was a better long term choice because he was a better quarterback. The Chargers were sitting at the number three slot in the draft and were trying to move up to get the second pick. Keep in mind the Chargers weren't that far removed from their 1994 Super Bowl season, so we thought that the team needed a franchise quarterback.

"Billy was doing his draft research as he always does, and being the scout that he is, felt that physically, Ryan Leaf had what it took to be a great quarterback. Billy prides himself in knowing players and personnel. Peyton Manning was very mechanical, while Leaf was the better athlete and had a better arm. At 6'5", he had Manning's size, but he was a better player. The offense they ran at Washington State had Leaf throwing the ball all over the field. He was coming off a year where he led Washington State to their first Rose Bowl in 67 years. It was an insane year this guy had. To this day, Peyton Manning's reputation is that he doesn't win the big one. He lost to Florida multiple times in college, and he's still doing it in the NFL. Ryan Leaf was raw. He really had only been a starting quarterback for two years in college, but everybody said he had far greater long term potential than Manning. No doubt. Billy really touted the guy. He was the Ryan Leaf champion in the beginning. Neither one of us were Peyton Manning fans at all. We both absolutely celebrated when Charles Woodson beat him out for the Heisman Trophy.

"When it became apparent that the Colts were going to take Manning, Chargers general manager Bobby Beathard then traded picks and return man Eric Metcalf so the team could move up just one slot in the draft, because they thought they were going to get the real prize in Leaf. So draft day came, the Chargers selected Leaf, and Billy and I were on the air just applauding the move. We couldn't wait for the Ryan Leaf era to begin. In the beginning, Billy and I were the guys who embraced Ryan. He wasn't the most personable guy, but we really didn't detect any major character flaws. Then before the season even began, sports columnist T.J. Simers wrote a scathing column about Leaf, talking about how he was a bad guy and some other things. Billy and I were taken aback and wondered where this was coming from. It didn't seem to be the guy that we had been talking to.

"Then it seemed that more and more writers were following TJ's lead, while Billy and I were the guys defending Leaf. So the season started, Leaf was the starting quarterback and the Chargers won their first two games. It's one of the few times it ever happened where an NFL quarterback won his first two games he started as a rookie. Billy and I were looking at everybody wondering what everybody was talking about. We just ignored them. We weren't going to let anybody make up our minds about this guy. We told Leaf to ignore Simers and not to listen to him. We were rooting for him and kind of took him under our wing. We thought this guy was going to be great. Then came Week 3. The Chargers went to Kansas City, and statistically, the game ranks among maybe the two or three worst games ever by a quarterback. Leaf was 1 for 15 for four yards, threw two interceptions and fumbled three times. It was so bad, there was no defending it. After the game, Billy and I figured it was only one game and it couldn't get any worse. Then just a few days later, with a TV camera rolling, Leaf just exploded on Jay Posner and got in his face about something he said about him. Junior Seau had to pull Leaf off of him. To make things worse, Leaf read off an apology to Posner that was written on a piece of paper. After he was done, he threw it into his locker. After that, we were all like 'Man, this guy's a complete ass.'

"This was a national story. The internet wasn't fully rolling at that point, but ESPN ran this full blast, over and over again. They were dying for this kind of video. Billy and I could no longer defend Leaf. He never recovered on the field or came up with any games to make us think the Kansas City game was a bad moment we could move on from. His attitude and play on the field both went south. Going into 1998, *XTRA 690* was no longer the Chargers' flagship station, and it was a little rough for us. Billy had been the color commentator for Chargers football for a couple years, and suddenly he wasn't anymore. We still had close ties with the team, so we felt that, with people piling on Leaf early, our attitude was 'Why don't you let this guy play. He'll silence his critics.' At least for two games, that's what happened. But after the Kansas City debacle and the

Posner fiasco, there was no saving the kid. It was such an ugly situation. It really was unbelievable. You kept thinking this kid's gotta wake up. He never did. From that point on, it was just an absolute freefall for Ryan Leaf and he just turned on everybody. After that, Billy and I started doing some background checks on Leaf. We even called his old high school, and everybody just hated this guy. It was unbelievable. We were duped more than anything else. Ryan Leaf's potential blinded many. But in the end, those that heeded the warning about what kind of guy he was were dead on the money. Everything about the Ryan Leaf story was a tragedy. It still is."

Steve is right. After the Jay Posner locker room incident, whenever Leaf did something really stupid, I would just shake my head and say 'Why did he do that? Here's a guy with a lot of ability, a big strong kid with a lot of money. What the heck is the matter with him?' The radio show callers in San Diego saw what Manning was doing for the Colts, and they saw what Leaf was doing with the Chargers. That was ugly.

When the Chargers finally had enough and released Leaf in early 2001, the feeling around San Diego was one of relief. He was out of our hair. It was almost like a 'by the way' sort of thing, but in our minds, he was already gone and out of the picture. The Chargers went 1-15 in 2000, landing the first pick in the 2001 NFL Draft, which they eventually traded to the Atlanta Falcons for a package of draft picks and wide receiver Tim Dwight. San Diego used one of those picks to draft running back LaDainian Tomlinson, and later in the draft they selected quarterback Drew Brees. In the 2004 NFL Draft, the Chargers selected quarterback Philip Rivers, so the sting has been somewhat lessened over the years in regards to the Ryan Leaf saga. After bouncing around with a few other teams, Leaf finally retired. He then became a quarterbacks coach for West Texas A&M and was later accused of burglarizing a player's home, apparently searching for prescription drugs. A few years later, Leaf was picked up and charged with burglary and drug possession after he allegedly broke into somebody's home and stole some prescription drugs. Days later, he was arrested again on similar charges!

When all was said and done, Ryan Leaf had a golden opportunity to be a household name, but for whatever reason, decided he didn't want to spend the time, effort and energy to become a good NFL quarterback. With the talent he had, he could have lasted 15 to 16 years in the league. I'm not saying he was going to be a Hall of Famer, but I think he could have had a good, solid career. Instead, he didn't apply himself, was just there to have a good time, and did not take his job seriously. He did a lot of things that were very immature and very childish, and now you see where his life has led him. Every year close to the NFL Draft, when there's some sports network special about the worst draft picks in NFL history, he's always at the top of those lists. It's not even close. Not just because he was once the number two overall pick, but because the Chargers absolutely broke the bank to get him.

To paraphrase former Chargers safety Rodney Harrison, Ryan Leaf "took the money and ran." He ran very fast and very hard. Now, all his money is probably gone, and he was recently released from jail after serving a prison sentence. Such a shame.

Ryan Leaf is one of the saddest cautionary tales in sports history.

CHAPTER 28

The Beginning of the End on the Left Coast

AFTER THE WHOLE Ryan Leaf debacle, the Chargers went through some lean years. This included that 1-15 season in 2000, which led to some controversy that was inadvertently started on my end during a radio broadcast that year.

One day, a caller on my show asked me what I would do to improve the Chargers. I flat out said the first thing I would do is trade Junior Seau, the Chargers linebacker and best defensive player in franchise history. It was nothing personal against Junior, who sadly passed away a few years ago. I had talked to two general managers from other clubs, and they also acknowledged that San Diego's rebuilding stage was going to be a long process. The team clearly needed more than a few players to get them back to respectability. The phone lines at the station blew up! In fact, the board operator half-jokingly told me I would need a police escort after my show ended. Years later, I said the same thing with Drew Brees after the Chargers drafted quarterback Philip Rivers and I got the same reaction. The fans of San Diego are probably still steamed about that one.

Unfortunately, the Chargers weren't the only organization in San Diego about to undergo a facelift. By 2002, I had spent a little more than six years with my fellow Loose Cannon Steve Hartman on *XTRA Sports 690*. The great success Steve and I had during this time was something I never could have dreamed of upon my arrival from Philadelphia. Unbeknownst to me, however, things were about to change drastically in the landscape of San Diego sports talk radio. Clear Channel had taken over *690* and wanted to primarily make it a Los Angeles-based station, which would become *XTRA Sports 690/1150* AM. In the process, they would divorce themselves from San Diego completely. Being an L.A. guy, Steve wanted to seize the opportunity.

In the meantime, I had heard that John Lynch Sr. was starting up a new station in San Diego. Despite the fact that Los Angeles is the number two radio market in the world, there were still a lot of question marks surrounding the move. Personally, I didn't want to leave San Diego at that particular juncture, and at the time, I thought John Lynch Sr. was a straight shooter. As a result, I decided not to go to L.A. and started working at Lynch Sr.'s new station. Because I would have been moved from San Diego to L.A., my old contract would have been voided. It never got that far in the negotiation process, but Steve told me the three-year deal I would have signed if I went to Los Angeles was worth a lot more money than I made in San Diego. Now I'm not always the most diplomatic guy, and in retrospect, I didn't handle that situation as well as I could have with Steve. It wasn't a great departure, and we didn't talk for about a year. To a certain extent, I regret not going to L.A. It was a union station and it probably cost me a few years of my pension, but you can't take back the decisions you make in life.

With my *XTRA Sports 690* days officially behind me, *The Mighty 1090 AM* became my new home. No longer a Loose Cannon, my new show was dubbed the "Too Much Show" and my new partner was Steve Mason. Steve had come over from Los Angeles and had worked in several radio outlets on the East and West Coasts. I worked with Steve for about a year at *1090*. Then one night, he called me at home and told me he was leaving the station. Personally, I think Steve's departure from *1090* was for monetary reasons. It's my opinion that he was promised certain things by the station, was not given those things, and got disillusioned with San Diego. If that was the case, it's really too bad. Steve Mason was a good guy and I enjoyed working with him. In fact, it was Steve Mason who helped me patch things up with Steve Hartman at the 2004 Super Bowl in Houston. The two of us broke bread, talked things out, and I'm proud to say Steve Hartman and I mended our fences. My next partner for nearly five years was a former producer named Darren Smith. I had a good relationship with Darren, but it wasn't like the Loose Cannons. Unlike Steve

Hartman, who had some input regarding who would take Chet Forte's place back in 1996, I had no input in regards to who my new partner would be at *1090*. I'm not saying whether I would or wouldn't have picked Darren as Steve Mason's replacement, but we auditioned a number of people after Steve left, and not once was I ever asked whether I thought Darren was a good fit or not.

That wasn't the only beef I had with *1090*. Another issue I faced during these years was having to constantly stress to John Lynch Sr. how we needed to talk more football. I knew the NFL was coming on strong. It was becoming the number one sport in the country! However, Lynch Sr. insisted we talk Padres, Padres, and more Padres. Even though *1090* was the Padres' flagship station, you can't manufacture stories if they don't exist. I realized we had to ride the NFL pony, but they didn't believe me and pretty much restricted me from saying anything negative about the Padres. If I would badmouth the team, the phone would ring with Lynch Sr. on the other end, telling me I couldn't do what I was doing. One day, the Padres got blown out by the San Francisco Giants and I went ballistic, blasting team owner John Moores and how he needed to be held accountable for the lack of success his team was having. The phone rang again and it was Lynch Sr., once again reminding me that *1090* was the home of the Padres. When the team acquired journeyman infielder Todd Walker at the 2006 trade deadline, I referred to the deal as "slop a la mode." I got in trouble for that, too. To a certain extent, Steve Hartman and I had to be careful what we said on *690*, but Lynch Sr. knew what he was getting when he brought me in to be part of the new station. He knew that I was a vocal guy and very opinionated. If I felt that the Padres brass weren't doing the right things, I was going to be vocal about it!

Whether there was any animosity towards the Chargers from Lynch Sr. is unknown from my perspective, but I do remember him telling people at the station's Christmas party back in 2007 that he hoped the Chargers got eliminated in the first round of the NFL Playoffs. Those remarks bothered me and I got ticked off that night. Whether we were the flagship station of the Chargers Padres? or not, football carried us through several months. Why would you say what he said? Ironically, the Chargers went all the way to the AFC Championship Game that year before losing to the New England Patriots, 21-12. That was the game Philip Rivers played with a torn ACL. After the run the Chargers put together that season, how could you possibly expect me to be excited about Padres baseball!? Lynch Sr. had spent so much money on the team and I understood that, but the only reason you'd talk about the Padres during the heart of football season would be if the team possibly made a trade. To be fair, the Padres did make the playoffs in 2005 and 2006, losing both times to the Cardinals in the NLDS. The '05 squad was 82-80. Not exactly world beaters. Two years later in 2007, they lost a one-game playoff to the red hot Colorado Rockies. The ending of the game involved a controversial play involving the Rockies Matt Holliday, who never touched home plate when he scored the winning run. I was on the radio and went crazy. That game really hurt. That was as good as it would get for those Padres teams during the rest of my time in San Diego. The next year in 2008, they lost 99 games.

As it turned out, 2008 wouldn't be a good year for the Padres or for yours truly. After 12 and a half years on San Diego radio, my career came to a screeching halt that December. With our country in a recession, the housing market was going south in a hurry, especially in San Diego. Our ratings at *1090* were fair, not great, and John Lynch Sr. came to me and said he wanted to redo my deal. I told John I was more than happy to do this, but I wanted my agent, Barry Axelrod, to handle it. John then offered me $100,000 a year over three years. Once again, I told John and his henchman, Gregg Wolfson, that I'm sure we could work something out. However, we needed to do this through Barry. As I later found out, John never even talked to Barry.

Then the next thing I knew, I was told that the role on my show was eliminated, Darren was going to continue by himself, and that I was terminated. When I reminded Wolfson that I still had a year left on my contract, he told me the station would give me two months' severance pay. When I asked about what happened to Lynch Sr.'s previous offer, Wolfson said it was off the table because I had "declined" that offer. When I told him they should have talked to Barry like I asked, Wolfson stressed to me that they couldn't waste any more time. That didn't fly with me. That didn't fly at all. They were just going to ignore my contract. I was a good soldier at that station, never complained about money, and within reason, did everything they wanted me to do. They thought I was some dumb, country bumpkin who wouldn't do anything about this. That's when I contacted San Diego-based attorneys Don McKillop and Guy Ricciardulli, who took the case on a contingency.

Don McKillop: "We only take cases that we know are good cases. After talking with Billy, we knew we had a good case. Billy was let go from the radio station, and they claimed the cause was based on the ratings of his show. At the time, he was partnered with Darren Smith, who he worked with for quite a long time before he got terminated. The termination was based on the show's ratings, but they kept Darren Smith, who was younger and making less money. We pursued them on a claim for breach of contract and age discrimination. They terminated the older member of the partnership making more money and kept the other member. Our position was, if the termination was based on ratings, why wouldn't they let go of Darren Smith at the same time? We pursued arbitration and took a lot of the deposition from the staff at *1090*. We then had a mediation and eventually settled the case. I'm confident that had we proceeded to arbitration, we would have prevailed. It was required in Billy's employment agreement to go to arbitration instead of filing in court. After a lot of discovery, we decided between the parties to go to mediation, and our arbitrator settled it formally. Although the mediation took about a day, we started talking to Billy about the case in February 2009. It was finally settled in July of that same year."

I would have taken the station's offer for $100,000 over those three years, as I planned on retiring after the contract expired. I also would have added to the deal that I wanted to be compensated $24,000 to $30,000 a year from age 66-70 for events and special appearances. By that time, I would have received my maximum Social Security benefits, still had a couple more years on my pension, and would have had some money coming in at the age of 70. It didn't happen that way, and that's the thing that hurt me the most. At the end of the day, I won the case, but the damage had been done.

The person I was and still am most disappointed about in all of this is John Lynch Sr., who recruited me twice before I finally made the big move from Philadelphia. Looking back, it's kind of ironic that the same person who brought me into San Diego pulled the rug out from under me in the end. There were people who took their shots at John a lot during my days in San Diego, but I still I defended him. I even followed him to *1090*, staying in San Diego after the radio station shake up that temporarily fractured my relationship with Steve Hartman. There were people who warned me to be careful about him before I even signed that contract, but I thought he was loyal to his people. Little did I know he would stab me in the back. John shook my hand at the end of the mediation, but in my opinion, it wasn't sincere. He wasn't an honest and sincere person. He was very devious. I really don't have a lot of respect for him. Of all the people I've dealt with in my almost 50-year career, there have been people who've done things to me that were pretty bad. John Lynch Sr. hit below the belt. It's no surprise at all that *1090* eventually showed him the door a few years later. From what I heard from several people, he was escorted out of the station by security.

Yes, San Diego had been a unique experience to say the very least.

And now it was over.

CHAPTER 29

And in the End...

WHEN I ARRIVED in San Diego back in the summer of 1996, I originally signed a three-year deal with *XTRA Sports 690 AM*. I thought life would begin again for me at 50, and that I'd eventually pack my bags and come back to Philly. However, life is what happens when you're busy making plans, and I ended up staying in San Diego for 12 and a half great years. Even though I hated the way things ended, it turned out to be an amazing run. I look back on those days quite a bit. I could go anywhere in that city and people would recognize my voice. You'd pinch yourself and say 'This is a guy from Sharon Hill, Pennsylvania who everybody recognizes.' When I go back and visit San Diego, everybody is still great to me.

I initially planned to stay in San Diego after my firing from *1090*, but in the midst of the lawsuit, I started doing some real soul searching and began to mull my next move. Even though it was a tough housing market in San Diego at the time, I was financially okay. Then around March 2009, my wife Corinne and I contemplated selling the house and moving back home. After giving it some more thought, we made it official and I came back to Philadelphia that June. I had to fly back out to San Diego to wrap up matters there, but after that, I was home for good.

In an ironic twist, the new management at *1090* offered me a deal to rejoin the station. Twice! However, I wasn't going to uproot my family again and I wouldn't have been able to see my grandkids consistently. Either way, it feels nice to be wanted, and it furthermore proves that I was never a poison pill at the station. Programming-operations manager Mike Shepard and Adelante Media Group CEO Jay Meyers are both good guys who I have a lot of respect for. If I needed a job and was desperate, it would be a different story. Don't get me wrong, I thought about it, but I felt that ship had sailed. In fact, I actually did some additional work with *1090* after I moved back to Philadelphia and my issue with the station was resolved.

Upon my return to Philadelphia, people suggested that I apply to some of the big sports talk radio stations in the area. I really didn't get any bites, but that's fine. I've found a new home at *WCHE 1520 AM* in West Chester, Pennsylvania. Station owner Jay Shur and general manager-program director Bill Mason have been tremendous to me. They love the content I bring to my hour-long show and let me do whatever I want to do on the program. These guys are real people, not "suits." I also do a show called "Jolly & The Loon" with radio personality Paul Jolovitz on Merrill Reese's radio station *WBCB 1490 AM.* Not only is Merrill a great broadcaster and administrator, he's a great friend. When you're down, Merrill Reese is the first guy to lift you up. I cannot say enough good things about him. He's an outstanding pro, but even more so, he's an outstanding person. In fact, I invited Merrill to my daughter's wedding and he even introduced the wedding party! The same goes for Bill White. They are two of the most wonderful human beings you could ever come across. They exude class from the word go.

If it all ended tomorrow, I've had a good, successful run and have no complaints, even after what happened in San Diego. Was I upset? Certainly. I know I still have a fastball and can get people out, but it's not like I have to be on top of the mountain again. There's no bitterness. None whatsoever. I'm as happy as a lark in Jellystone Park.

I remember when WFIL became WPVI-TV/Channel 6 and all of the old records were getting thrown away. I happened to come across my old application, which read *"He will not advance past a clerical position in television."*

50 years later, I'm still here. That has to count for something.

It's been quite a ride.

Closing Remarks

by Steve Hartman

Let me give you a little background as to how the whole "Philly" Billy San Diego experience started. I was previously working with legendary Monday Night Football director Chet Forte. In 1991, we began building the first major sports station on the West Coast, *XTRA Sports 690 AM*. Our update guy was Jim Rome, before he went out and did anything on his own. Not only were we the biggest station on the West Coast, it was ahead of *WFAN* in New York and *WIP* in Philadelphia. Chet and I had the morning show, Jim Rome moved to the midday show, and we had Lee "Hacksaw" Hamilton on the afternoon drive. We owned San Diego, we owned Orange County, we owned Los Angeles. We had it all.

Then on May 18, 1996, Chet Forte died of a heart attack at 60 years old. Not only was I suddenly left without a partner, but my partner was dead. We knew Billy from his work with Ourlads' NFL Draft Guide. We were the flagship station of the Chargers, so we would bring in Billy to be our draft expert along with Hacksaw. After the death of Chet, I had to figure out who was going to be my new partner. Chris "Mad Dog" Russo was considered, but he was getting paid too much money to leave the East Coast. After considering some ex-athletes, John Lynch Sr., the father of former NFL player John Lynch, suggested Billy. The question was whether Billy would leave Philadelphia and move all the way to San Diego. So we did a couple of audition shows. The biggest similarity Billy had to Chet was that he was from the East Coast. A lot of transplants in Southern California liked the fact that Chet had an East Coast flavor, and they got the same with Billy. Another thing I loved about Billy from the get-go was that he was insanely connected with a lot of general managers in the NFL. I felt like Billy was it. It wasn't even close.

The initial response was very positive, and then it sort of took a turn south when everybody realized that Billy was not Chet Forte, who was extremely popular. In those days, the only line of communication other than people calling into the show was the fax machine. So we had faxes rolling in, and they weren't kind to Billy. 'This guy sucks. He's terrible.' Blah, blah, blah. So I grabbed Billy and told him that he'd have to trust me on what I was about to do next. We got back from the commercial break and we literally read the faxes live on the air. There was one that said 'You suck.' Here's another one: 'You're the worst thing ever in radio.' I read these faxes that were just slaying Billy live on the air, one after another. Of course, Billy's a hyper sensitive guy, and he asked me why I was doing this. My thought process actually worked out, because eventually, people were sending faxes encouraging him and telling others to give him a chance. I realized I sort of had to reorganize my role on the show and play the heavy, because I really wanted people to like Billy.

The thing about Billy is, in his world, there's nothing but sports. Nothing else exists. On the night before 9/11, Billy and I had done an appearance at a bar for Monday Night Football. Billy didn't live far from me, so he asked me if I could pick him up for work the next morning. So I got up the next morning at 7 am and turned on the television right around the time the plane flew into the Pentagon. I went to pick up Billy and he got into my car. And I asked him 'Can you believe what's happening in New York right now?' His response was 'Yeah, the Yankees are friggin' blowin' it in the AL East.' He was watching classic sports that morning and had no idea that our country was under attack. When George Harrison of the Beatles passed away several months later, I asked Bill if he was familiar with his music, and he referred to him as Dr. Pepper, instead of Sgt. Pepper! One time we were covering the Bob Hope Desert Classic in Palm Desert, and I introduced Billy to the late Glenn Frey of the Eagles (the band, not the football team). When Glenn walked away, he thought it was Glen Campbell! That same day, actor Samuel L. Jackson came over to say hello. I explained to Billy who Samuel was so he could introduce him after the commercial break. He then introduced him as Samuel L. Adams. Samuel wasn't laughing, but the audience was roaring with laughter. If you aren't a sports figure, Billy has no clue who you are. You can't script this stuff. It was pure gold to me as his broadcast partner.

One time, we decided to cover the Pro Football Hall of Fame induction ceremonies on a trip back from a show we did in Boston. Prior to my radio career, I worked for the Raiders in public relations, and that was the year Howie Long, Joe Montana, Ronnie Lott and Dan Rooney were getting inducted to the Hall. We thought it would be cool to go to Canton, do some interviews with those guys, and spend a few days there. The radio station wasn't going to pay for anything, so Bill suggested we stay with his aunt who lives in Akron. We got in late, around one o'clock in the morning, and we arrived at this little 800-square foot house. Bill started banging on the door, and I was worried about him waking up this 90-year old woman in the middle of the night. The door opens, and this little old lady opens the door, looks at Bill and says 'Boy, did you get old!' I almost fell over laughing for 15 minutes at this woman deadpanning. She was a hoot. These "accommodations" Billy arranged for us saw me having to sleep in the daughter's bed of a childhood friend Billy spent summers with in Akron. I was thinking 'You got me sleeping in this guy's daughter's bed?!' These were the kinds of things about Billy that were priceless.

Billy was never intimidated by anybody and was not afraid of confrontation. Chet Forte and I were labeled the Loose Cannons. I left it to the listeners to think whether or not Billy was worthy of the moniker. It was obvious from day one that he *was* in every sense of the word. I remember once when the Arizona Diamondbacks were in town for a series against the Padres. Randy Johnson had a ridiculous stretch where he didn't get any wins in four starts, despite giving up one run over that span. He got zero hitting support, so Bill and I went up to him at his locker and asked if it bothered him that the team wasn't scoring for him. Billy and I both have loud voices, so as we asked the question, Matt Williams, who was about halfway across the locker room, yelled out 'What kind of horseshit question is that?' When we both turned to him to inform him we weren't talking to him, Williams, who was a notorious asshole, came up to Billy, and the two of them went back and forth yelling at each other. Randy, who wasn't the warmest guy, either, basically stood out of the way. When push came to shove, Billy was always ready to jump on in.

During our time together on the radio as the Loose Cannons, Billy and I always went to the Super Bowl, and we were so aggressive in trying to get guys to interview. We took no prisoners and we were going to get what we wanted. During Super Bowl XXXI, which featured the Green Bay Packers and the New England Patriots, Billy was the only person to get an exclusive one-on-one interview with Reggie White. Outside of a group situation, nobody was going to get close to Reggie at that Super

Bowl. Because of Reggie's friendship with Billy in Philadelphia, Billy got it done. Two Super Bowls later, Billy's relationship with former Eagles quarterback Randall Cunningham resulted in one of the all-time classic interviews. After the great year Randall had with the Vikings in 1998, he was one of the finalists for NFL Player of the Year. So Billy started talking with him and we congratulated him on the year he had. Randall's response for all seven questions we asked him was exactly the same: "I have to thank my lord and savior Jesus Christ for the season I had."

During our days at *XTRA Sports 690*, we were an absolute power-house. Who knows what would've happened if Billy changed his decision to not to come to Los Angeles. In 1997, Clear Channel had taken over *690*. At the same time, they also decided to buy the radio rights to the Los Angeles Dodgers. In the process, they took *1150*, a Los Angeles signal, and essentially created a sister station. We were still *XTRA Sports 690*, but there was now an *XTRA Sports 1150*, the home of the Dodgers. What Clear Channel decided to do was split the sports stations. They thought in time, people in LA would listen to *1150*, and people in San Diego would listen to *690*. It never happened. People never stopped listening to me and Billy in Los Angeles.

On October 31, 2002, Billy and I got called in to speak with the station's program director after our show. In the meeting, he informed the both of us that we were finished. *690* and *1150* were going to be merged into a superstation and everything would be phased out. *690* was dead, and everything was going to move to Los Angeles. A survey taken in LA clearly showed that our program was the one most listened to. They wanted me to go to LA and dump Bill because unlike me, he wasn't an LA guy. I fought tooth and nail to keep Billy. The show was successful, I was with him for six and a half years, and there was no reason to break up this team. Eventually, they agreed to keep Billy. We made a trip to LA, met with the sales staff, it was all set. In February 2003, Billy and I did our show. I told him I got my contract done, and he implied he was getting his done. When we walked out the door and I said goodbye to Bill, however, he looked at me sheepishly and sort of nervously. He didn't say anything. Later that night, my station manager called me and told me Bill had just quit. I called Billy to ask him what was going on, and he was very nervous. Apparently, he didn't know how to tell me he didn't want to move to Los Angeles. It was unfortunate that things happened. But after a while, we both moved on, it all worked out, and we have long since mended fences.

I've literally never known anybody like Billy. There is nobody else in the world like him. I thought I was a sports fanatic to the nth degree, but that's nothing compared to Billy. Other than the world of sports, there's nothing else he cares about, which is the beautiful thing about him. Who else flies to Japan just to spot a game for around $300 bucks?! Just absolutely nuts. It isn't like anything I've seen in my entire life. Billy would say such outrageous things to where I literally could not script the guy. And then, if he said something goofy and off-the-wall crazy, I would just repeat it and magnify it. I couldn't understand why Billy continued to work as a stat guy, because how he took root in Southern California and became a big star is really because of his fanaticism for this kind of work. What really made Billy a legend in San Diego was the 'Werndl Wire,' a segment I created for him. In the early stages of the internet, Billy would rifle off three or four breaking NFL stories through his contacts he had with NFL general managers. It was wildly popular. Everyone could not wait every day for the 'Werndl Wire.' Billy was totally devoted to it, he worked his ass off, he got information. That was Bill Werndl at his absolute best. Tremendous stuff.

There isn't anything I don't remember - good, bad, or ugly - about my six and a half years with Billy. As far as a two-man radio show goes, I actually worked with Billy longer than anybody. I still go on the radio with him whenever he calls me. I love Billy, and I was extremely protective of him. He's one of my all-time favorites.

-Steve Hartman
July 2016

Bill Werndl Acknowledgements

I'D LIKE TO thank:

My wife, Corinne Werndl; my daughter, Ashleigh and her husband, Brandon South; my grandchildren—McKenzie and Mitchell; my stepson, Vic DiMarco; sister-in-law, Rosie Anescheck; stepdaughter Leslie and her husband, Anthony Boccio, their children— Gia, Liana and Anthony III; my cousin, Janice Thornton and family; cousins Jerry and Jane Werndl and their children—Jerry, Steve, and Jackie; cousins Bob and Dorothy Crissey; Angela Anderson and family; Wayne Wiley and family; Bill White; Merrill Reese; Larry Kane; Bruce Conly and family; Bill Shupper; Michael Dementri; Dei Lynam; Ukee Washington; Bill Gallagher; Barry Axelrod; John Boggs; Jim Ryan; James Lofton; Dean Spanos; Bill Johnston; Warren Miller; Theo Epstein; Jack Evans; Geoff Harris; Fred Staffieri; Dom Anile; John Spagnola; Kevin Reilly; Dick Coury; Dodgers' manager Dave Roberts; Zach Hill; Sonny Vacarro; Larry Lucchino; Cindy Webster; Mark "Frog" Carfagno; Gil Sadie; Tom Donahoe; Phil Nevin; Dick Allen; John Lynch; Jim McKenzie; my good friends Joe and Susie Natoli of Akron, Ohio; Jim and Jeri Morrison; Jim Solano; Lew Klein; Pete Kouris; Howard Kesselman; Bill Friel; Denise Gardier and family; Les Keiter; Chuck Bednarik; Stan Hochman; Joe Pellegrino; Don Tollefson; Steve Levy; Charlie Swift; Al Pollard; Stan Walters; Herb Adderley; Jim Barniak; Bill Bergey; Harold Carmichael; Mike Quick; Mark Loretta; Don McKillop; Guy Ricciardulli; Jack Edelstein; Jerry Rossett; Al Meltzer; Jim "Sports" Kelly; Joe Fowler; Ron Burke; Michael Barkann; Mel Proctor; Skip Carey; Ron Franklin; Mike Gottfried; Alan Nesbitt; Mel Kampmann; Dean Tyler; Jack Ferrante; Paul Hornung; Bud Long; Mike Glickenhaus;

Lee Hamilton; Jim Laslavic; Bill Campbell; Joe Tutino; Brian Wilson; Bill Pugh; Jack Evans; Carl Peterson; Ken Dunek; Mark Chlebowski; Eric Allen; Johnny Sample; Tom Cardella; Paul Jolovitz; Steve Mason; Darren Smith; Herman Gassaway; Tim Sabean; Tom McKinley; Joe McPeak; Jim Steeg; Ed Placey; Sean Learman; Darren Balsley; John Sadek; Bruce Clark; Randy Moss; Kevin Harlan; Don Henderson; Bill Bradshaw; Jim Gallagher; Don DiJulia; Chick McElrone; Jim Murray; Matt Mirro; Mike Samsel; Pat Dion; Paul Holmgren; Speedy Morris; Phil Martelli; Joe Crawford; Ted and Joan Shaw; Michele Wright; Jay Shur; Bill Mason; Gary Papa; Scott Palmer; Kevin Newlin; Angelo Cataldi; Matt Vasgersian; Fred Gaudelli; Bruce Bochy; Steve Hartman; the staff at WCHE; all my friends from Sharon Hill, Pennsylvania; my ex-wife—the late Patricia Conan.

And last but not least, my parents—William and Mary Werndl, and my old neighbor, Mr. Gottschalk.

Joe Vallee Acknowledgements

I'LL NEVER FORGET the day I first met Bill Werndl.

It was during the summer of 2013. Several years earlier, I had struck up a friendship with Philadelphia broadcasting legend Larry Kane after I gave him some press for his Beatles book *Ticket to Ride* on my website, Philly2Philly.com. When I reached out to Larry and sent him a copy of my book, *A Snowball's Chance: Philly Fires Back Against the National Media*, he liked it so much that he made the book's premise the subject of one of his weekly shows on Comcast, and invited me on as a guest to discuss it with him and several other sports panelists.

After I arrived at the Comcast studios' green room the day we were shooting the show, the producer introduced me to Bill, who was one of the panelists. Bill shook my hand and was rather inquisitive, asking me a little about my background and why I was there. When I told him we would be discussing my book, he looked at me in a very quizzical manner and started asking me about particular events and incidents in Philly sports history that he thought might be included in my book. I really didn't know if Bill was grilling me or if that was just his way. As I sat at the studio desk ready to start taping the show, I thought to myself 'Oh boy. What is a half hour show going to be like with this guy?'

When things finally got underway, Bill stole the show, and I was rather amused. He didn't break character from our meeting in the green room, and his enthusiasm and passion were on full display for the entire Delaware Valley to see. Not only was Bill extremely knowledgeable, he was hilarious! SportsRadio 94 WIP's Al Morganti and Paul Jolovitz were also on the panel with me, and in between commercials, we couldn't contain our laughter!

After the show, Bill approached me in the parking lot and actually apologized to me in case I thought he came on too strong or stole any of my thunder during the show. When I told him it wasn't an issue at all, we exchanged numbers. About a week later, he offered to have me on his radio show at *WCHE* in West Chester, Pennsylvania to promote my book. A few days later when I was on the air with him, Bill hyped *A Snowball's Chance* like it was the greatest story ever told. When I called him to thank him later that day, he mentioned to me that he had been thinking about writing a book himself, and he asked me if I would be interested in helping him write it. It was an absolute honor, but being that I wasn't too familiar with Bill, my first reaction was to meet with him to see if we had enough material. Over the next year, he shared with me some incredibly engaging and inside stories from his phenomenal career, and the book you're reading right now is the result. In all honesty, writing *'No Curveballs'* never really felt like work to me. The two of us would just casually meet up at Pappone's Pizza near the Granite Run Mall, shoot the breeze, and I'd let the tape recorder run. As time went on and I began to put these stories into a document, I really began to appreciate everything Bill has accomplished in his career as well as his friendship. He even had me speak to his class he teaches at Widener University, and practically convinced his entire class to buy my book!

I never doubted that Bill valued what I was doing for him. Every time we would hang up after confirming a meeting, Bill would always end the call with the same words: "Joe, you're a good man, and I really appreciate you doing this for me." Well Bill, it takes one to know one. You're a good man yourself, and I really appreciate you entrusting me with the task of putting your amazing career into words for everybody to see. If the book is half as successful as you have been, then the sky's the limit!

I'd also like to thank **Bill White**, whose accomplishments in the game of baseball have been matched by very few. I was a Phillies fan growing up in South Jersey, but when we first got cable television, it was always a pleasure listening to Bill broadcast Yankees games on WPIX/Channel

11. As if a great playing and broadcasting career weren't enough, Bill then became National League President! His time spent writing the foreword for this book will always be appreciated. You're a class act, Bill. Thank you!

I'd also like to thank the late, great **Stan Hochman**. Stan came to the launch party for my first book, *A Snowball's Chance: Philly Fires Back Against the National Media*, and gave us a glowing review of the book in the newspaper. He was as generous as could be, and a nice friendship developed between the two of us. Shortly after his write-up, I found myself talking to Stan regularly. He would fill me in on the plays he would see during his trips to New York with his wife, Gloria, and I would let him know what projects I was working on. Whenever I had a question, or generally wanted to pick his brain, Stan readily provided me with anything I needed, and was so engaging while doing it. Sadly, we lost Stan in April 2015. When I spoke with Gloria at his service, she told me that Stan mentioned my name on several occasions. That really meant a lot to me and it still does. I'm truly honored that this book features his insights. For my money, Stan was Philadelphia's best sports writer ever. Thank you, Stan! You are missed.

Don McKillop, thank you for your time and for sharing some great scuba diving stories! You kept us on the straight and narrow and made sure we dotted the i's and crossed the t's.

Many thanks also go out to **Steve Hartman**, "Philly" Billy's former co-host and fellow Loose Cannon in San Diego. Steve was also very generous and readily accessible with his stories and his time. His closing remarks in the book are absolutely classic. I know I've told you this before, but thanks again, Steve!

I'd also like to thank **Al Meltzer, Top Kepler, Ashleigh South, Corrine Werndl, Harry Booth, Merrill Reese, Chris Wheeler, Ken Dunek, Dick Vermeil, Fred Gaudelli, Matt Vasgersian, Angelo Cataldi, Carl Peterson** and **Bruce Bochy**, who all offered valuable insight for this book and/or contributed some great stories and kind words.

Special thanks to **Steve Olenski** for some insightful recommendations, the immortal **Jon Evoy,** the quintessential marketing pro, and **Diane Cooney,** my friend and Philly2Philly writer who can adjust manuscript fonts with the best of them!

I've known **Ryan Downs** since we were sophomores at St. Joseph's University. One random night of studying for an English test turned into a friendship that's lasted 18 years and counting. Ryan's writing was instrumental in the success of our book, *A Snowball's Chance*, so when he took a look at some of the chapters I sent him for this book and really liked what he read, I knew I was on the right track. Downsy, you're always there in a pinch, right 'Down the Hall.' Thanks for steering me in the right direction. Francis would be proud. Your influence and suggestions were invaluable. Let's start thinking about a sequel for *Snowball's!*

To **Matt Goldberg**, who has editing abilities that would land him in the Editor's Hall of Fame, if such a thing existed. When you look at a book for parts of four years, your eyes are shot, and you need a new set of eyes. Matt was that new set of eyes and then some (despite the fact that I've been needling him to get glasses for years!). Matt sees things while reading a manuscript that most humans simply don't see, and I'm extremely grateful that he saw them. If you need someone to look at your final manuscript, if no one else can help, and if you can find him, maybe you can hire Matt Goldberg. Thanks Matt!

Check him out at: tipofthegoldberg.com

To **Billy Vargus**, my other co-writer from *A Snowball's Chance*, for simply being Billy Vargus!

To **Kyle Hudson:** Webmaster, marketer and video man extraordinaire. Thanks for all your help with everything! Kyle has a time machine (yes, you heard right). You can check it out at www.letsbuildatimemachine.com

To my parents, **Joe and Shirley Vallee**, for always supporting me in any production I'm involved in that has the potential to drive everybody crazy, as well as my sister, **Nicky Vallee.** Having another writer in the family indeed has its advantages! Thanks for lending us the microphone, too!

And finally, to all the Joe Vallee supporters out there who've stuck by me and continue to encourage and inspire me every day. You know who you are. Thank you!

About the Authors

BILL WERNDL is a man of many talents, as well as several nicknames. If you know him from Philadelphia, you may know him as "The Loon." If you're from the West Coast, you know him as "Philly" Billy. No matter what name you know him by, it's safe to say that Bill's successful career in sports that spans almost 50 years is matched by very few.

Just months after starting in the mailroom at WFIL Radio (the future WPVI/Channel 6) in 1966, Bill was promoted to the newsreel. In 1974, he became the first full-time sports producer in the Philadelphia market. Along the way, Bill established friendships with the Philadelphia Flyers Broad Street Bullies, Philadelphia Eagles coach Dick Vermeil, baseball's all-time hit king and former Philadelphia Phillie Pete Rose and countless others. During his 30-year stint in the City of Brotherly Love, Bill covered more than 3,000 stories, including the Philadelphia 76ers' NBA championship seasons of 1967 and 1983, as well as both Flyers' Stanley Cup parades in 1974 and 1975.

In addition to his work in television, Bill was also a long-time spotter for the Philadelphia Eagles radio broadcasts, as well as a co-host for Eagles pre and postgame shows on WYSP radio. During his long and varied career, Bill has spotted more than 800 football games, including the "shortest day ever spent in Japan" back in 1993. Along the way, he has worked for every major network, which includes CBS, ABC/ESPN, NBC and FOX, covering some of the biggest college football games ever played while working with such notable sports broadcasters as Ron Jaworski, Bill Campbell, Johnny Sample, "Big Al" Meltzer and Jim "Sports" Kelly.

After years of working behind the scenes, Bill received the offer of a lifetime to work sports talk radio in San Diego, California. Immediately after arriving, Bill became a talk radio sensation, and was given the nickname "Philly" Billy by his on-air partner, Steve Hartman. The two were known as the Loose Cannons on *XTRA 690 AM*, and their show became the number one-rated sports talk show in all of Southern California. During his time in San Diego, Bill covered the 1998 World Series featuring the San Diego Padres, San Diego State basketball and football, was a color analyst for the San Diego Chargers, covered golf tournaments (including the Bob Hope Classic and Torrey Pines) and was a color analyst for the San Diego Chargers. Bill also reunited with baseball great Ted Williams and forged relationships with Padres Hall of Fame legend Tony Gwynn, former Sixers Hall of Fame coach Alex Hannum and many more. After six and a half years at *XTRA Sports 690 AM*, Bill moved up the dial to *The Mighty 1090 AM*, before returning to Philadelphia in 2009. Since his return, Bill has appeared as a panelist on numerous media outlets, including The NFL Network and Philadelphia's Comcast SportsNet. You can currently catch up with Bill on *WCHE 1520* AM in West Chester, Pennsylvania, and *WBCB 1490* AM in Levittown, Pennsylvania.

Bill's list of accomplishments doesn't do his career justice. He's simply one of the most diverse and knowledgeable personalities in the world of sports.

Bill currently resides in Valley Township, Chester County, Pennsylvania with his wife, Corinne.

 **Joe Vallee's** love for sports began as a child growing up in the 1980s. With his family having been full or partial season ticket holders for all four major Philadelphia sports teams during certain parts of his youth, Joe was able to experience the good, the bad, the ugly, and the absolute heartbreak that too often comes with being a Philadelphia sports fan.

A former Phillies bat boy, Joe is always open to sharing stories about his encounters with the likes of Mike Schmidt, Darren Daulton, John Kruk, and memories of a not so pleasant meeting with Lenny Dykstra. Joe is a graduate of Bishop Eustace Preparatory High School in Pennsauken, New Jersey. While attending St. Joseph's University, Joe hosted his own radio show and graduated with a degree in English and a minor in Business. After an internship fell through at a local sports station just prior to graduation, Joe continued to work his way up in the family business at Vallee and Bowe Cadillac and Oldsmobile in Woodbury, New Jersey, before its closing in 2006.

Joe is the co-founder of the Philadelphia-based website Philly2Philly.com. The site officially launched in June, 2009, and reached more than two million views in just the first two years. Joe was also the brainchild behind the book *A Snowball's Chance: Philly Fires Back Against the National Media*, which he wrote along with several sports writers from Philly2Philly.com. The book was published in 2013 and has been met with critical and commercial success.

Joe has played a major role in the launch of the *Rainbow Rabbit Anti-Bullying Educational Program*, which is based on a character created by his grandfather, Arthur Vallee, who was one of the first Disney animators. The program is currently being utilized by various educational institutions throughout the Tri-State area. He is also a musician, having played drums in practically every venue in the Tri-State area for better parts of the last 20 years, as well as releasing two albums and an EP with multiple groups. Joe was featured on *97.5 FM The Fanatic* Dream Job contest, has served as guest host on *The Artie Clear Show* with Artie Clear, and has broadcast news segments for *The Daily* on the Apple iPad. Joe's voice can also be heard on numerous KYW News Radio commercials, as well as spots for Activision and Potomac State University. He has also been an occasional sports contributor to FOX 29's *Good Day Philadelphia*, a writer for *JerseyMan Magazine*, and digital media manager for CBS Philly/WOGL.com.

Joe currently resides in South Jersey.

Sources

Ch. 2

1. Meltzer, A., & Lyons, R. S. (2012). Wilt Chamberlain Tells All...for the Final Time. *Big Al: Fifty years of adventures in sports broadcasting* (p. 155). Philadelphia, PA: Camino Books.

Works Cited:

Ch. 2

1. Ramsay, Jack. "The Game Plan: Making Decisions." *Dr. Jack's Leadership Lessons Learned from a Lifetime in Basketball*. Hoboken, N.J.: J. Wiley & Sons, 2004. 210-211. Print.

Ch. 5

1. Nightengale, B. (2014, December 14). Dick Allen's hard road may take Hall of Fame turn. Retrieved January 31, 2015, from:

   http://www.usatoday.com/story/sports/mlb/2014/12/02/dick-allen-hall-of-fame-phillies/19798077/.

Ch. 13

1. Bruton, M. (1988, September 25). Toney Limps Into Battle Of Words With 76ers. Retrieved February 1, 2015, from:

   http://articles.chicagotribune.com/1988-09-25/sports/8802020321_1_sixers-drug-test-racial-insult

Ch. 21

1. Miller, R. (2015, August 6). New bombshell: Pete Rose accused of statutory rape; hit king denies claim. Retrieved January 10, 2016, from:

   http://www.nj.com/phillies/index.ssf/2015/08/pete_rose_denies_allegations_of_statutory_rape_by.html

2. Erardi, J. (2007, March 18). Dowd: Some nights, Rose didn't bet on Reds. Retrieved January 31, 2015, from:

   http://usatoday30.usatoday.com/sports/baseball/2007-03-15-rose-dowd_N.htm

3. Schmidt, M. (2015, December 14). Dear Pete Rose: It's Still a No. Sincerely, Baseball. Retrieved December 17, 2015, from:

   http://www.nytimes.com/2015/12/15/sports/baseball/pete-rose-ban-mlb-commissioner-rob-manfred.html?_r=0

Ch. 24

1. McCarron, A. (2012, December 4). Tommy Lasorda defends Mike Piazza, says there's 'no proof' ex-Mets catcher used performance-enhancing drugs . . Retrieved July 19, 2014, from:

   http://www.nydailynews.com/sports/baseball/mets/piazza-played-game-clean-lasorda-article-1.1213393

2. Booth, S. (2010, December 16). De-constructing the Piazza trade. Retrieved July 19, 2014, from:

   http://www.hardballtimes.com/de-constructing-the-piazza-trade/

Made in the USA
San Bernardino, CA
11 March 2017